Wasted

A Sober Journey through Drunken Ireland

Wasted

A Sober Journey through Drunken Ireland

Brian O'Connell

Gill & Macmillan

Gill & Macmillan Ltd
Hume Avenue, Park West, Dublin 12
with associated companies throughout the world
www.gillmacmillan.ie

© Brian O'Connell 2009
978 07171 4599 7

Typography design by Make Communication
Print origination by O'K Graphic Design, Dublin
Printed by ColourBooks Ltd, Dublin

This book is typeset in 11/14 pt Minion.

The paper used in this book comes from the wood pulp of
managed forests. For every tree felled, at least one tree is
planted, thereby renewing natural resources.

A CIP catalogue record for this book is available from the
British Library.

5 4 3 2 1

Dedicated to the memory of Rose O'Connell

Contents

Acknowledgments

To Mam and Dad for keeping the faith.

Óran for being all any father could ask for in a son.

Sophie for love and friendship.

Damien, Sinead and Aoife for putting up with me during the 'lost' years.

John 'Granda' O'Connell and Peg O'Donnell for paving the family way.

Mannix Berry for opening the door all those years back.

Fergal Tobin for his belief from the outset, constant encouragement and professionalism.

John Leahy for a huge amount of time and support. Fellow salesman Aidan Mulcahy, Brian Carey, Faith O'Grady for her valuable advice and support, Gordon Deegan, Nick Kennedy for the poetic eye, Therese Tierney for calling up, Ray Scannell for friendship and an appreciation of fine cake, Shane Hegarty for swapping notes, Miriam Donohoe for all her support, Shane Malone for encouragement and solid advice, Rachel Andrews for notes, Fintan O'Toole, Caroline Walsh, Barry O'Keeffe, Conor Goodman, Carmel Daly, Hugh Linehan, and all at the *Irish Times* for guidance, advice and an income, John and Christina Kelly, Eoin Ó Cathain, Theresa and Caroline Cavanagh, Rosaleen Quinlan, Richard Fitzpatrick, Fawn Allen for sharing some of the journey, Dr Chris Luke, Tony McCarthy and all at Forefront, Tom Donnelly, Ryan Tubridy and all at the 'Tubridy Show', Colm Moore and 96 FM, Cianna Campbell, Joe and Grace Carey, Eileen Sweeney, the Fahy family, Neil Pearson, Mary Bohan, Denis O'Connell, Ciara Dwyer, Thomas Power, Fiona Kearney, Fergal and all at The Cornerhouse Bar in Cork, John Kennedy, Liam Heylin, Danny Maher, Pat Keogh and family, Joe and Mary O'Connell and family,

Jim O'Dowd and family, the Hehir family, Christy McNamara, Ann Sweeney, Una and Diarmuid Clarke, Madeline Johnston, Sara Keating, Steve, Trevor, Shay Howe, Eoin Vaughan, Professor Joe Barry, Colette Sheridan, Dr Stanton Peele, Ronan Farren, Barry O'Sullivan, Gerry Collison for taking a punt on me, Cilla Kotey, Dr Bhamjee, Dr Alex Michel and Niamh, Geraldine Hartnett and all at the Aislinn Centre, Frances Black, Robbie Breen, Deirdre Rennison Kunz, Nicki Howard, Neil Ryan, Esther Kallen, Mark Nixon, Teresa Daly, Mary Coughlan, Declan Doherty, Mike Darcy, Eibhlin Roche and the Guinness Archives, Eoin Fahy, Will O'Connell, Cork City Library, Knud Hedeager Nielsen, Gerard and Marie and family, Jean Doyle, John Egan, Dr Brian Girvin, Dr Mary Tilki, John Doocey, Donal Ó Drisceoil, Lorraine O'Connell, The Shannon Bar, Danish Tourist Board, Greg Canty, Deirdre Waldron, Doreen O'Mahony and all at Fuzion PR, Martina Carroll, Niall Toibin, Des Bishop, Cathal Murray, Ger and Jemma, Paddy O'Gorman, Kathleen Fitzpatrick, Paul Bugler, Judy Murphy, Pauline Scanlon, Donogh Hennessy, Michael McSweeney, Tabor Lodge, Knight of Glin, Mark O'Halloran, Nuala O'Faolain, Ursula Earley, Paul Durcan, John Creedon, Jimmy MacCarthy, Edel O'Connell, Fred, Sinead Harrington, Brendan and Lucy Fitzgerald, Jack L, Marian Egan, Tim Vaughan, Joe Dermody, Emma Forrester, Ger Fitzgibbon, Vic Merriman, Fr Micheál Mac Gréil, Professor John A. Murphy, the Irish Pioneer Movement, Seamus Heaney and all the staff at the Kingsley Hotel.

Introduction

It seems strange saying this now, having invested the last year of my life writing and researching this book, but I never consciously planned on writing about either my own or Ireland's association with alcohol. Same way, I suppose, I never intentionally set out to develop a drinking problem. Both just happened organically, taking me by surprise, leading me along a more scenic, albeit bumpier, route. The seed for this writing lies in an *Irish Times* article I wrote in 2008, which in turn followed a radio interview with Dave Fanning on the 'Tubridy Show' a little time earlier. I owe thanks to Tom Donnelly in RTÉ Radio for the platform to begin with and Shane Hegarty in the *Irish Times* for encouraging me to turn those initial comments into print.

The reaction to both media outings, and to my thoughts on living sober in Ireland, seemed to strike a chord. I received dozens of letters and emails from a wide range of people, from 18-year-old teenagers to 80-year-old clergy, expressing support and telling me of their own struggles. Several of the letters and cards went unsigned, and simply offered messages of mutual understanding. I remember being at a social function some weeks after the *Irish Times* article appeared, and someone whom I had never met before told me of his own battles with alcohol, and the fact he felt unable to admit it or deal with it effectively. He was a respected member of his community, known as a 'heavy drinker', he said, and facilitated as such. He felt unable to discuss his inner torment with family or friends. We chatted for a while and then he returned to the bar. The image of him—bulk hunched and back turned—putting his arm around the shoulder of a fellow drinker as he took his seat at the counter stuck with me.

Following this, I began to reflect on secrecy, alcohol and Irish society. How emotionally open and upfront have we really become as a society? Is it still taboo to admit defeat to something like alcohol in Ireland, and impossible not to feel socially scarred as a result? What difficulties arise as a result of the interaction between society and sobriety in twenty-first-century Ireland? Are problem drinkers born or do they develop and evolve over time? Is there a place for the non-drinker in Irish social life? These were all the initial questions, flirting for answers in the back of my mind. Both of those personal media outings came three years into my sobriety, at a time when I was very much enjoying life, both personal and professional. It's worth pointing out that sobriety was never something I kept hidden or under wraps. From the start, I was quite comfortable with the fact that I had sought help for my drinking, much the same way a diabetic seeks insulin. Having said that, I had been careful, with much of my writing, not to fall into the confessional, first-person genre of journalism, which has been gradually diluted by unchecked ego since the days of Hunter S. Thompson and the everyday descriptive poetry of Robert Lowell.

When fashion journalists spend a night on the streets, so they can write about how it would feel for *them* to be homeless (minus their haute couture), then you know conscience-driven journalism has taken a wrong turn somewhere. I feel the need to justify myself, then, in the face of a confessional journalism culture, where shock and awe sometimes replace probing and insight as the determining factors. We also live in an age where rehab has gone very public, with 'personalities' frequently stepping in and out of treatment, from where their tell-all stories are offered to the highest bidder. Behavioural crucifixion and salvation sell—just tune into Jonathan Ross any Friday night if you're looking for proof.

This was never intended as an academic endeavour, more a teasing out of some of the issues behind Ireland's drinking culture through my own personal insights. My reasons for laying down my thoughts were as much determined by the society I live in as by any lingering desire or need to make public my personal self or to mark a break with my past. My security with sobriety seemed to climax at a time when Ireland's problematic drinking patterns had been soaring unchecked for almost a decade. It's not that I felt a duty, but

I felt qualified to examine some of the reasons for our problem drinking and how it is being addressed. That, coupled with the fact I was also just plain curious.

That's not to say I don't have reservations about exercising what I hope will be interpreted as emotional honesty. I'm conscious of family and friends reading aspects of this publication and not being wholly comfortable with my revelations. I'm conscious of my son picking this up as a teenager and having to deal with my shortcomings as a father during my drinking and how that may subsequently impact on him emotionally. Perhaps the guilt and shame of abusing alcohol never quite leave you, and there's an inclination to keep those feelings hidden or suppressed. It's something I have thought long and hard about—the dangers of offloading my story at any cost and of being labelled as the guy who pillaged his problem past for a book. I'm wary, then, of becoming a one-issue candidate who hurts the feelings of others needlessly and recklessly on the road to redemption. These are all issues I have taken into account before embarking on this examination.

Yet there is, in my view, far too much secrecy around the subjects of alcoholism and problem drinking in Ireland of 2009. There are too many stories that remain untold and far too much anxiety and stress and trouble that problem drinkers endure and cannot relay because society is the way it is. The irony is that in my personal life I'm careful not to allow my sobriety to become a defining characteristic. And yet, here I am writing about it! In the end, I guess it came down to the fact that I'm not the person I describe in the first two chapters any more, and haven't been for a very long time. Hopefully those who know me will recognise that. And the old cliché abounds: if retelling my struggle with alcohol offers insight to someone, one person even, currently in the depths of that struggle, then the work will have been worthwhile.

I have tried also to collate some of the reports, studies and statistics available in relation to Ireland's current relationship with alcohol. While the information is constantly changing and being updated, some key facts remain. Firstly, that overall alcohol consumption grew faster in Ireland than anywhere else in Europe between 1996 and 2003. The rise of the off-licence, accounting for just 19 per cent of sales in 1991 and more than 35 per cent in 2006, is another noticeable trend, changing our drinking patterns to a more insular, domestic practice. The change in our drinking patterns has also been fuelled by the rise in consumption of wine, which grew fourfold between 1985 and 2003. Other statistics and analysis, such as the rise in alcohol-related illness, spikes in binge-drinking levels among the young and the rise in alcohol-related suicide, are contained in later chapters.

During the course of the research for this book, I received an email from Dr Stanton Peele, one of the world's foremost addiction thinkers. He told me he had read what I had written in the *Irish Times*. His probing reply took me a little by surprise. 'I'm glad you've stopped drinking, if that makes you happy,' he said, 'but rather than being a revelation to the Irish—that they drink too much—this is of one piece with the Irish binge-purge sensibility, and actually reinforces their underlying alcohol pathology. You probably don't want to read my book, where I say, "If you see the choice as being one between abstinence and excess, you've already lost the battle."'

As time has gone on, I've come to see sobriety less as a clinical or psychological choice and more as a lifestyle one, like cutting out meat or sweet foods. That way, I manage to sidestep all the alcoholic definition debates and all the abstinence versus moderation dilemmas that stalk the mind of many a problem drinker in Ireland.

I may have already lost the battle, as Dr Peele suggests, but I'm enjoying the struggle nevertheless.

His point fails, though, to fully grasp the Irish cultural and historical experience. Colonisation, hardship, religious repression, emotional need, greed and economic giddiness are all contributory factors to the Irish experience and relationship with alcohol. For many in this country, drinking excessively helps numb that experience, and has done so for generations. To paraphrase Homer Simpson, in Ireland, alcohol is often the cause of and solution to all of life's problems.

My personal opinion is that it is only when we have a sincere national discourse around some of the issues behind our problem drinking that a new relationship with alcohol can begin to assert itself. It won't, in my view, come about by importing a café culture, or by limiting or tailoring the current drinking culture by exclusively legislative means or information campaigns. It will come about only by a change of mindset, by a deeper understanding of why the Irish drink the way they do, and what can be done to tackle some of the underlying reasons for our behaviour with alcohol.

A UK-based employment specialist I met on holidays was telling me about his experience working with high-flying executives. He couldn't get his head around the fact that often when he put forward Irish clients for interview with Irish employers, they would meet in a bar and, in his words, 'have five or six Guinness to break the ice'. Some of the jobs they were going for had salaries of upwards of £100,000 per annum, and going on the lash before signing on the dotted line was the culturally done thing. It didn't happen with other nationalities, he noted. It's this accepted embedded relationship between the Irish and alcohol that is the core of our societal issues with drink, and I hope that some of that reveals itself in this narrative.

I recently read about Chris Matthews—a liberal political pundit on MSNBC, and a proud Irish-American. On the MSNBC morning show, responding to a joke by Mika Brzezinski about his drinking at a prominent Irish social event, Matthews declared, 'Despite the ethnic stereotype, I haven't had a drink since 1994.' The problem is, though: this *is* the Irish cultural stereotype. As Dr Peele notes, 'Addiction thinker George Vaillant found that Irish-Americans in Boston were seven times as likely to become alcoholics as Italian, Greek and Jewish Americans—at the same time as they were more likely to abstain.'

The observation appears to be backed up here by a recent Department of Health study, which found that Ireland is the European country with the lowest daily drinking rate and the highest binge-drinking rate. Only two percent of Irish men drink daily, while nearly half binge weekly. This is the virtual reverse of drinking patterns by Italians, for instance. Abstinence and excess are familiar bedfellows in Ireland's relationship with alcohol. We opt for cut out before cut down. How many of us, for instance, have woken up after a heavy night to vow, 'Never again'?

There also exists an often tense relationship between sobriety and socialising in Ireland. One of my preferred bars in Cork, and also one of the oldest in the city centre, serves sandwiches throughout the day. I tend to pop in regularly, enjoy sitting at the bar chatting with staff or local regulars. But after 7 p.m., the bar stops serving coffee and tea. Why is that? Is it saying that the night is the sole preserve of the drinking classes? Is it saying that my money is okay during the day, when alcohol sales are off peak, but come the dark, I'm persona non grata? It's a small point, but a point to be made nonetheless. This mindset needs to change so that the distinction between day and night is blurred, and public houses (those that are left) can concern themselves less with excess and more with enjoyment, experience and tangible social engagement. Last St Patrick's Day in Dublin, I organised to meet two friends who don't drink or take drugs any more. We were determined to mark the national day of Irishness, and set ourselves the task of getting a cup of coffee post-9 p.m. in the city centre. Bewleys duly obliged, but given the night that was in it, they closed at 9.30 p.m. Business was quiet. Two of us went looking for a cup of coffee in Temple Bar. Practically every coffee machine had been turned off since 6 p.m. Bar workers shook their heads, looking at us as if we were from a different planet. In many ways we were.

Staying sober and having what might be termed 'a fun night out' are often mutually exclusive for Irish people. A sober night is to be endured rather than enjoyed. In company, you're a lift home, a finder of bags and coats, a shoulder to cry on. With the advent of late-night bars, the art of conversation has been further muted, overdubbed by slurs and sound systems. Irish publicans have confused overbearingly loud music with atmosphere. I'm beginning to sound like your parents. I know. And that's the other thing with this sobriety lark—it's hard not to over-moralise, testing to remain non-judgmental. It's difficult to offer insight without sounding like you're casting a shadow from the moral high ground. To comment without patronising. Over the coming pages, I have attempted to lay down a recollection of my own journey from adolescent experimentation to problem drinking and beyond. Following from that there is an engagement with the wider issues of alcohol abuse and Irish society. Drinkers, like those I encountered in London and Tipperary, can be at once deluded and insightful, warm and revolting. It was my intention to portray that world in an authentic manner, interfering as little as possible in its telling.

Along the way countless persons have helped me with publication and I owe them a huge debt of gratitude. Fergal Tobin at Gill & Macmillan was the first publisher to pick up the phone and broach the subject of turning my thoughts into a book. Others such as John Leahy, Dr Chris Luke, the Night Ravens in Copenhagen, Mannix Berry and Catriona Molineaux, Shane Malone, Sophie Johnston, Professor Joe Barry, Faith O'Grady and many more, all gave freely of their time and I am hugely thankful to them for their contributions and observations. As for those who told me their own stories, the people I met in London and Tipperary, in the Aislinn Centre in Kilkenny or casually along the way, I remain full of admiration for their honesty and daily struggle. Others who allowed their stories and insight to weave through the narrative—Mary Coughlan, Mark O'Halloran, Niall Toibin, John Leahy, Frances Black and Des Bishop—added enormously to the variety of the text and were very giving of their time and patience.

Even after spending a year examining the subject of alcohol abuse and consulting widely on the topic, I'm still unclear as to why I ended up a 'problem drinker'. I'm not sure the pathology matters, though, as much as the personal approach to dealing with the issue. Sometimes, we can get too caught up in the 'why' rather than dealing with the 'what now'. I'm conscious, too, that I have taken a particular editorial line when talking about the relationship between the Irish and alcohol. Many of those interviewed had acute difficulties with alcohol. Of course not everyone who drinks runs into problems. Moderate drinking is a fine means of social interaction. I'd be at it myself if I was able and there are plenty in Ireland, from individual publicans to large brewing companies, able to articulate the merits of such socialising. For this publication, though, my interest lay more in the point where moderate drinking becomes problem drinking, both on a personal and societal level, and what the consequences of that change are and how it can be dealt with.

In my personal life I realise I have been incredibly fortunate. My struggles have given me a different understanding of life in Ireland—something of an outsider's lens, perhaps. I only hope I have done the subject justice and offered some added understanding of what, or who, drives us to drink the way we do.

Brian O'Connell
7 April 2009

Chapter 1
Taken to the Sup

The first time I got drunk was 1991. I know this because after a naggin of Bacardi, I thought I was a fighter pilot who sang U2's hit single 'One' (released in November that year) while simultaneously and indiscriminately bombarding the urban sprawl below—in this case Stephen Corcoran's first-floor landing—with the remnants of a snack box from Enzo's takeaway. Analyse that.

I remember little else, except a feeling of otherworldliness, of having pushed through the fur coats at the back of my mind and entered a new exciting universe, where the drink and I shared the throne. Growing up in a town like Ennis, where one local swimming pool had signs stating, 'No Heavy Petting in the Deep End' and graffiti such as 'Heavy Metle, Loud and Poud', there wasn't much else to do besides getting out of it. In fact, practically every conversation from the age of about 14 onwards revolved around drink or, more to the point, how to get it. You were judged by how many pints you could hold, where you could get served, how sick you got and what the consequences were. You talked about the easiest off-licence to get served in, what bars and nightclubs accepted fake IDs, and what were the best spirits to mix together. There were buses organised to nightclubs in neighbouring towns, which turned into rampaging drink tours of places like Gort and Lahinch. There were teenage discos where drink was hidden in urinals hours beforehand. There were cans in the cinema, bottles at dawn on scouting weekends. There was even a healthy bootleg market, where alcohol and cigarettes which were stolen from local grocers were sold at knockdown rates. Everything, and I mean everything, revolved around drink.

Looking back, my drinking career was more Pádraig Harrington than Tiger Woods, a steady rise as opposed to a dramatic and alarming early introduction. In fact, most Irish teenagers would have had the same type of experiences as I had. There was no real self-destruct button in evidence at that point, and my adolescent boozing would have been considered routine by Irish standards. Faking ID cards, siphoning a bit of spirits from the drinks cabinet at home or slowly building up my tolerance levels from two pints of Carling to three—it was all pretty normal stuff.

There were plenty of weekend mornings when I woke with vomit strewn sheets, or had to struggle to recall whose mouth my tongue had found itself resting in the previous night. Lucky girl. Ennis was well known for people getting into bars from about the age of 15 onwards—the general attitude was that it was better for youngsters to be in the pubs than in fields somewhere. Ennis was also known as a strong drinking town which prided itself on the number of pubs per capita and the co-dependency between traditional music, craic and pints.

Farmers on market day filled the bars of the Market, revellers from all over the county filled the narrow streets all weekend, and tourists wandered about bemused by the free-for-all that passed for acceptable nightlife.

It seems, too, on one level, the generally accepting societal response to underage drinking in the area has changed little since the early nineties. Some months back, one local newspaper carried the headline 'Kids on the Booze', after a 17-year-old in court named three outlets in the town where alcohol was freely available. Local publican Declan Brandon, whose premises was not one of those named, and who has tried to promote music in his venue in the town for decades, was quoted as saying the issue of underage drinking was a very hard one to police, and compounded by the fact that 'every house is like a pub or off-licence at this stage. There is far too much alcohol around the place. There should be far more restrictions on the availability of alcohol outside pubs.' He's right, of course, as the crushed-can-littered fields and estates around Ennis can testify.

The local nightclub was The Queens, and the main ambition of any discerning Ennis youth from early adolescence was to conjure ways to get past the bouncers and enter what seemed like hallowed ground. IDs were passed down from older brothers, or, with the advent of basic home computers, some were made and sold. Some tried their luck booking into the hotel adjacent for the night or holding the hand of a far older girl on the way in. Once inside, it was all about kissing girls and drinking pints. Later, thanks mainly to Tom Cruise, cocktails entered the fray. Drinking away from bars, or bush drinking, as it was known, was as popular when you were of legal age as it was through adolescence and beyond. The choice of location was either the rail tracks adjacent to the town, or the girls' convent, which had the added comfort of bus shelters. Years later, fellow Ennis native Mark O'Halloran told me that much of the inspiration for his film *Garage*, in which youths gather on rail tracks to drink cans, was taken from growing up in Ennis. Invariably three or four cans would be downed before hitting the bars between 10 p.m. and 11 p.m.—some of the group would have been in their thirties with good regular incomes and perhaps married with kids, but they were still drawn to the outdoor boozing. It was both a non-conformist and, more to the point, a financial thing. After a quick pit stop in one of the town's many bars, the general form was to try to blag your way into one of the town's nightclubs, where stealing drink became part and parcel of the night out. This was done by nonchalantly joining a group with a table of drink piled high, and passing a full pint backwards to an accomplice waiting yards away who could then quickly make a getaway. On the dance floor, 'Cotton Eye Joe', 'Dirty Dancing' and 'Come on Eileen' provided the backing tracks.

From time to time a new Garda drive in the town would see a number of bars raided and fines imposed, but generally it never lasted too long. Drugs had yet to make their way wholesale into rural communities, and the general attitude seemed to be that this sort of mass alcohol abuse was part of the fabric for any market town. On the rare occasions you went out for dinner, you booked a table early—say seven or half past—so that you'd have it over with by 9 p.m., when the real socialising could start.

It's not that there was much else to do—no arthouse cinema, theatre, art galleries, few if any gyms, restaurants were still of the beef-or-salmon variety, and dinner parties were something you wore a tuxedo for. Welcome to 1980s Ireland, then.

It was sort of like that community in 'The Wicker Man'— everyone knows something is not right, but all are complicit and reliant upon continuing the wrongs through the next generation in order to keep the social fabric intact. In other words, once the problem was contained within the community it was accepted and fertilised. The bars and nightclubs seemed happy enough to be cultivating their future customers young, while parents saw it as a rite of passage for early adolescents to have a pint.

Many youngsters were taken to the bar by their parents first, at 15 or 16, and given their first pint. For the majority this heralded the arrival of adulthood.

This societal acceptance existed, probably, in every other town in Ireland too, and would eventually lead Ireland to have one of the highest rates of binge-drinking in Europe and an alarming level of suicide among under-25s. It didn't take a genius to spot the warning signs—every social function, wedding, birthday, christening, birth, death and celebration in Ireland revolved around the pub and pub life, and still does to a certain extent. For young adults, especially growing up in a small close-knit community like Ennis, the majority of formative experiences were filtered through an alcoholic gauze. I know it was that way for me. I look back at debs nights where I was lying on the ground getting sick, on post-match underage celebrations where trainers and players held up the bar. Alcohol soaked the fabric of pretty much every aspect of life in a town like Ennis and very few people seemed concerned about doing anything about it.

———

With secondary school out of the way, I set my sights on university and headed for University College Cork, where I enrolled in Arts, the academic equivalent of hedging your bets. I first got accommodation in digs, with an elderly lady near the university. Initially college life was a rollercoaster of free drink, beat-the-clock promotions, hazy afternoons and missed morning lectures. My mind was adjusting to the new academic light, trapped between small-town mentality and medium-city freedom. I quickly got into the swing of things, bought a pair of dungarees, dyed my hair red and settled in for an extended party. Oasis and Blur were waging a Britpop war and Pulp were heralding common people. David Gray was playing introspective ditties to a few hundred students in bars on Barrack Street and sounding more despondent each time, while Sir Henry's nightclub was witnessing the peak of the Ecstasy-fuelled dance scene. I bought my first bottle of wine, ate in my first restaurant without my parents present, and became acquainted with Sophocles and shots, often at the same time.

The digs came to an abrupt end when I fell asleep across the kindly lady's bathroom door while trying to get sick one night. This had the effect of denying her access to her morning denture routine. I told my mother the food was terrible and the room cold, and she called the lady to say I wouldn't be coming back. The kindly lady responded by telling my mother I had the beginnings of a serious drinking problem. We all laughed, and I settled into a newly built townhouse behind an off-licence and within a stone's throw of the student nightclub quarter.

Drink of choice in those days was bottles of lager or flagons of cider at home (mostly Linden Village or Old Somerset or other such vinegars with questionable cider complexes), while pints and shots were opted for towards the end of the night. Drink was cheap—this was still the time of legally reduced prices and promotions in bars where shots were free or pints half price. I always had a student job, so whatever spare cash I earned was invested in socialising. There was an inevitable tension involved in engaging with this more upfront and adult student life. I began learning to cook (pork chops on a bed of instant rice) and buying a few bottles of Carling to accompany the cooking—sometimes the Carling doubled up as a sauté. I thought it was posh. In retrospect it was more of a means of masking inadequacy.

Tuesday, Wednesday and Thursday were the student nights, while the temptation to blow the week's money on a Sunday night was ever present. I flirted with both socialism and Republicanism, combining nothing for everyone with dying for Ireland. Neither cause lasted very long. Drugs were mainly limited to hash and weed and because money was tight and supply was expensive, the quantities involved were small.

There was never a moment when I thought drinking three or four nights a week was cause for concern. In many ways it wasn't. Society didn't frown upon it, parents never questioned it and friends were all doing the same, if not more. Not much room for a reality check there, then. The first summer after college was spent in Cape Cod, as was the subsequent one, and in both cases drinking took on a daily regularity. I got work in an old hippie store called Yellow Orange, on Main Street in Falmouth, which sold Beatles T-shirts and Indian jewellery. I spent two summers behind the till, getting an education in the 1960s counterculture three decades after the event, and got to know an assortment of drifters who used the shop as a hangout. Included was Chris, an ex-fisherman, by this stage a heroin addict who had HIV/AIDS and sold the shop his monthly supply of uppers and downers in order to feed his habit. Others, such as Happy, a dope addict, or Christine, an amateur hairdresser, would stop by and buy the pills for $2 a go, asking for 'blue' or 'pink' toilet paper, depending on which ones they wanted. Steve, the owner, who missed out on Woodstock because all his staff took the day off, was glad of the company behind the counter and let me have the run of the place. I had thoughts of staying on and taking over the shop, perhaps writing the Great American Novel or picking up work on a fishing trawler out of Woods Hole in the off season. Steve introduced me to Eddie, an Irish-American mobster whose father had been shot dead by the Mafia in Boston on his tenth birthday. Eddie was on the Cape getting away from a life of hustling, and sold grass to keep things ticking over. I bought it in enough quantities to make sure I didn't have to pay for my own use, while Eddie would lecture me from time to time—'Hey Bryannn, you make sure you call your mudder in Oireland every week, ya hear?'

Another guy who came into the shop was Brian, an Irish-American who never worked a day in his life, living off his wife's income and eating in the local Chinese restaurant every day. He carried a photograph in his wallet of his dead father lying in his coffin, which always struck me as very odd.

Last I heard, Chris died, Happy was destitute, having moved from grass to crack, Christine was placed in a psychiatric hospital for murdering her daughter, and Brian still eats in the same Chinese restaurant every day. The shop is now a laundry store, with Steve working administration for a power-tripping college graduate, having failed to make astute investments down through the years. His only regret is not closing the shop for Woodstock.

Those summers were seen as time off from college, and so anything went and was excused. Bottles of Michelob, shots of tequila, bags of grass and insect bites were the extent to which I engaged with wider American culture outside Falmouth. For my nineteenth birthday, I decided to pierce my nose, DIY style. Several bottles of beer later and I applied an ice pack to the right nostril while smearing the whole area in Preparation H, which numbed the skin. A safety pin culled from behind a couch did the piercing, and from then on my right nostril was the proud owner of a gold stud, which grew up to be a silver ring when college started back. Presumably, by doing this I was rejecting conformity, although if I had my time back, I'd much rather have a scar-free nostril than rail against the 'system'.

My social thinking was all skewed, confirmed when I had to come back early from the States to repeat one of my subjects, which, appropriately enough, was sociology. Without having handed in any course work, I had gotten a respectable 23 per cent in my end-of-year exams. Not quite Noam Chomsky, but not a bad return for having missed every Friday morning seminar since the academic year began. I repeated and got the exam and was back in time to take my place on the annual rag week booze cruise. My only other memories of that rag week were dressing up as a student nurse for the Rags Ball and being thrown out of the nightclub for doing lines of speed in the female toilets.

Of my three years as an undergraduate I only have selective memories. I'm slightly wary of writers (James N. Frey take a bow) who can recall whole episodes involving their past drunken or drugged selves. If you indulged enough, then you shouldn't be able to remember! My attitude to drugs was that I could take or leave them. Invariably, of course, I took them, mostly cannabis and the occasional brew of magic mushrooms, later on ecstasy, cocaine, MDMA, acid and speed. There were some fellow students who entered Sir Henry's nightclub in first year only to re-emerge years later, 3 stone lighter and a lot more paranoid. I exposed myself to the dance scene in limited bursts, maybe every second Sunday night or on bank holiday weekends. I still had a fear of what drugs could do, and had seen several Ennis natives whose lives were destroyed young enough for me to realise I needed to creep up slowly on this particular animal.

There were exceptions, of course, including a heavy weekend in Amsterdam with a trainee doctor who was always up for a night out. We were staying with a Canadian friend, and had partied through the night in anticipation of the weekend's delights in the Dutch hedonistic oasis—Amsterdamaged, as we liked to call it. The three days there are now distilled in my mind to about four or five freeze frames. On day one we sourced herbal Ecstasy tablets and some cocaine from a local street chemist. The cocaine had the same effect as an anaesthetic from a dentist, albeit with a splitting headache thrown in for good measure. We got it into our heads that the herbal pills were having no effect so doubled up on dosage. The rest, as they say, is a bit of a blur. I remember ending up at a squat party in a former embassy somewhere and walking past neo-Nazis training their alsatian to attack members of the public. 'Come to Amsterdam and suppress the memories for a lifetime' should be the Dutch Tourist Board hook.

Other memories flash back every now and then—getting hit by a car outside Sir Henry's nightclub while on Ecstasy, limping off before the Guards arrived and spending the remainder of the night rolling around the Mardyke Cricket Pitch. Generally I felt socially awkward and found getting drunk or stoned a way to sidestep those feelings. I never would have seen it that way; at the time I was just doing whatever everyone else was.

———

Knuckling down in the second year of my studies, I finished the year with a respectable result, enough to suggest I had a shot at a decent degree. I was living with a girl at the time, a childhood sweetheart from the end of our schooldays in Ennis, and the stability of that relationship had an impact in limiting multiple benders in any given week. I had vague notions of becoming a teacher, so it was important to make some bit of an impression with second year's grades in order to secure the postgraduate course. In the main, I felt academically slight. Perhaps it came from being surrounded by a new intellectual discourse. Before attending university, my reading was mainly limited to Stephen King novels and whatever was demanded on the Leaving Cert curriculum. Hopkins appealed, so too Kavanagh, and on a personal level, I could relate to Othello's emotional frailty. I didn't know much about New Romanticism, right and left political argument, postcolonial theory or Bob Dylan. I probably couldn't even have told you what the main difference between Communism and capitalism was. I struggled with the apostrophe (still do!), and given that I was the first in my family to go down the academic road, I found it difficult to relay my experiences when home. Dislocated, both physically and psychologically, would be how best to describe it. Ours wasn't a bookish house in any event, which isn't a criticism, just a statement of fact. I was often struck by the reality that my dad worked hard in those early years to be able to keep the family finances on track and send me to college. Yet, the more time I spent in university, the further away from him in outlook and experience I got. We get on well now, but it took time, and in a way, and I guess this is the same for many parents of his generation, he was enabling the distance between us by virtue of the fact he was doing an honourable thing and financing my studies. Zadie Smith put it best when writing on her relationship with her father, and the feeling of alienation brought about by furthering her studies—'It was university wot dunnit,' she remarked.

At the time I could also be desperately socially awkward (what Irish person isn't at some level?). Walking into lecture theatres late was a major ordeal, and so too was walking past groups of colleagues in the bar and having to speak in small tutorial groups. It came from a feeling of inadequacy which would later be suppressed by the faux camaraderie of the bar scene. Back then, though, I was unsure and idealistic. Later in this book, Des Bishop talks about the generations of shame and guilt Irish people carry around with them, of how much of a wounded society we Irish are. Perhaps there was some of that, an inner feeling that here I was in university, debating the constructs of Beowulf or Banville's *Book of Evidence*, when only a few generations earlier my ancestors struggled for their very existence. Both my parents' families were from rural areas of west Clare, and would have had to contend with eviction, famine, war, and religious extremism. Perhaps, and not to get too Jungian on you here, that collective energy needed venting at some point, or was passed through the generations needing an outlet. Or maybe I was just unlucky—maybe I had emotional issues I didn't fully address and they hid like dormant fleas, waiting for the right personal habit to come along which they could attach themselves to and achieve liberty of sorts. Whatever the reasons, my drinking during those years changed and became more and more a badge of who I was and how I thought.

———

In final year I managed to rediscover quite a bit of self-discipline and from January that year onwards, I socialised very little. Course work was going well, complemented by two drama courses, which allowed for performance-based modules. Studying history sparked an interest in Irish land agitation, specifically the west Clare region where my ancestors had farmed. For my final year undergraduate thesis I focused on the Vandeleur Estate, part of the Kilrush Union, where a series of evictions occurred in the mid-nineteenth century. Halfway through, a history professor took me aside, enquiring whether or not I had thought of a career in academia. Of course I hadn't but said it would be something that appealed. And why wouldn't it, with the chance to spend a few more years milling about campus, living the student life? It became clear during the final year that I was headed for a good result, and still with vague notions of teaching at the end of it. I fell in with a good group, where academic competition was high, and we all strove for the elusive first-class degree, egging each other on. After the exams I headed to Edinburgh for a summer, where my drinking returned to pre-final-year levels, although this time there was an edge to it not present in previous years. Whiskey, and more specifically Canadian Club, became my drink of choice; I often downed shot after shot between rounds or on my own when no one else was looking. It enabled more erratic behaviour and blackouts became more and more frequent. I worked in a Mexican restaurant, usually in the mornings and evenings. In the afternoon, in fact every afternoon, I went to the Green Tree Bar, and found camaraderie there among the regulars at the counter, which appealed to me throughout my drinking life. Every day, the regulars participated in the Channel 4 game show 'Countdown', with military-style concentration— whoever got the conundrum was assured free drinks for the rest of the evening. I got it once, and it was a great day indeed. I longed to return to America and one night/early morning came home from an all-day whiskey session, packed my bags and informed my room-mates, including my girlfriend at the time, that I was heading for Boston and would see them all at Christmas in Ennis.

I had £45 and a passport in my pocket and it was close to 2 a.m. The cab driver dropped me to the departures terminal and wished me luck. A national airline had a flight to Boston the next day, so I queued at the check-in desk and waited for it to open. My plan was to tell them I had received very bad news from Amerikay, and that it was imperative I got on the next flight. To me, the plan was foolproof. While waiting for the desk to open, I fell asleep, and awoke several hours later, in the airport, with no recollection of how I got there or why I was queuing for a flight to Boston. A taxi ride later and I was back in bed, trying to sleep off the rest of my hangover, before my flatmates had got up for breakfast. Boston would have to wait.

The summer's drinking was fuelled by a variety of odd jobs—handing out flyers at nightclubs, waiting tables, working in factories. At the start of the summer, a few others and myself managed to bluff our way onto the British welfare system, and once every two weeks we took a bus to a local employment office to claim £88 benefit. This had usually been drunk by the time we arrived back to our rented accommodation.

The feelings of social awkwardness present since early adolescence accelerated during this period. I felt like I had something to say, but couldn't find ways of saying it. I never fully fitted in with whatever group I happened to be with, whether it was the daily drinkers on the Cowgate or the artists taking part in the Festival. I leaned on alcohol more and more as a means of unlocking social situations, of easing myself into company. It was a self-confidence thing. Perhaps it's an Irish thing. Every Sunday night we headed to Taste, a weekly event at the Honeycomb nightclub, and began experimenting more with Ecstasy. One, maybe two pills at most. The atmosphere was part hedonistic, part quasi-spiritual, summed up by the fact that doormen searched you down on arrival and then hugged you afterwards! I had vague notions that I should be part of some creative group—an actor, maybe, or a writer. The Dublin actor Mannix Flynn was in town that summer with his one-man show *Talking to the Wall*, and afterwards in the bar over vodkas and orange juice he got me thinking politically. The acting seed was planted in my head. Mainly, though, I honed my skill as a drinker. Scottish society welcomed the daily drinker into its open arms—every night there was a party, or even a quiet night in with plenty of stimulants.

The night of my twenty-first birthday was one of the first when

I began to eye alcohol suspiciously. A party had been organised to celebrate my coming of age, and I left early, whiskey fuelled, with a regular in the bar where I was working. I fell out of her bed, got up to go to the toilet and for some reason answered her phone, which was ringing. On the line was her boyfriend.

The rest of the summer was like that—chaotic and shambolic. I was becoming paranoid and increasingly erratic, and began a relationship of sorts with someone I shouldn't have begun a relationship of sorts with, if you know what I mean. My final exam results arrived in August and the hard work and abstinence had paid off. I was a few percentage points off a first-class degree, and had my choice of postgraduate courses. This further vindicated a hedonistic lifestyle. I now had an academic base to my drinking. I was Behan and Baudelaire all rolled into one. To celebrate I had half a Guinness with a shot of Canadian Club nestling in it and lit a £2 cigar. As Paul Calf noted, 'You can't buy class.' The next night I took my first acid trip, and it was one of those great nights when the entire world was all right. Shop aisles moulded into one, pots and pans danced Disney-like across kitchen floors, roses smiled and winked as I looked out in the morning. A good friend's tooth fell out, and left traces as it flew across the room. The comedown was in a downstairs jazz joint, my only memory of which is singing 'Me and Bobby McGee' with the band and waking up in someone's doorway.

By this stage the signs of what were to become major issues in my life were present. Drink was beginning to tease my morality, mess with my finances and lead to behavioural changes. It led to extreme paranoia in relationships, to unfaithfulness, and blurred the lines between the right thing to do and the wrong. Things like getting sick in a friend's apartment and walking out the door next morning, not bothering to clean it up—that's a sign. Drinking on my own all day and night and walking home bare-chested, shouting at passersby—another sign. Not keeping in touch with family except when finances were low—all indications of behaviour to come. It's difficult sometimes to relay the effect alcohol can have on you to another person—no one really knows the anguish and torment which swirl around in the head of a developing problem drinker. All society sees is the *bon vivant*, the engaging, entertaining you presented outwardly. It's also sometimes not the big signs that point to problems. For example, I once went a year not calling my grandparents—partly because of shame, and partly because, well, alcohol makes you self-obsessed. To someone on the outside of my life, outside my environment, that might not sound like a hanging offence. But all my summers were spent in part on my grandparents' farm, and most Sundays we visited. To suddenly not keep in contact—it was unexplainable behaviour. There were no arguments that led to my communication breakdown, just a total acceleration of self-serving obsession. With one grandparent left alive now, I look back on that period horrified. It still rankles with me. It might not be the destitute-on-the-streets story alcoholism sometimes results in, but to me, if you had told me years earlier that I would ignore family for a year for absolutely no reason, I wouldn't have believed it.

——

The history department in University College Cork, lured by the strength of my undergraduate work on land agitation in west Clare, offered me a Master's scholarship, paying my fees and giving me a monthly allowance. In return I would have to do some tutoring. I flicked a coin, literally, during one drunken afternoon drinking sangria on Cockburn Street in Edinburgh. Heads, I'd stay away from Ireland and maybe explore Europe more, or train to be a chef. I enjoyed the theatrics of commercial kitchens, if not the booze-fuelled comedowns after a night's work. Tails, I'd return to Cork, make a fist of academia and carry on with student life. Nineteenth-century Irish history was big at the time, and I had delivered a good undergraduate paper on aspects of the land struggle, which I felt an emotional connection to. The coin landed on tails, and I headed for Cork and a world of student loans, scholarships, daytime drinking and declining health. Not that Edinburgh would have been much different. Within weeks of starting my postgraduate I quickly realised I was out of my depth. Part of the deal was that I would have to teach third-year history students some of the finer points of eighteenth-century Irish and nineteenth-century European social history. In effect, I was now responsible for about 14 per cent of 80 history students' final year degree. As part of this process I would have to correct exam papers, complement course teaching, and be punctual and professional. I was 21 years old. My routine began to involve more and more daytime drinking, often with essays or course work deadlines missed, as I downed pints of Carlsberg accompanied by side orders of dry roasted peanuts in Cissy Young's Bar off College Road. I applied for and got a student loan, which facilitated more daytime drinking, while the lack of supervision a research Master's gives allowed me to go weeks, if not months, without any contact with my college supervisors. In essence, doing a postgraduate by research was all about giving me a licence to continue the exploits of college socialising for another two years.

My tutoring approach was shambolic—at one point I showed a video about the Irish land wars, which started 100 years after my course material finished—and this to students about to do their final year exams. Suffice to say, I wasn't exactly CS Lewis developing lifelong friendships with impressionable young minds eager to mine my intellect. During these years I had fewer and fewer ties with Ennis—Cork became my adopted homeland, taking me by the hand and introducing me to the world of sex, drink and indie music. Half way through the two-year Masters, close to Christmas, and following a period of sustained drinking, I began to feel ill. I was living in a Dickensian hovel—the type of accommodation where one wrong turn out of the bathroom upstairs and you ended up on the footpath. My diet consisted of alcohol, Capri-Suns (for vitamin c) and toasted sandwiches, and I headed home to Ennis with severe stomach pains. A few days later I was admitted to hospital and woke after Christmas in intensive care. The surgical staff had operated expecting to find an appendix that needed removing, but instead found a digestive system in need of some

TLC. At the time I couldn't really bring myself to tell the medical staff or my family that my system was faltering due to excessive drinking. So they carried out a whole range of tests, thinking for a time it might have been Crohn's disease. It was most likely a bout of ulcerative colitis, brought on by poor diet and lifestyle. In hospital, I passed the time hanging out with an English man who lived in Kerry and was in intensive care with a heart scare. He also had some great weed and as soon as I was able to hobble around, I joined him for a daily smoke in the small church on the hospital grounds. Medicine indeed.

Coming out of hospital I took things easy for the first few weeks, but soon after was back on the booze like before. The illness bought me time with college authorities, who were beginning to suspect I wasn't the great academic hope after all. After 13 months of postgraduate studies, I hadn't delivered a single line of my expected 40,000 words. In truth, I was getting tired of the pettiness of college life and having to photocopy an assistant lecturer's research notes by way of repaying my scholarship.

Around this time I took a job in the bar in the Everyman Palace Theatre on MacCurtain Street. Without my knowing it, my life choices were being determined by my dependence on, or need to be close to, a ready supply of alcohol.

I never for one minute contemplated socialising without alcohol and had this theory that I really only became myself after a few drinks. To my mind, there was no other way to tap into the inner me, who was far more interesting and appealing than the boring, socially awkward, sober self being presented. I had had an interest in acting since college days, appearing in a number of productions in the Granary Theatre. So the Everyman also gave me a chance to blag my way onto the stage. This was a time before late-night licences, when theatres had the advantage of being able to remain open later than nightclubs on weekend nights, or any night of the week for that matter, once a 'performance' was on in the bar area.

The late-night bar in the Everyman quickly attracted a tanked-up troupe of musicians and actors, of spoofers and drinkers. And that was only the bar staff. People like the late ballet master David Gordon became regulars. Dave hosted many a party in his flat at number 10 Roman Street, where pints of sherry and rum flowed. If a ballet group were in town, inevitably they ended up at Dave's, where young Russian ballerinas skirted across the sticky tiles to Dusty Springfield. It was hedonistic and heady, and a million miles from the rail tracks in Ennis. Dave once moved to the flat downstairs, 10A, and when I asked why, he replied, with acerbic wit, 'Oh, because I didn't like the neighbourhood, dahling.' It was that kind of vibe.

Because we didn't start till late on a Saturday night, often I was well oiled behind the bar during work, but so was everyone else. Many nights the drinking only really started after the last customer had left. This was probably the beginning of the most consistent period of my drinking, where tolerance levels rose and other areas of my life began to take second place to getting sozzled. I got a few small parts on the Everyman stage, decided I was the next Liam Neeson, ditched the postgraduate studies and the world of academia and waited for Hollywood to call. Surprisingly, the phone never rang.

In the years that followed I worked various jobs to make ends meet, including nighttime work in a cash-and-carry and weekend shifts impersonating Charlie Chaplin at children's parties. Things shifted in my personal life when, at the age of 23, I became a father. My son had barely entered the world when I was wetting his head, downing shots bleary-eyed, while baby and mother tried to get to sleep. I was out of it—a combination of the pressures leading up to the event and the copious amount of free drink offered by well-meaning acquaintances after. I ended up in hospital for two days, thanks to a run-down system which shouted stop. It was a pattern that would repeat itself later. Rather than embrace the responsibilities of fatherhood head on, I sought refuge in drinking binges, mostly at weekends and almost always with consequence. I had just about held onto friends from college, but my behaviour when drunk became more erratic, including running around the backyard naked when guests came over for dinner (I still can't figure that one out), and getting quite abusive and incoherent on nights out. I was unfaithful and untrustworthy and blackouts were becoming a regular occurrence. More and more I was getting frustrated with my personal and professional life. I started to blame others—luck, fate and circumstance—for the lack of opportunities afforded to me.

At the time, it seemed everyone was getting work in the information technology industry, and so I thought if I got myself on a career ladder, life would level out. Therefore, I signed up to do a programming course through FÁS, and half way through was offered a job as a computer programmer with a new startup company, which is just as well because I would have failed the course hands down had I stayed. My only contribution to the company was producing their annual pantomime, after which they realised I was no threat to Bill Gates and had to let me go. I began substitute teaching, mostly primary schools, and enjoyed the short days and lack of ongoing responsibility life as a replacement teacher brought with it. I also began to write articles and started to be published on a regular basis for the *Irish Examiner*, after the editor there, Tim Vaughan, took a punt on me. The media world was an attractive one, with liquid lunches and brewery launches still a feature of the scene. I got pally with a few editors who had the use of company credit cards, and long afternoons often turned into two-day binges. And yet no one at any point told me to cut down on my drinking. There was lots of other advice about getting a qualification or perhaps rethinking my domestic situation, but never once did someone refer to my drinking as cause for concern.

Several years in, the relationship with the mother of my child ended; I moved into an apartment I clearly couldn't afford, and lost myself in weekly drinking sprees and a replaying of my adolescence. I began dabbling in the music industry, and set up a company to promote acts around the country. I took particular interest in securing the drinks rider for the acts I was promoting, far more than in helping cultivate their rhythm. The lifestyle I fell into meant I was on the road four or five nights a week, which in turn gave me further licence to drink on a daily basis and be paid for it. My personality began to take on a nasty, ego-driven and arrogant slant.

On one occasion I was responsible for promoting a gig in a venue in the southeast, and had booked into a plush five-star castle after, where a girl I had met in a nightclub a few weeks earlier was to join me. It was all pie-in-the-sky stuff, running before crawling and all that. I had a meagre income, had probably lost my shirt on that night's gig, and there I was splashing out on an overnight in a plush resort. It was all about the pretence. A few drinks after the gig had ended, we headed for the hotel, which was accessible only by a private car ferry. A night porter had been waiting all night for us to arrive and once we approached the quay, the ferry began moving across the bay to meet us. The both of us were well tanked and the night was foggy so we drove towards the water's edge, except we misjudged it, and suddenly the car began filling with water. We scrambled out the back windows, up to our knees in muck and estuary water. The girl I was with had to call her ex-husband, who in turn called the car insurance company and organised for the vehicle to be towed out of the river. We arrived in the castle, dripping wet, covered in mud, demanding champagne. I thought I had arrived.

Throughout this period relations with my son were occasional at best and indifferent at worst. My finances were shambolic and I began to borrow heavily from the banks to support my fledgling music business. The Celtic Tiger was roaring loudly and financial institutions were only too happy to hand out loans based on the skimpiest of business plans. One bank manger in Cork signed off on a sizeable overdraft without needing me to call into the bank in person! I don't want it to sound like I'm blaming my financial mess-ups on the banking sector, but the fact is they were looser with the money than at probably any other time in the history of the State. Then again, I could be very convincing. The apartment I was renting ended in acrimony when I missed payments and moved into a shared house. The next two years were a haze of weeklong drinking sprees, all-night parties, and increasing loathing and self-hate. My parents had to bail me out of the music industry when I accrued debts to the tune of €20,000. My drink of choice was often double tequilas and pineapple juice, accompanied by steadily increasing amounts of cocaine and Ecstasy, often mid-week. Journalism offered me some level of income, but I was frequently behind on bills and child maintenance payments, and often missed deadlines and turned up at interviews the worse for wear. I passed it off by pretending I could turn things around at any moment if I really, really wanted.

The image portrayed of a hedonistic lifestyle is one of attractive 24-hour party people, living on the edge, rejecting 'Normal Street' and not wanting it any other way. The reality is often much starker, incorporating mental anguish, social paranoia, feelings of worthlessness and self-loathing. I was in a series of chaotic relationships, was afraid to answer the phone or even walk into a shop and relied on alcohol more as a means of avoiding reality and numbing day-to-day experience. I started getting blackouts at an early age, perhaps my first one on the night of my school's debs when a neighbour carried me home and I lay beside a bus getting sick while all the attendees watched. I could remember none of it the next morning, so quite early in my drinking, blackouts became a normal part of a night out. There were times when waking up I had to double-take, to quickly scan the recesses of my mind in order to piece together where I was and how I had gotten there. Moving between houses, my home life was in constant flux. I had certain places I stayed when I was late on rent, or had bills to pay, or needed time away, or wanted someone to lie beside. I began to develop regular night sweats. The first half-hour waking in the morning was the worst as dehydration intensified and parts of the night revealed themselves in periodic flashbacks. There was also the backtracking over finances. Financing drinking is a system in itself—a chaotic monetary world where everything and nothing can be rationalised. If it was a choice between food and drink, between rent and a night out, there was usually no contest.

During this period—indeed, throughout my drinking life—I

lived in some pretty squalid flats and houses. Perhaps in reaction to those days, I seldom go two or three days now without changing sheets. In the drinking days, though, there was no such order. It was all stained sheets, matted carpets and body odour, scraps of paper littering the ground, clothes kept in different houses and a shoebox the sum total of a decade's possessions. I think the only items I managed to hold onto were a well-thumbed collection of Paul Durcan's poetry and a Neil Young album—fragments of a decade of existence. And I didn't really see anything wrong with that.

The extent of your ambition—be it material, professional, social—is narrowed as alcohol and the impulse to self-medicate take over. Each time I moved home, I threw out whatever little I had accumulated. It was a way of starting anew, of attempting to reinvent myself. But it never quite worked, and the standard of accommodation I stayed in deteriorated over the course of four to five years. I had no savings, couldn't get it together to learn how to drive a car and was reliant on family to supplement whatever little income I had.

It was a shambolic life; a meandering, chancing, shell of an existence, and it takes it out of you psychologically.

But, throughout all this time, from that first drink on Stephen Corcoran's landing to the last, through multiple house moves and failed relationships, I never seriously thought that drink was an issue. I put my shortcomings and lack of progress in life down to emotional naivety. I put it down to having energy or drive that remained constantly unfulfilled. I put it down to intellectual shortcomings, to feelings of inadequacy and unrealistic expectations. At various points, I blamed the Famine, the Brits, the Church and my ancestry. I put it down to bad luck and lack of opportunity. But what I didn't put it down to was the one constant throughout all this period, the one ever-present aspect of my life, which I could always turn to in a crisis. I never pointed my finger at the gargle, the sauce, the hooch or the soup. It was always somebody or something else's fault. In my mind, the drink made things better, not worse.

Chapter 2
I said, 'Yes, Yes, Yes'

I'm not sure what came first—the excess or the exasperation. Both seemed to develop in tandem, to take flight together. But what I do know is that the crunch came in late summer 2004, when I was 28 years old. The writing had been on the wall for a year or so previously. Life had become chaotic. I couldn't be on my own for very long, and was barely clinging to the remainder of a once-promising media career. If I'm honest, my son took second place to my social life. I spent my time dodging a widening circle of ex-friends who wanted nothing more to do with me. Five years after leaving secondary school, I'd gone from being a scholarship student at University College Cork to stealing sausage rolls at the hot food counter at Tesco, just so I could save money for alcohol. I had it down to an art form. My usual tactic was to go into Tesco and pick up a shopping basket. I would then walk around the store filling the basket, as if I was doing my weekly shopping. Half way through, I stopped at the hot food counter and got a few chicken drumsticks, sausage rolls and maybe potato wedges. These were eaten on my way around, before depositing the basket with an employee and asking him/her to mind it while I went outside to withdraw more money. 'You only come in for one thing and suddenly you have a basket full,' I remember telling one dubious employee. I never returned with the money and this became a weekly, sometimes daily, occurrence. Thankfully, I was never apprehended—I suspect the embarrassment of having to go down because of a few drumsticks and a flaky sausage roll wouldn't have lent me much cred on the inside.

Towards the end, the highs were still fulfilling, but the lows were now more commonplace. Panic attacks began to set in, and I struggled to bring myself to look in the mirror. I drank on the breakdown of relationships. I drank on not being able to provide a proper home environment for my son. I drank out of loneliness. I drank because of insecurity, unfulfillment and arrogance. I drank because everyone else did. I drank to fit in. I drank out of frustration. I drank to feel normal. I drank and drank and drank and drank.

If I could get away without paying for anything that didn't involve alcohol, I did, and most of the time I owed money to someone or other. I surrounded myself with male and female companions in the same boat, hiding from some aspect of life. Two episodes brought home to me that the party had to stop. The first was at the end of a two-day drink-and-drug bender, which ended up at a get-together at a friend's house after closing hours. I was waiting on a delivery of Ecstasy, to keep the party going, when I witnessed a death. It was one of those shocking and traumatic, time-stood-still moments almost too monumental to take account of. To be honest, my first thoughts were whether or not I should still take the chemical delivery. Afterwards, I drank for two days— any excuse—and went to the funeral and sympathised with the family in a dazed state. Many months later, I gave a witness statement to Gardaí and broke down, in a windowless room with a sergeant nearing retirement scribbling frantically. Only then did I deal with what I had seen, did I realise the extent to which my life had become out of control and how fragile emotionally I was. It was a telling moment that brought me some way towards self-realisation.

The second moment that sticks out was in October 2004, at a World Cup qualifying soccer match in Paris. A group of us had decided to go to the game, taking the ferry over and driving down to Paris via Normandy. The drinking on the ferry was shocking, kind of like being at a Wolfe Tones concert for 20 hours. The 'best fans in the world' tag was nonsense—it was a drunken free-for-all.

Teenagers slept in the cinema cradling bottles of vodka; ferry staff were abused repeatedly, while the ship's internal PA system was taken over by drunks shouting obscenities. Marauding groups searched the cabins below for an empty bed to lie down in, while vomit and beer redecorated the carpets and decks. We found a quietish bar and sipped away nicely for the journey—the party had begun. I even managed a chorus of 'Boys in Green' and 'A Nation Once Again'. I was with older friends at the time, and was in a financial mess, barely scraping together what little money I could in the week previous to have enough to get through the couple of days' drinking in Paris. I overcame financial shortfalls by buying cheap bottles of wine. So while the others sat in restaurants or drank in bars, I hung around outside on the steps and drank, or joined them later with a bottle of wine concealed up my sleeve.

Inevitably, though, I was broke half way through the three-day trip, and so, one night, while my roommate slept, I helped myself to €100 from his wallet. I can still see myself doing it, carefully reaching under his bed for the wallet, expertly opening the button clasp that held it closed and sliding out one of the larger notes. Of that group, he's the only one I'm still in contact with and I've never been able to admit what I did. Although I'm sure he was aware of it next morning. It didn't really matter to me, though; I would have done anything to be able to continue drinking. Would have fucked over anyone, and not thought twice about it. There were countless other incidents, including getting barred from late-night clubs, abusing people verbally and not having any recollection next morning, and messing up relationships through serial infidelity.

The French weekend got to me, though. It got to me because I was with a group, all with stable relationships and steady incomes. For that weekend, at least, they were on the same level as me, out for a laugh and a good drink. Yet once the weekend ended they continued with their lives and I continued with mine. I had probably spent my week's rent and child maintenance and would spend the next week or two playing catchup, ducking and diving to try to cover the excess. It made me realise that my 'friends' could dip in and out of my life and take part in the gregarious bits. I was stuck with it 24/7. I couldn't opt out of it periodically. I remained unfulfilled, while they were laying life-markers—getting promoted, having children, buying houses. And yet, if you ask any of them today should I have stopped drinking, they will probably say I shouldn't have. But, as I've said, no one knows really the true torment of the mind of a problem drinker. You don't really even realise it yourself until long after the last hangover.

On several occasions I didn't turn up to collect my son as expected on Saturday mornings. My time with him was now condensed to 8-hour periods on a Saturday or Sunday—the stereotypical McDonald's dad. Because I didn't have a proper room for him in whatever house I happened to be staying in, I would drop him back again in the evening. My timekeeping and sense of days became more erratic. I was a father in name only, nothing of a moral guide and an increasing emotional void. This lasted for maybe two years, and looking back, I find it impossible to reconcile myself now to that vacant father figure I had become. And of course I drank on the shame and the guilt of that.

I recycled stories I had heard and passed them off as my own. I was a fraud. A phoney. A fantasist. It's alarming the depths to which human self-delusion can sink. I pretended to be writing a book, a sort of novel based on fact, or an 'observational take on Ireland's underbelly'. Other times, I assumed the guise of a big-shot music promoter, when the reality was that I had lost a small fortune due to negligence and bad management and chaotic bookkeeping. With no transport, when I was in the music game I would take a bus to gigs which I was promoting. If someone called me while I was en route, I'd pretend my car had broken down or that I had missed the train and was now having to endure the 'nightmare of a bus journey!' I'd say it out loud so the other people on the bus would be able to hear me. Yes, I was one of those incredibly annoying public-transport-grudging travellers. That's how screwed your head gets! The reality was that a car I did part own had been repossessed when I had left it into a garage for repairs and didn't have the money to retrieve it. It was embarrassing for my family, as a neighbour in Clare who owned a garage had organised the finance a year or so earlier. And now he had to call the finance company to arrange for it to be collected. His words were 'That fella can't even buy a breakfast. You'd better take it away.'

Of course there was a dawning realisation that I couldn't continue life the way it was. Living the type of life I did, you become increasingly isolated and there are few avenues left open to you. I thought about moving abroad (most problem drinkers do at some point), toyed with the idea of returning to college and finally tried to resurrect my media career.

An editor in Clare took a chance on me and gave me a few days a week working in a local newspaper. It would be a chance to wipe the slate clean, get away from Cork for a bit and have a regular income.

I was to start in Ennis on a Monday morning. Because relations with my family had broken down, I planned to leave Cork on Sunday afternoon and stay in a B&B in Ennis. A few media friends and a girl I was seeing at the time suggested meeting in the HI-B bar in Cork for a few last jars and a toast to new beginnings. The HI-B is a curious spot, with the eccentric owner Brian O'Donnell at the helm, barring everyone from coffee drinkers to mobile phone owners. (I once heard him shout 'SPACE INVADERS' at a couple who had been sitting on the only couch in the pub and nursing one drink for two hours.) It had a core group of daytime professional drinkers, and was a perfect oasis in the middle of an afternoon.

My plan was to have two drinks and make an afternoon bus, which would have me in Ennis for early evening, leaving plenty of time to get accommodation for the week sorted. Two drinks became three and the crowd got bigger and the bus time got later and later. I was now intent on making the last bus, at 7.25 p.m., which would have me in Ennis for half ten or thereabouts. By 8 p.m. I was still ordering drinks and had been drinking steadily for five hours. Not exactly ideal preparation for your first morning in a new job. At 9 p.m. I said my goodbyes, convinced my female companion to come with me, walked out the door and hailed a taxi on Patrick Street in Cork.

'Where we off to, lads?' the driver asked.

'Ennis, please,' I said, 'or Power's Pub in Clarecastle if we make last orders.'

The job lasted a matter of days, and I was back in Cork, drinking with the same media colleagues who a week earlier had toasted my departure. It was farcical. My living situation at this time was still chaotic. I had left a house where I was sharing in order to rent a place on my own, but a month or so in I arrived home to find the locks had been changed. I was already several weeks behind on the rent, and the letting agency decided to take action. After that, I stayed in different locations, mostly spare rooms, and kept whatever possessions I had held onto under the stairs of a friend's house. I used to change clothes and freshen up in public toilets, generally art galleries or theatres, washing my hair in the sink and giving under my arms a wipe with toilet soap and paper. When staff began to recognise me, I made up a story about the plumbing at home being on the blink. I did this for a few weeks, especially if I was in the middle of a bender and felt rough. Warped needs must.

——

One day, my parents, with whom relations had been strained for several months, called and told me they wanted to see me. I met them at St Finbarr's Hospital in Cork, where the rest of my family had arranged for a treatment counsellor to help them confront my drinking. I sat there, silent, as they expressed their concerns. None of them knew me any more. My brothers and sisters had no real relationship with me. They wanted to know if I was willing to do something about it. Would I go back on my own the following week and provide a urine sample? I probably would have tried anything at that stage. I had become 'sick and tired of being sick and tired', as the manual says, and I wanted out. After the consultation, my family headed for Clare and I went on a two-day pub crawl, ending up getting barred from my local late-night bar and crying my eyes out on a side street as dawn broke. As an 11-year-old child, watching JR Ewing in 'Dallas' reach for a crystal decanter full of whiskey and pour, you don't anticipate that that initial spark will lead to such inglorious finales. I knew myself at that point the game was up. I had been full of increasing self-loathing in the preceding weeks, would wake up with a sudden shock of anguish, frantically trying to remember the night previous or rampage through my pockets to find out how much money I had left. But it was the paranoia, the self-hatred and the insecurity that comes with heavy drinking that is rarely spoken of which got to me most of all. It's the feeling deep down that you know you're better than the existence you've settled for, but you know also that alcohol keeps those thoughts at bay. It waters the self-denial. It can also be a hell of a lot of fun, don't get me wrong. I had some great nights, days and early mornings because of alcohol and whatever else went with it. And if my parents hadn't intervened, who knows, I might even still be there in the land of mid-week benders and bullshit. I'd like to think, though, I'd have crawled out of the hole myself at some stage. Few people ever said to me, 'You should do something about your drinking,' but the thing is you end up surrounding yourself with the type of people who you know won't be upfront with you. You depend on them and vice versa. In Ireland, we have such a high tolerance for the problem drinker, and in the circles I was moving—arts and media—it's accepted even more.

I took on board what my family had said. I was the eldest and somehow meant to lead by example, yet here were my younger brother and sisters giving it to me straight. They didn't have a brother anymore. They couldn't believe a word I said. They said I had no interest in them and they were right. I had become completely self obsessed—my pub friends were my family by that time. It's pathetic and shameful to think back on it, but it's the truth.

I admitted that I was drinking too much and that it was a problem and gave a commitment to returning to the treatment service the following week. In the room with a family counsellor, I began discussing my life and how out of control it had become. By this stage, I had recently been evicted from another house I was renting, again after only six weeks, for non-payment of rent. I found this out one night, when I had persuaded a girl to come back for coffee and perhaps some third-leg boogey, only to realise all the locks had been changed. Having tried and failed to scale the outside wall, she quickly left in a cab and I settled into the coal shed. George Clooney eat your heart out. When I was sober and had some clarity on the situation, I was aware that alcohol had wreaked havoc on my life and my headspace. I knew that whatever difficulties life would have thrown up in the normal course of things were compounded 100 per cent by my overdependence on the booze.

But, as the definition goes, insanity is doing the same thing over and over and expecting different results. I kept waiting for my life to get going, and it never really did.

I remembered a boat trip to Croatia the previous summer. It was an organised trip and I was the only single person on a boat of couples for a week. Every night, when the captain went to bed, I would help myself to the tap of beer in the main galley. It got to the point where I even poured drinks for the rest of the passengers. But something happened on that trip. I became more withdrawn, more depressed. I was prone to crying in the middle of the day on my own. Looking back, I probably had something of a mini-breakdown half way between Split and Dubrovnik. I called my mother and told her I wanted out, that the life I was living had to give. I cried and apologised.

She organised for me to take a call from my local GP in Ennis, who told me to call to a doctor soon as I got home. I did and arrived in her surgery in a mess. She said she felt really sorry for me, gave me sleeping medication and advised me to call Alcoholics Anonymous. I called, arranged to go to a meeting, and expected to be cured by the time it finished. Some of it I could relate to—the emotional toll it takes, the madness and mayhem, the skewed logic. But much of it I just couldn't sit through—the acquired dialogue, the nostalgia and so on. I left and never went back. Six months of drinking later I was in a prefab on the grounds of St Finbarr's hospital and it was only then that I finally began owning up to my problems. I discussed my living situation and the type of friends I

was hanging around with. I talked about the panic attacks and the morbid thoughts. The counsellors listened compassionately, and following two or three meetings decided that outpatient treatment wasn't going to work for me. I was still moving in social circles where drink was freely available and partying was ongoing. Although I had managed to stay off the drink for over a week, it was only a matter of time before I would fall back into it again, they suggested. They asked would I commit to rehab for a month. To paraphrase the poet, I said, 'Yes, Yes, Yes.'

Mid-November 2004, and a friend dropped me off at Tabor Lodge Treatment Centre in West Cork, with a bag full of books and a head full of belligerence. To be honest, I was glad of the time out, of fresh sheets, three square meals a day and the chance to start over. My life had become one long hangover, punctuated by bouts of self-pity and short flashes of self-realisation. In Tabor Lodge, I wasn't quite as bad as other cases; some had been to jail, others begged on the streets, while one guy snatched handbags from old ladies. Yet all of them had been at my stage on the way up, and I could relate to enough of it to know I needed to be there. The thing with alcohol or any other dependence is that it is a progressive disease. I had an insight into the future, brother, and it was murky.

I met others in treatment I could relate to and we all sort of undertook this voyage of honesty together. It was a relief to be away from the mayhem of my life for a prolonged spell. A relief, too, to get something of a second chance with family and friends. For four weeks we had daily counselling sessions, where we accounted for our actions and looked at ways to prevent them recurring. I struggled with the word 'alcoholic' and began to question the tenets of Alcoholic Anonymous. We were shown a video of a priest on the 'Late Late Show' years earlier who took a broad definition—if drinking causes you problems, then you are an alcoholic. Christ, I thought, no one in Ireland was safe! Addiction treatment was searingly honest, and offered a multifaceted approach to understanding how my life had gotten so out of control. Yet I wasn't quite willing to buy into the one-size-fits-all formula necessary for addiction treatment. I found compulsory AA meetings tough going and couldn't relate to the adopted diction and repetitive slogans. How many of these stories were borrowed from each other, I wondered? We're a nostalgic race at the best of times; throw sentimentality into the mix and it felt, to me at least, like romantic war stories. That's a personal opinion, said in the knowledge that AA is the only thing that works for so many people.

What rehab gave me, most of all, was structure and space. There was daily meditation, and long walks in the surrounding country lanes, several hundred yards from the wooded centre. Three weeks in, several of us were taken to Kinsale for an AA meeting and that was as much contact with the outside world as we had up to that point. I could take phone calls, but noticeably, few of my 'friends' picked up the phone.

It wasn't without its lighter moments either—I established strong friendships, some of which endure to the present day. Several compulsive gamblers were part of the group, and often, serving dinner, I asked if their preference was for 'Beef or Salmon', a well-known racehorse at the time. Games of football at break time pitted the alcoholics against the drug addicts, while the first Friday night in the centre we were allowed watch a movie as a way of dealing with the weekend edginess. The choice, ironically enough, was *The Shawshank Redemption*. The most popular book doing the rounds in the centre, after the AA manual, was Howard Mark's *Mr Nice*, his account of his years as one of Europe's largest soft-drug dealers. Not exactly ideal reading for a bunch of addicts trying to turn their lives around, is it?

The toughest parts were when family members came to the centre to speak frankly about how my drinking had affected their lives. Or when I had to read out among the group what family and friends had to say about my drinking. There was nowhere to hide in those moments, which, of course, is exactly the point. As a group we confronted each other daily, probing our fellow addicts, and comparing and contrasting their stories with our own. It was a genuinely cathartic experience and a nurturing time spent bonding with people from outside my social and moral circle. In many ways it reaffirmed for me the universality of human experience.

For some people, the fact that I was attempting to give up drink meant the natural end of our friendship—if you could call it that. I remember one friend, who took me aside just as I was committing to the 28-day residential treatment programme. We met in a Cork bar at evening time, and he'd come up specially from the countryside to deliver his verdict. His take on it was that once I went in for treatment, it would always be a negative mark on my medical records and go against me in future life. He urged me to reconsider. All I needed was regular work, he said. A nine-to-five and everything would be fine. Needless to say, we haven't stayed in touch. There were others who drifted away naturally, and in many cases, I only realised afterwards the extent to which certain friendships were based around alcohol and how little I had in common with those people once I left that life behind. The natural break with many of these associations came on entering rehab and there were very few of those friendships I look back on as being of value.

Studies show that only a small percentage of addicts, some say one third, others say it's as low as 15 per cent, come out of treatment and remain sober or clean. Of the group of 18 people I was in treatment with, incorporating overeaters, gamblers, drug addicts and alcoholics, I know that some have committed suicide, others are in jail, and perhaps four or five maximum have remained on the straight and narrow.

I was one of the lucky ones. While I have every respect for Alcoholics Anonymous, I determined to stay sober largely of my own accord, and somehow it worked. I didn't have the staying power for weekly meetings or group sharing. I felt I had given up alcohol to leave that world and its experiences behind. There was also a religious aspect to the movement, mainly Catholic, which I didn't share, and while the association points out they are appealing to a God of 'your own understanding', I felt it was kind of like Sinn Féin saying they were not part of the IRA. But within AA are some incredible people, with amazing insights. Few other social groupings or organisations have the ability, through dialogue, to effect such change in their members, and I would encourage anyone in need to at least give it a try. After a month of treatment, two days before Christmas in 2004, I left Tabor Lodge. It was surreal re-engaging with Christmas decorations, packed streets and the reality of having to forage for myself again.

The key to my sustained sobriety was that I got lucky very quickly. Work opportunities came along within weeks of rehab ending, which enabled me to draw a clear link between sobriety and professional fulfilment. It also gave me the space to start afresh with friends and family and allowed me the breathing space to put things right in my personal life. A clear distinction was emerging between life with alcohol and life without. I could pay the rent. My son stayed over. I got a cat and went back playing golf. Simple things. The other key was that I managed to rent a nice house, a little outside the town centre, and a friend who had a similar outlook on life at the time rented a room. So we both became buffers for each other's sobriety, and for a year it was all staying in watching the television with Ballygowan and biscuits. That time away from socialising, though, was needed. I had to get to know myself again without the luxury of alcohol to access my emotions. Somehow, it worked out. My advice to anyone who feels addiction is taking over his or her life is to abandon ego and seek help. There is an alternative life available; it just takes a little while to find it, that's all.

When I look back now, my introduction to alcohol came through the usual routes—the odd bottle of Harp here or sips of Bacardi there. I'm not quite sure why my formative experiences led to issues in later life. All I know is that by the time my late twenties came around I'd come to rely more and more on alcohol as a means of social and personal interaction. The counsellors in rehab pointed to the fact that being the first in my family to pursue academia may have been a trigger. Others felt that becoming a father in my early twenties also had something to do with it, while my genetic makeup also played its part. I'm not sure any of those explanations are in any way valid. For me, I drank because I could, and more often than not because it made me feel better about myself. Simple as that, really. It was when it stopped making me feel better that things began to unravel. On reflection, my addiction was not particularly severe. I had no ongoing health problems, no criminal convictions, and at its height, I still had a few people around who were willing to invest their time in me. I didn't need a drink first thing in the morning and could go days, perhaps even a week, without it.

Some months back, I called a respected French journalist in Paris, asking for some contacts for a later chapter. I mentioned I was writing a book following experiences I wrote about in the *Irish Times* article. 'Oh yeah, I read that article—I didn't think you were an alcoholic, though,' she said.

So am I an alcoholic, then? Well, it depends on who's asking. The term 'alcoholic' has much more severe connotations in Ireland than in the United States, say. To be called an alcoholic in Ireland, a person has to be at the very rock bottom, at such a low point that society is no longer willing to tolerate their presence at the national party. So, in that context, in the extreme definition of the term, I probably don't fit the definition. But if an alcoholic is someone for whom drinking causes problems, then hands up, that's me. I'm more inclined towards the phrase 'problem drinker'—it has less social stigma and more practical connotations. And anyway, what's definition got to do with it?

As time has gone on and I've begun to fit into a life without alcohol, I'm less concerned with how many drinks I had at the height of my drinking. I'm less concerned with what grade of seriousness my problem was at. I'm less concerned with what people may think and with labelling.

What I know is this. When I left rehab, two days before Christmas in 2004, I had €60 in my pocket. I went from there to a mattress on the floor of a friend's spare room with two broken springs shooting up through the middle. I wouldn't have gotten so much as a stamp from the bank. My media career was in the doldrums. I had to re-engage with fatherhood responsibly. I was left with a handful of friends. In a social setting I had little to offer—my confidence was shot, I was still paranoid and had yet to feel wholly comfortable walking down the street.

Now, five years on, I'm a homeowner, with a wonderful career, a great family, a beautiful son, a partner, I enjoy conversation and I like me. I actually like me. So again, was I an alcoholic? I honestly don't know. But what I do know is that none of the things in my life right now were appearing on the horizon while I was falling out of late-night bars several nights a week. I know also that living a sober life is not that big a deal. It's a readjustment, sure, but it's very do-able readjustment if you get a break or two along the way. Having said that, living in Ireland it's easy to be carried along by the feeling that everyone else seemed to be drinking the same amount as I was and didn't have an issue. If you allow those thoughts to play themselves out, it can be dangerous. Even now when I say to people I don't drink because it was a problem, most people want to know how much I used to drink. They want to be able to quantify it in numerical terms. We have an obsession with quantity in Ireland when it comes to alcohol—how many pints? Was it every day? Did you spend much money? What was the most you ever drank?

But that line of questioning misses the point. It's the psychological debris that goes along with heavy drinking that wreaks most havoc on the individual. It's the feeling of worthlessness, the compromised morality, the loss of self and identity. Those are the things inside the mind of every problem drinker to a greater or lesser extent. I was never one to hide bottles under toilets or behind cupboards, because I didn't have to. I lived in a society that encourages you to be upfront about your excessive drinking.

In fact, there are probably thousands of people living the same sort of life I led and functioning away, seemingly content. For me, though, it got to a point where alcohol laid siege to my morality and sense of self-worth. I realised that at a young age, leaving plenty time to start afresh without too much irreparable damage to confront. Others are not so lucky.

Much of the time, I had an inner voice trying to convince me I was too young to have a drink problem. Sometimes I wondered if it wasn't all in my head. Perhaps if I got a nice girlfriend, or change of location, it would all be fine. When dependence becomes an issue, you start making all sorts of side deals with your fading conscience: maybe you can just cut down. Stick to the weekends or cut out spirits and just drink at home. An alcoholic is someone on a bridge with a brown paper bag and you start trying to convince yourself you're not nearly as bad as *those* people. But there will always be extremes in any illness, and it's up to the individual which stage you want to identify with.

When my career began to take off once again, as a journalist I was very conscious of speaking publicly about my views on alcohol and my personal experience. There are too many 'one-person' journalists in the world without me adding to the genre, I felt. But as time went on I felt compelled to make my views known, to not hide behind the fact that I drank and now don't. Although I have been careful not to let my sobriety become the dominant theme in my life, and even writing this, I'm conscious that I could become easily stereotyped as the ex-drinker willing to exploit his experience for a story. I also don't want to define myself simply by virtue of the fact that I don't drink.

So while I'm wary of adding to the canon of rehab stories churned out on an almost weekly basis, the interaction between sobriety and society in twenty-first-century Ireland remains a hush-hush affair. If you're sober in Ireland, the general message is to keep it to yourself and not spoil things for the rest of society. My reasons for putting my story down are simple: for years, I advanced my dependence on alcohol in a very public forum, whether it was staggering out of a bar mid-afternoon or turning up at a media launch the worse for wear. And now I'm supposed to keep schtum because I don't do any of that any more. Because now I don't fit the stereotype, and perhaps that makes people uncomfortable.

It's been five years since I spat out the hooch and turned my back on the world of libation. Five years, and not so much as a Bailey's cheesecake has passed my lips. While the first few months were undoubtedly tough going, now I don't have time to think about going out and getting hammered. I have seen and witnessed a different Ireland. It takes a bit of getting used to, and some situations I'll never be wholly comfortable with.

What I've found is that late-night socialising in Ireland is not exactly a spectator sport. When I do go out, it gets to a point, usually after 11 p.m. and before 12 p.m., when I make my excuses and leave. I don't like the smell of bars at closing time. I don't like spilled beer or soggy beer mats. I don't like elbows and staggering, pub talk and cover bands. All the things I would have loved about bars—the escapism, the camaraderie and the craic—I can't quite relate to anymore. If anything it's a little self-isolating. And I am first to admit, especially for the first year of my sobriety, I sometimes tended to shut myself off from the world. It's a hell of a lot easier than remaining socially active. Part of that is because I feel comfortable in my own skin now and enjoy the more mundane aspects of life.

But self-isolation is a danger, particularly in Ireland, where the pub, or more specifically alcohol, still plays such a central role. It's one of the reasons why AA meetings often become such a huge social outlet for some people in recovery. In many ways, they're recreating the best aspects of the pub in a dry setting. Compulsive 12-steppers or ex-addicts addicted to recovery, they exist, sure. When I rang Tabor Lodge and told them of my decision not to continue with weekly counselling and AA meetings, I remember them telling me it was the first step on the road to relapsing. They have to say that—it's a blanket approach. I get it. But deep down I think I knew that this was one I needed to work through on my own.

Sometimes, when I am out, I'm met with curiosity—the journalist who doesn't drink. Other times people feel self-conscious around me, and feel like I'm judging them purely by virtue of my sobriety. Maybe I am. And maybe it's hard not to. I find weddings hardest and least fun of all. There's a hedonistic attitude at weddings in Ireland. I've lost count of the number of times I've been at a wedding where people at the table will tell each other how drunk they're going to get. There's the church, the meal, a few speeches and then anything goes and conversation slips out the side door unnoticed. Perhaps it's because weddings are in a way a display of deep affection or romantic emotion and as a nation we need to get inebriated in order to be comfortable around those types of feelings, expressions and emotions.

Visiting relations in Galway recently, we went looking for a local bar to watch a soccer match. Entering the bar, early on a Sunday, one of the locals was fairly well on, wearing a knitted Aran hat and conducting several conversations at once. He'd clearly had a late one the night before and had an early start that morning to help recuperate. It turns out he was, until recently, the local bachelor in the village, who held up the bar most nights. He had his own seat at the bar, one of those kings-of-the-counter types. One night a lady sat on his seat while he was in the toilet. 'That's my seat,' he said on his return, and they hit it off. (Try turning that into an opera.) Anyway, they got married, and one of the conditions of the marriage was that he kept a handle on the drinking. The day we met him was the day after his wedding. It was 12.30 p.m. on a Sunday and he was completely inebriated. Not exactly a precursor to wedded bliss, is it?

——

My drink of choice these days is a sparkling water. If it's the weekend, I might ask for a dash of lime. You know, push the boat out. If people ask, I normally say I used to drink but was in danger of becoming a cliché, so I knocked it on the head. I sometimes go months without going to a bar. It's not that I consciously avoid the social scene, just that I have other priorities in my life now. I have never gone to a disco since I got sober. I don't see the point and have only been in late bars for afternoon coffee.

At the heart of the Irish experience, there is a need to filter the way we experience the world, be it through drink or drugs. Why is that? We're in danger of drinking ourselves into a national stupor. Reality alone is not enough, and issues of self-esteem, mixed with our newfound arrogance and recent deflation, have created an Ireland on an endless bender. My payback for living in this Ireland is to leave it as much as possible. In other countries, no one can point to the person standing at the bar drinking a sparkling water and say for certain, 'That's the alcoholic.' Can the same be said of Ireland? We have an all-or-nothing mentality that is playing itself out seemingly unchecked. Or perhaps I'm being overly sensitive, applying my own black-and-white relationship with alcohol to what should be a case of personal moderation for everyone. I'm more interested, though, in how Irish society copes with its problem drinkers. I'm interested in how they drink and why and what the consequences are. I started out on this book wanting to hear what the government is doing about it, what the health sector thinks and what happens in other countries. I want to hear how drinkers become drinkers, what make them tick and, for those who have given it up, how they find living in Ireland since getting sober. I was on a radio show recently and the researchers had gone onto the streets of Dublin to speak to people about drinking.

They asked one girl, 'Would you go out with someone who doesn't drink?

Her reply was 'No way.'

In how many other countries in the world would you get that type of response?

Abuse of alcohol caused me to lose my way, but also allowed me to find out who I am. The way I viewed the world had been filtered from the age of 15 onwards through alcohol, so in a very real sense, giving it up meant a re-engagement with adolescence. Relationships, conversation, weekends, sex, love and living all had to be re-learned.

I'd be lying, too, if I said I didn't think about reintroducing alcohol to my life from time to time, although it's rare. I counteract those thoughts by thinking back to when there was no real material or emotional buffer to prevent my drinking from becoming a problem. I didn't really know how to be a parent. I didn't know how to be a partner. I didn't know how to make a living. I had no money and no home. Now I have all those things, and have a tight control over my life. So, surely, the logic goes that if I was to start having an occasional gin and tonic, or a glass of good wine with a nice meal, what harm could it do? It's a debate not entirely resolved, except I think about what I have, and compare it to what I had, and don't feel prepared to take the risk. I also don't know what added benefit it would bring to my life. It might make certain social settings more informal, but it's not my fault that we Irish rely so much on alcohol as a means of social interaction. It's hard not to feel sometimes like I'm damaged goods or tainted stock or that there is an emotional lack at the core of my issues surrounding alcohol. Perhaps there's some truth in that. Alcohol is a mood-altering substance. It helps numb experience, helps fertilise fantasy and alter behaviour. But whatever the reasons for my drinking getting out of control, I'm glad I went through that experience. It's made me who I am today, to quote the cliché.

I used to dread the thought of going on holidays in the early stages of my sobriety. To me holidays were all about a licence to start drinking earlier and for longer. And as for interacting with locals, or dealing with social groupings, forget it—I could never have thought it possible without some form of Dutch courage. Now, though (cue birdsong), I have a newfound confidence, am constantly fascinated by new cultures and experiences, and have the clarity of mind to process those experiences.

In the last four years I have been all over the world, from eastern Congo to Mozambique, Kolkata to Tasmania. It's ironic, but now I wonder how the hell did I ever travel and take in another culture while I was drinking? I can't imagine waking up with a hangover, trying to negotiate a foreign tourist trail or simply plan a day's events. I've a newfound confidence now and am capable of a type of honest human interaction I never had before. I feel genuinely privileged. Relations with my family have never been better; I'm financially secure and personally content. More than that, though, I can look myself in the mirror again. In fact, I quite like what I see.

Sure, life can still throw its curveballs, but I'm far better able to bat them away *sans* alcohol. Life is probably less extreme and more on an even keel these days. Are there times when I want to express the darker side? Sure. Because I spent so many years screwing up my career, or fumbling about trying to find one that suited me, I have a tendency to overwork now. It can become an obsession and

I have to keep it in check. Genuinely, though, alcohol, or the pursuit of it, which for so many years was my *raison d'être*, rarely enters my head now. I feel like I've filed that aspect of my personality away, and, like I've said, look on it more as a lifestyle choice than a clinical or psychological one.

Having said that, there are still tricky moments, and times when I can feel alienated by Irish society to such an extent that assimilation would appear the easier option. Travelling abroad also still brings its own problems, especially on media trips, with any amount of free drink on offer. The thoughts begin to creep back. I could just have one final lash at it and no one would know. I wonder if I still have the same tolerance levels I had at the height of my drinking. It's not like you can unravel all the good things in your life in a 24-hour bender, is it? So what harm would it be to have one final hurrah? The feeling is there also when I'm out with friends at a good restaurant and they labour over the wine choices before selecting a fruity little red or a crispy white vintage.

I often compare my urges to that scene in the film *A Beautiful Mind* when Professor John Nash is attempting to recover from the delusions that have plagued his life. One hallucination, a little girl, still haunts him, and waits at the end of his college steps, arms outstretched, asking to be allowed back into his life. For me, alcohol is always there with its hands out, asking for one final embrace. I just choose to ignore it.

Des Bishop, Comedian

I was nineteen when I stopped drinking. I was probably about seventeen when I first said, 'I don't think I can actually drink.' In between there were a few stopping periods and during those periods when I tried to go out and socialise it was really uncomfortable.

In retrospect I was still trying to live a drinker's life, just not drinking. It's kind of miserable, really, plus I wasn't making any new friends with like-minded interests. Back then, most of my friends were pretty much one hundred per cent focused on drinking. After nineteen, when I stopped properly, I did stop going out for a while, but only for three or four months. Then when I moved back to Cork and got some new friends from the non-drinking side of things, we started going out together. We established a new thing which was nightclubs.

We went to nightclubs because we could dance all night and drinking didn't really come into it. Drinking in a nightclub didn't have the same allure as that nine o'clock in a smoky pub on a Saturday evening feeling. I guess that's kind of alluring. We just wanted to dance and have a good time. There was something quite easy about not drinking and dancing all night.

If you are to ask me what makes a problem drinker, well, there's a massive industry trying to answer that! Everyone has their own opinion. I mean, there is a lot of alcoholism in my family—I won't single out anyone—but generation after generation there's buckets of alcoholics. I would say seventy-five per cent of my relations have said that they have a problem.

My mother told me when I was fourteen that I was definitely going to become an alcoholic because she could see it already. This was after some evidence to suggest it was already happening, mind. She didn't just take me aside out of the blue and say, 'Son, you're going to be an alcoholic'! I didn't think much about it. It was one of the things going on around that time which led to me coming to Ireland.

In terms of the big question, I know that it can be an energy thing. It's kind of in families; whether it's genetic or not I don't know. With alcoholics or people who have a problem with drink, there is a lot of searching going on. Often they're looking for something more than is on offer and they find a bit of relief in booze. That journey takes them to a dark place. Even if you take the booze out of it, that search, or lack of something within a person, gets passed on from generation to generation.

Whether it manifests itself as shame, or some parent in middle-class families harbouring a kind of dysfunctional ambition, or the way you become overaware of yourself socially or the way that your family appears becomes the most important thing.

All these things I find to be quite abnormal and unhealthy. There are all these sort of energies bandying around the place with people who are searching for something that is not on offer. Often people are trying to escape this sense that something is not quite right and I guess it comes out in so many different ways. Definitely with alcoholics and addicts, most of them would express something along the lines of growing up with the sense that something is not quite right.

I definitely think in various different ways that's the energy that gets put out in a house. No one is aware of it, and it's not like parents decide, 'Well, what I'm going to do, I'm definitely going to make my child feel bad for no reason whatsoever!' It just tends to happen.

The term 'alcoholic', in America people don't have a problem with the word. Somebody who decides they drink way too much wine after their dinner and it is a problem in their lives can call themselves an alcoholic without any labelling going on. So for me, I don't have a problem with the term. Then again I'm thirteen and a half years without drinking. I'm thirteen and a half years having discussions like this. I'm thirteen and a half years surrounded by people who have no problem calling themselves alcoholics.

I went to Alcoholics Anonymous and Narcotics Anonymous and

I have stayed actively involved in those places to this day. I got a whole new rack of friends. The greatest thing is a lot of the people that I drank with disappeared, but a lot of them didn't because after a while after I re-established myself as a human being. The people that were just genuine friends, and we weren't just bound solely by drink, they're all still good friends of mine today. I guess one of the ways I established myself is that I found a new life and new interests. More important, I really tried to challenge and remain vigilant around the things that were behind my drinking.

In a way I agree with you that the term 'alcoholic' has become redundant because alcohol is not the problem; addiction is not even the problem. None of these things were actually the problem. The problem is, people have things running around in them that motivate their behaviour.

When you take away the drugs and alcohol there are still other things that can creep up in your life that become a problem so I was constantly trying to be vigilant through all of those things. I lead a pretty normal life—it's not like every day I'm trying to focus on whether or not a situation is a negative or positive thing in my life. But, at the same time, I don't take for granted that I have a tendency towards taking things a little bit too far, for whatever reason, it just naturally kicks up in me. So I have to remain on top of all those things.

But also, without realising it, my lifestyle is completely different. I find that for many people in their thirties, their lifestyle is a little more mature and less centred around going out and getting pissed anyway.

I was never really exasperated living in Ireland sober, mainly because I very quickly established a new lifestyle which had nothing to do with the pub. When we went to the pub, it was to meet girls and that was the only reason. We quickly discovered that life doesn't have to be catered around the pub at all. People always say, 'Is it not really hard in Ireland?' I say no, you only perceive it as being hard because you don't look at all the other options, and that comes from social conditioning.

Having said that, though . . . I love going to the pub now. Sometimes there's nothing I like more than being down in west Clare. There's a great pub in Lisdoonvarna that does hot smoked salmon. I can sit in there and have a cup of tea—I'll even talk to an auld fella at the bar who probably is an alcoholic (none of my business). I love that too, but at the same time it is one of many things and places I would go to. It's easier now anyway; there are so many more cafés.

When people think about a social life they still often think about going to the pub. I think there are definitely greater options there now. We never thought we needed more options in those early years of not drinking. We drove down to west Cork and did stuff all the time, like going down to the Buddhist retreat centre, and did different things. And then you meet new people and you realise there so many things you can do.

I have to say now, I'm touring around all the time and I'm on my own looking for places to go and hide away for an hour or two, there's definitely more cafes. Even in pubs, you'll always get a decent bit of lunch and you'll always get a real cup of coffee now, whereas fifteen years ago it was always the instant type in the cup. Now it's decent coffee and probably more comfortable seats and the sense that fifty per cent of the people are there to read the paper and have a sandwich and not to get inebriated.

I think sometimes people have a foggy notion of nostalgia. People are constantly going on about how it wasn't like this twenty years ago and all of that. I came here in 1990 and I remember being blown away by the social life. I loved the drinking but was too young to get access to bars. When I went away with my cousins to parties, I was blown away by the amount of drinking, especially by adults.

I couldn't believe the amount of drinking they were all doing. It was a million miles from what I had I grown up in. My parents didn't drink, but even the Americans that I knew that did drink—never would they have ever been that inebriated around their children. There were ferocious amounts of drinking in Ireland when I came here. And people say it wasn't like this years ago, and I would say,

'What are you talking about?!'

They say young people didn't drink, but that's because they didn't have any money. They couldn't wait to do what the adults were doing. I sometimes question this nostalgia around the healthiness of drinking—there was so much darkness in Ireland in that time that people were trying to escape that I would question those memories.

I remember when I was in school someone came in to talk to us about booze. But it's usually the same thing, some alcoholic tells their story. A lot of the time teenagers can't identify with that. I mean, it worked out for me as I remember going up to the guy when I was eighteen and saying, 'Take me to an AA meeting!'

I was particularly bad. Really what you need to do is to get it into kids' heads that later on if it starts to become a problem they might think about what they learned at an earlier stage.

When I went in to the priest in our school after the alcoholic came to talk to us, I asked to leave early on the following Friday to be able to go to an AA meeting. He said, 'But you can't be an alcoholic, you're too young.'

The problem is that there is not enough talking about it, but then again, like, what can teachers say? The majority of those teachers, and this is not a judgment, probably find that their social life centres around alcohol, so what advice are they going to give?

Most of those kids are thinking, 'I can't wait to go to college so I can properly, like, give it a lash,' that's what they're thinking. It's really much more of a societal shift that needs to happen.

The government are focusing on all the wrong things. They're focusing on alcohol advertising and they constantly push this thing that the problem is young people drinking. Like as if that's the fucking problem. Just because those problems are maybe more apparent and those problems are out there on the street, people think it's an outrage.

So suddenly it's all about alcohol advertising and drinks sponsorship in sport? As if any regulation is really going to make any difference—like . . . pub closing times and so on. All the time they're trying to chaperone people's drinking—it's not going to happen. It's like the Bull McCabe trying to fight back the ocean—it isn't going to have an effect.

I think the focus should be so much more on people's social and emotional health around drinking. I'd love to see somebody put out an advertisement here saying:

'Irish people: Feeling like you lack self-confidence? Feeling like you have a social awkwardness? Feeling like you always thought there was something niggling inside you that says, "I'm not quite good enough?" Ever had those feelings? Those are probably the things you're drinking off . . .'

I find most people, if you get them into an honest situation where it is quiet, they will admit loads of things to you that they're not comfortable with about themselves. But if you're in a cycle going out every weekend and getting pissed, everything is meaningless in a way, or if there is any supposedly meaningful discourse it's usually full of debate. But there's nothing quiet or a bit honest there.

I've been all over the world and I've never seen a society with more blatant dysfunction on show than Ireland. Ireland is a wounded society.

Now, with the recession, it's like the end of our adolescence. Ireland had a long childhood where it had this discipline factor coming in from all these negative sources, and then all of a sudden you get fifteen years of liberation and people are acting out all over the place, which is totally fine.

But now you're going to have to stop, realise, right, we're heading into adulthood here, let's get real. Let's see where we're really at.

So I do think Irish society is really wounded. And I mean, I love it and never want to leave. I can totally identify with the wounding! But I think if they focused a little more on how everybody is wounded and a little bit less on how everyone is being themselves in a wounded situation we would get somewhere.

It has little to do with drink and everything to do with hundreds of years of people being adversely affected by the elements.

I mean, do people not think that there was a spiritual continuum if you had your culture ripped from underneath you? And then you have emigration and after the Famine, one hundred and fifty years of ridiculous guidance from the Church, riddled with shame and feeling bad about everything, to the point by the 1930s and '40s, you have a completely stifled society. That's not that long ago. And all these things are out there. I'm not trying to assign blame, but that's what's in society, let alone families, where you have internal dysfunction and abuse and so on. I believe that if you were able to discern the percentage of population in Ireland with family issues, it would be higher in Ireland than in so many other countries in the world. That's a total assumption, by the way, and if I turn out to be wrong in the future, then I'll be first to admit I got it wrong.

Getting back to my own personal story, I very rarely talk publicly about my association with either AA or NA. They're both pretty un-boastful organisations.

People within it can be judgmental but actually the organisation itself is not that judgmental. I hear the cliché thrown about of members being addicted to recovery and so on, but that is not the case. I'm not addicted to recovery. I'm thirteen years sober and live a totally open life. I help others when I can. I go to meetings go to talk about today. Everybody needs support and there's no real addiction in that. Some people go to play bridge as a social outlet—I go to meetings as a social outlet. I go to meetings to see my friends and to talk about real things that are going on in my life today. Together we are kind of driving each other, you know, to some sort of ideal or belief that there is something more we can do to make our lives better.

I'm no defender of NA and AA and in a sense I've heard all the things that people use to criticise those organisations. I say they are just as valid as the things I'll say against what is said. I think . . . there are many ways to engage in being a non-drinker and staying clean. Definitely the formula of NA and AA, which are voluntary organisations that exist all over the world, is a seriously healthy one.

If you asked me about this ten years ago, I would have said nothing else really works and if you don't do it this way you're probably hiding out. I don't believe any of that any more. I just believe that it really works for me. It works for a lot of others and it's a really healthy way, but at the same time I believe that there are loads of other ways.

But just in terms of people saying you get addicted to recovery and all these things, that is pretty much nonsense. You see, you can get addicted to anything. That can't stop you going down a path— people would say, 'Oh, well, then you shouldn't exercise when you get clean because then you can get addicted to exercise.' Yeah, but you could *not* get addicted to it too, and even if you did start to overexercise eventually you would reach a rock bottom of that.

The point is that if you go by the guides of the fellowship it guides you away from anything like it becoming the dominant theme in your life. Those organisations don't exist to suck you in, they actually exist to give you freedom, and so if you end up in a situation where it becomes the dominant theme in your life, then you're not doing it right.

That viewpoint about the fellowship, though, is out there and is a kind of short-term observance of what you think might be going on. People don't really know what it's about when they say that. And sure there are some people that are hiding out in AA or NA, but good luck to them, it's up to them. That's not because AA did that to them, it's just because they decide after a couple of months that they want to replicate the pub in an AA group. What are you going to do? Take them out? It's whatever people want it to be.

When I think back, I was so bloody young when I stopped drinking that I don't see professional fulfilment playing a role in my sobriety. Academically I had to repeat first year and even sober I again failed sociology. That's because I was back in college, where I was a part-time student and a full-time person trying to get my life back in order. Making new friends with the intention of going to meetings or going away for weekends became my full-time concerns for a while. But I don't regret that.

It was someone I met through recovery that got me into comedy. I never did a gig when I was drinking—I was nearly three years sober when I did my first gig here in Cork.

Not that I think recovery got me into comedy, but I do think that the way you open yourself up to a new energy, a new road, all those things came from that turn I took.

I believe the energies in your life happen as a result of you taking action and you build up this momentum. I do believe that everything that led to this path came from the momentum of not drinking.

Being sober in Irish society is not something that overly concerns me. On one level you always get the 'Why don't you drink?' comments, often from people that are probably a little uncomfortable with their drinking. They either tend to push you away or else they sort of want to half-engage with you about it, without telling you anything. But you half-know what they're saying and it can be awkward because maybe you're out in [a] social setting just trying to have a good time.

In my twenties, a lot of the time buddies of mine who were drinkers and might be going out on a big session wouldn't call me, which was totally fine. But then, at the same time, they're bonding a lot with that, so your relationships tend to get strained because there's this bonding thing that you don't have and feel separate to.

I think, though, that bonding becomes less important as you get older. What becomes more important is getting together and playing a game of squash or a game of golf and maybe going over to the house for dinner or maybe going away a bit more.

For instance, I couldn't imagine travelling nowadays, or going on holidays, and drinking. I would be on my own in Thailand and the night maybe would start out great, but later I'd be throwing a table across the room or some chaotic thing that would come over me. Then in the morning you'd wake up in a hostel and you'd have to leave the town because you are the insane one that nobody cares about. So I couldn't even imagine what that would be like.

Not drinking, I don't ever feel like I'm missing anything. I don't see what the big deal is—I don't get it. Obviously when I was drinking, I didn't think about any of this. I just thought that I want to drink and I didn't have any questions in my head. Nowadays I often look at people and say, 'What do you think is fun about this at all?' There's nothing in this. But once you're in that cycle you don't question it. Drinking is such an overrated thing, it's not even funny. It's amazing how much energy is given to it in this country.

In the world of performing and arts, there is this myth out there if you stop your suffering your creativity gets knocked back. I don't know anyone in my personal experience whose life has not got infinitely better, more productive and more creative, when they stopped drinking. I could name loads of people—when they stopped drinking their creativity blossomed. Then, on another level, it's not a uniquely Irish thing. It's a strange ideal that people would idealise or put on a pedestal this constant of the romantic version of the suffering artist or the lonely drinking figure. Only in Ireland would you idolise or consider it a goal to become someone who is miserable and suffering. I think when people hold up that ideal they don't realise that behind the Brendan Behans and Patrick Kavanaghs there is ferocious pain that these people will probably never experience. There's nothing romantic about it.

People hold up Shane MacGowan as this oracle. I find Shane MacGowan so sad that it makes me cry sometimes. I find it even sadder that people would enable this Greek tragedy to continue in public view.

I find that terrible. Alcoholism to me is a brutal, brutal disease that destroys families. Yet people can hold up these figures as if they are heroes. To me, they're not heroes. And they're not villains either—they're just sad, sad characters.

If a writer needs a few glasses of wine to write, then how insecure do you have to be in your own creativity to think that it comes from three glasses of wine?

As if you never have an idea when on a train after your first cup of coffee that wasn't as valid as the idea someone comes up with after three glasses of wine. What I would say is that that writer is probably riddled with fear and self-doubt and totally critical in his own head, which we all struggle with in terms of creativity. The censorship that goes on in our own mind with this committee that doesn't exist, telling us that things are shit. The writer who needs drink to write probably can't shut them off until he has three glasses of wine. But it's easy to shut them off if you learn how to do it. That's just a confidence thing. It's the same as someone saying to me, 'Oh, well, I started drinking because I didn't have the confidence to talk to women and once I had a few pints, I could talk to women. Little did I know that twenty years later I'd be getting kicked out of my house, my children crying and so on.' You hear that story in so many different ways.

The thing about life is it is so much more exhilarating to find out how to challenge your fears without substance. Yet with addicts, every day you're dousing yourself and taking away the joy of life by saying, 'I use this to get me through it.' But it doesn't have to be like that.

Chapter 3
A Day in the Life

It's 10 a.m. on Monday morning in a rural village in north Tipperary. The owner of the bar is putting on the kettle, stocking the shelves and getting ready for his morning shift of regulars. Every bar has them—the core group of daytime drinkers who prop up the bar and the profits and are first in and often last out. There are only two bars left in the village now—the drink-driving/smoking ban has seen to the closure of others, or perhaps the area was overpopulated by public houses in the past.

I hadn't spent a day in a bar for a few years and wanted to observe a group of daytime drinkers in a traditional Irish setting. Looking back, there was a time I could think of nothing better to do with a day than plonk myself on a high stool. Often I'd start off with a white wine (to convince myself I wasn't drinking, because wine, as any regular drinker will tell you, isn't alcohol at all), switch to pints mid-afternoon and finish the evening with gin and tonics or tequilas and grapefruit. If the truth be told, I was a little apprehensive and slightly edgy at the prospect of entering a bar again for a whole day. For the first year after giving up the drink, I didn't really set foot inside a bar, beyond a quick hello and perhaps a mineral. I was worried who might see me and afraid that someone could misinterpret the situation and get word out I was back on the gargle. Even now, almost five years on, I have a two- or three-hour limit on how long I can spend in a bar. Having said that, there is one bar I feel totally comfortable in (cue prepaid endorsement)—the Corner House on Coburg Street in Cork. It's a funny one because I would have done a fair bit of drinking in the bar in the past. But I feel relaxed there because most of the staff and regulars know my story and so the tension when I approach the bar isn't there as it might be in other places (begin Cheers soundtrack—'Making your way in the world today . . .'). If I ordered a pint, in other words, there would be raised eyebrows and a disapproving reaction (*everybody*: 'Taking a break from all your worries sure would help a lot'). The bartenders are safekeepers of my sobriety by virtue of the fact that they are aware of my circumstances (chorus: 'Where everybody knows your name'). Also, Fergal, the owner, does a great pot of coffee with a free chocolate thrown in. And if that doesn't grab you, he only charges €1.50 for a Ballygowan (and that includes a dash of lime). Carlsberg definitely don't do sober joints, but if they did . . .

In most places, there's a seemingly carefree abandon to the life of a daytime drinker, with the pub like a kindly uncle who wraps his arms around you and protects you from the outside world. Call it safety in declining numbers. The life of the daytime drinker, though, is one of avoidance, of dodging calls and dinners, of skewed budgeting and yesterday's clothes. It's a life of empty retching and remorse, of diarrhoea, headaches, hangovers, holding on to emotions you should have let go of a long time ago and lost causes. The smoking ban has interrupted that closed world, brought the daytime drinker outside the intoxicated womb for nicotine inhales, holding him up against regular life. I used to notice it most outside the early houses near Cork's Union Quay. Charlie's Bar, for instance, where early-morning drinkers were forced to take their cigarette breaks outside the door, in the heart of the business and legal district. Many of them would have been familiar with the family law courts around the corner or the maintenance payments office next door. And here they were, being forced to display their antisocial antics in front of society. Charlie's quickly added a smoking room at the back of the bar, thereby eliminating the need for early-morning punters to see or be seen. The hidden life of the daytime drinker could remain hidden for another while longer.

The drinking in the bar on the Monday morning I visited was progressive and steady. Four regulars stood or sat at the bar—one of them going through four pints of Carlsberg in 46 minutes, while another had six large bottles of Guinness in a little over an hour. They weren't exactly sipping it, in other words. The conversation was of bicycles left behind after a night's drinking, of neighbouring villages where bars close at 3 p.m. on a Sunday, and memories of a regular who had passed away weeks earlier. Some of them kept their money in glasses cases, while others carefully counted out loose change—leftover debris from the weekend's drinking. I was told a story of one regular who went to a local doctor with a pain in his side. It was suggested by the medic that this could be his liver in need of help.

'How many units of alcohol would you have a week?' asked the doctor. 'Jesus, I don't know,' said the regular, 'maybe a hundred?'

'You realise 2 units makes up one pint?'

'Better make that a hundred and fifty, so.'

(This reminded me of a similar tale from Mallow in Cork, of a hardened drinker visiting his GP with severe stomach pains. The doctor, knowing full well what lay behind his patient's medical problems, asked, 'How many pints would you drink in an evening?'

'No idea, Doctor,' came the reply.

'Could we say three or four?' probed the medic.

'Jesus, I'd spill that in a night,' came the reply.)

The bar was traditional in form and function—a lounge in one part and a small bar in another, with room for a pool table and plenty big enough to cater for functions. Old LPs vied for wall space with GAA snapshots from intercounty and local teams. In all, the bar caters for up to 20 steady daytime drinkers, some of whom clock in early and might return at different intervals throughout the day. By 1.30 p.m., the racing channel was turned on and bets were being placed. The clientele were made up of a patchwork of ruddy, lined faces, patched jackets, unkempt hair and shaky hands. Mostly the age profile was over 40, single, and hardened, with only one female popping in for a coffee while I was present. There was a steady stream walking in and out, answering phones, churning bottom lips, perhaps trying to erase things to do from their memories as they faced into another fresh pint.

They looked pained and pleasured and, if I'm honest, part of me would have loved to have pulled my barstool close, swapped my tea for a crisp, cold pint of Carlsberg and joined in the craic. I began to visualise that moment of holy transition from the remnants of one pint to a freshly poured one. The feeling as the beer began to settle into an empty stomach, having taken time to get comfortable in its surroundings. The writer Eugene O'Brien has a line in the play *Eden*, when one of the characters is having the first pint of the morning after a heavy night and remarks that the new beer is meeting the old beer and both are getting on just fine. I could see that moment in the faces of the regulars, as that first-mouthful grimace turned to a grin, and the shakes began to recede.

The barmaid was like Nurse Ratched, carefully measuring out the medicine (mostly large bottles of stout) with the inmates (regulars) chatting amicably through the dispensing.

The inmates in this case were all bad teeth and tense expressions, unfurling crumpled notes, checking watches and grabbing the barmaid's eye in a sort of wink-and-elbow language of transaction. Few of them asked for a drink by name, their liquid leanings known intimately to the staff behind the dispensary.

By 2.17 p.m., one of the regulars, now on his sixth pint of the day, was close to not being offered any more.

'Have you anything to tell me?' he asked the bar worker.

'No, have you?' came the reply, as he was given his last pint.

He had been in the bar since 10.50 a.m. that morning and was beginning to get a little what we might call rowdy. Perhaps sensing he had become centre of attention, he made his first statement of the day:

'Do you remember back the years, there was a show, "Some Mothers Do 'Ave 'Em"?'

'I do,' I said.

'Well by Christ she had a right one when she had me!'

I couldn't argue with him, really.

While I was sitting there wondering whether I should introduce myself or remain in the background observing, one guy walked over and asked how the book was going. My cover was blown (aside from the fake glasses and nose, the tape recorder and frantic note-taking probably gave the game away).

Without prompting, 'John' began to tell me his life story, beginning with the blunt fact that he had tried to take his own life three times over the past few years. The last time was in Dungarvan, he said, when he had to be fished out of the water. While he was telling me his story, his mobile rang every few minutes—his 18-year-old daughter trying to get him home. Five years earlier his relationship with his daughter's mother had broken up. Had he ever tried to knock the drink on the head, I asked.

'I managed to stay off the drink for about nine weeks after I had residential treatment; that's as long as I ever lasted.'

A fortnight earlier, John had again tried to stay off the booze, but broke out and was now on his fourth day of solid drinking. He had a rising list of medical conditions, including a swollen heart, and his daughter was partly calling to ensure he took his medication and didn't miss an appointment with a specialist later in the week. He had missed the previous two appointments. 'The doctor told me it's not entirely my fault,' he said, 'it's more the country I live in. I know everything my daughter is saying is right but I can't hear her because of the drink. Once I get a taste for it, that's it.'

He worked here and there wherever he could, but arthritis prevented him from working a regular week. He sounded resigned to his fate. 'Treatment wouldn't work for me, I tried it,' he said.

When I asked him how many drinks per day he got through, he said he wasn't able to answer. 'I might work a few hours and help out around the place here and then I could drink for another few hours. My daughter is on the phone saying I will have to go back to treatment, but I can't relate to the people in there. A lot of the men are violent with the drink but not me. Looking back on my life, drink just got the better of me.'

The fact that 'John' was willing to speak openly about his addiction and his attempts to tackle it confirmed something I have noticed over the past few years—that drinkers were becoming more open about alcohol-associated illnesses. The bar worker and wife of the owner confirmed as much, when I brought up the subject with her. 'I don't think there is as much of a stigma anymore. I know the lads in during the day will still slag about it. Some of them might have been in psychiatric wards but will see that more for depression rather than drink. I think the stigma thing is going.'

Getting treatment is one thing, though; being able to remain sober after treatment is the tricky part. 'It's extremely hard if they don't have supports,' said the bar worker, 'unless a wife or someone is getting onto you about it, it is a real battle. If you have a job and stuff then fine, you may be able to make it. The difference is that you need to have another life outside of the pub. For guys who don't have another outlet, what are you going to do? Are you going to say is it worth my while to sit here? I imagine if I was in their place I would be thinking, so what will I do, sit at home seven nights a week?'

The question of how these regulars finance their drinking lifestyle is beginning to resonate more, now that the economic boom has been left behind. But where there's a wino, there's a way. 'One of the guys coming into us is drinking some amount at the moment and I've been thinking, where is he getting the money?' said the bar worker. 'Someone told me he is selling cigarettes on the black market. A lot of people are on the dole and they work cash in hand. This worked very well before the recession and they'd get a few jobs from a builder and get very well paid. So if they work two days [a] week, it'd be enough. Lately one of the guys worked a bank holiday Monday and he said to me, "I never worked a Monday in my life, not to mention a bank holiday!" That will tell you how bad it's gone. But that's how they fund it, they're milking a system and these people are all on rent allowance and so on. Those that have kids, I can't say I ever see the kids suffer financially. I don't know how they fund things like that—Christmas comes and is sorted, and so are communions and confirmations. I don't know whether they borrow money but you don't see them skint very often. Lately a bit, perhaps, but I hadn't seen it for years.'

John's approach stayed with me. As an ex-drinker you're constantly having to stop yourself assuming the moral high ground and judging. You forget sometimes how ridiculous the plight of the problem drinker is and the lack of control and awareness a serial drinker has. Sometimes I drive past bars where daytime drinkers are congregated and want to open the window and call them all fucking losers. Fuck them and the added strain on the health system. Fuck them and the chips on their shoulders. Fuck them and their stories of being passed over for jobs or screwed by ex-wives. Fuck them and their farts, their stale breath, their yellow teeth. Fuck them.

I get angry, not because of them (although you'd hardly know it!), but because I wasted so much of my own existence, of my life, thinking there was some benefit from sitting on a high stool for large chunks of the day and theorising. You forget the hold drink can have over someone, how utterly powerless an addict can be over the forces of alcohol.

You forget about the reality you construct for yourself, about the skewed thinking and the insane list of priorities. Even monetary values are broken down into units—€50 was 10 pints, or the bones of a session. Anything less and you needed a Plan B, a backup.

I got money from everywhere, from overdrafts to credit cards, from term loans to bounced cheques. Without a bank account thanks to credit problems, I would cash cheques wherever I could, from local shops to pawn merchants. Christmas and birthday presents often found their way into pawn shops—anything to keep the session going.

It's an insane way of living, a hand-to-glass-to-mouth existence, and you sometimes forget about the logistics of daytime drinking and what a full-time occupation it is.

By 3.30 p.m. only one of the regulars was left, nodding off (his first sleep in 24 hours), in the corner of the bar. Tickets for the annual Christmas Lotto were flying all afternoon as the majority of the early-morning regulars made their way home for a few hours' rest. Some headed to an off-licence for a naggin to help them through the rest of the day. The drinker's smell, a mix of tobacco and old jumpers, left the bar for the first time.

I got a chance to talk with the owner who has been working here for 27 years. The crackdown on drink-driving has significantly impacted on the older locals moving from village to village and having a few drinks on their way, he told me. The younger people are now only into 'quick' ones, and are often only seen when he has a function in the bar. 'They're into the shots and so on, although I have a more settled crowd here. You see it going on at parties and that and they tend to get oblivious to what's going on around them. It's mostly eighteen- and nineteen-year-olds and their drink of choice has become spirits. When I was younger, and it's not all that long ago, you'd like a pint and rarely touched spirits.'

I like the owner—he has his own health problems, which he has tackled head on with an overhaul of his diet and a positive outlook. Anecdotally, locals had told me of the manner in which he looks after his problem drinkers—of him going the extra mile to make sure they paid their rent or didn't drink every penny they had. I noticed myself that he was careful not to give some of the regulars spirits and made sure they didn't do anything foolish and get too out of hand. There was healthy respect among the regulars towards him and I got the feeling it went both ways, and not in a superficial, 'I'll take every penny you have and pretend to be your friend' kind of way.

I was interested to get his take on the difference between the problem drinker and the regular one.

'That's a hard question to answer. Every pub has a few regulars. You would have the lad in here, as you saw, on a Monday all day and he is probably a problem drinker. My definition of a problem would be when they don't go to work and things like that.

'Some of the lads might be on the dole and waiting for the cheque on Thursday so they can be in here.

'A lot of the lads are separated and they have problems. In terms of the money they might have nixers on the side and things like that. I wouldn't have too many problem drinkers, I would say, I have a few heavy drinkers and you'd ask yourself are they alcoholics too? They probably are. I notice, too, that girls are drinking much more now. They would now go for drinks on the top shelf and things like that.'

I couldn't help feeling, though, that the owner was complicit in the destructive lives of his daytime drinkers. He recognised some of them had problems, sure, but wasn't he fuelling the issues in their lives by serving them alcohol every day? Wasn't there a conflict there?

'I find that hard,' he said, 'but I suppose I am a kind of a counsellor here as well. That's especially true in a small village, where you know too much of what's . . . going on. Part of my job is listening a lot and you have to try and help. Of course, I am aware of what is happening and it can be a conflict sometimes, but that's the nature of the job.'

When asked why he thinks some people drink more than others, the owner said a lot of it, in his opinion, is down to loneliness. Although the nature of conversation in the pubs is changing, he says, and the community aspect of the bar is being eroded.

'The culture of drinking has changed an awful lot [in] the last few years. The pub is still the focal point of many communities and for many individuals—you still have the banter and the craic, just not as much, and you don't get the groups of people coming in. That's what I like about the pubs, you know what's going on, both good and bad, and it's all discussed in the pub. A lot of the time it goes in one ear and out the other—you can't be listening to everything!'

The owner said he looked forward to the day when he could bring his own son or daughter into the bar for the first drink— already, he said, they would have a glass at Christmas. 'Eighteen or nineteen is the right age for a drink in a bar; I'm not into the idea of kids drinking in a pub at fourteen, fifteen or sixteen.'

One thing he says he has noticed in the past decade is that many of his regulars will now drink at home, something that was unheard of in previous times.

'Growing up, we never had drink in the house. I only see it here in that there is a bottle bank right across the road and I see people dumping stuff there. It has increased steadily in recent years and probably accelerated when the smoking ban came in. That kick-started it. For anyone who smoked it was a big culture shock. I know one person in particular who hasn't come into a pub since. He's not local here, but will only go into a pub if there is an occasion, such as an anniversary or that, now.'

We continued to chat about changing traditions. The owner pointed to the fact that a neighbouring village had 20 bars at one point and is left with four now.

'I think the pub will always be there in rural Ireland,' he said, 'but the numbers are declining and I can see a lot more closing. Pubs in the real country areas on their own find it very hard. The Guards are closing in on them and locals have to go to a place where they can get a lift home or villages where they can walk.'

Not one to stand still, the bar has started to do food this year in an effort to broaden out their daytime trade. 'You have to move on with the times, definitely, and food really is a must if you're going to keep the people, even for a funeral or anything like that. You feel that if you don't [there's] a danger that the local trade could be lost because they'll go somewhere else. In Ireland our culture is very much pub orientated and I enjoy it. Having said that, you don't get the big functions like you used to get years ago. Think about christenings, for instance, and only a small minority now come in and have a function.'

The demographic of the daytime drinkers in the bar was very much bachelor and Irish, with few women and fewer still foreign nationals. I remarked to the owner that it seemed out of step with the changing culture outside, of the new multiethnic Ireland which has emerged. He then told me a story that happened a few months earlier.

'I had an experience with a guy who had a room rented upstairs. He was training to be a doctor and was from eastern Europe. He worked as a stable lad for a trainer over the road. A very nice fellow, and he told me his story and showed me pictures of his wife and his child. He was still far off becoming qualified as a doctor but he ran short of money and he wanted to spend three years here to make enough money to build his house and finish college. So he was on his second year here and he went home for Christmas and his wife was to come back with him and the child. He was at home for a month when he came back. I think his wife wouldn't come back— she wanted him to come home but he knew another year or two would see him through. So he had money saved up and he started drinking a lot, bottles of vodka and so on. Maybe he was depressed at being up there without his family.

He was a very nice chap, a young lad, maybe twenty-seven or twenty-eight. You wouldn't get foreigners in here that often. Him and a friend would come in and play pool and so on and have a few beers. But they started drinking heavy upstairs and you'd see him drinking bottles and carrying empty ones over to the bottle bank. It was beer and spirits mostly they drank. The only big spirit-drinkers we would have were after funerals or something, when fellas would have a few shots. But this lad just got into a routine of drinking and was buying it locally in shopping centres. He went on for months, and one day, he just fell down up there and died. He actually died there. He drank himself to death. We put a few quid together to get his body home.'

I found the story quite shocking. When I first visited the bar, weeks earlier, one of the regulars had died the weekend before and there was a post-wake of sorts happening. The man who died had cancer, I think, and other health complications. Every week the bar owner would take him out of hospital and bring him down to the bar for a drink. He had gone from being a solid drinker to barely being able to hold two pints towards the end. It was my first introduction to the bar—locals talking with fond memories of this man who drank with them, who worried with them and who, by his presence, allowed them to continue their lives beside the counter. And now he was dead and no one was making a link between the unhealthy lifestyle of the daytime drinker and his premature death.

To be honest, I found the whole scene quite depressing. Not that it is in any way unique—bars all over Ireland have similar scenarios, and I guess at least with the bar I visited there was a conscience at work behind the taps.

That evening the owner's wife invited me for dinner. We sat down for a chat in the living room of their large home, on a gated site across the road from the bar. Try as I could to suppress the thoughts, I was struck by the probable dichotomy between the landlord's home and that of some of his customers. Many of them, I imagined, slept in weeks-old sheets, tin-can-boiled eggs the extent of their culinary exploits. In contrast, the owner's home was well kept, family orientated, spacious and comfy. Not that it was his fault that he had done all right over the years. He doesn't have the problem. But the thought struck me that drink provided him with a nice family home and environment, whereas for many of his customers, it broke up what families and homes they had.

His wife told me she had worked in an office until her husband's illness forced her to take a career break. Now she does the morning shift in the bar, dispensing the morning dosage to sickly patients. She brought an outsider's eye to the daytime trade and her preconceived ideas on the type of people who drink during the day had changed dramatically since taking over the morning shift.

'I worked in a bar years ago, before I ever got married, but only started working back behind the counter a while ago. It's only now I'm getting used to the daytime crowd. Before, I would . . . only have worked when we were really busy and it was nighttime and you're hardly talking to people, just throwing out the drink to customers. I used to hate the idea of daytime work. But now that I have been in there I got to know the people and actually I enjoy it. I really enjoy their company. Some of them are very witty and I guess I take a different view of it now.'

Reflecting on Irish culture, we got chatting about the extent to which a problem drinker can be assimilated into Irish society before being found out. Or, if he has been found out, he is carried along by the crowd and it's not seen as a big problem. 'It's looked on as an acceptable thing to get pissed in Ireland and nobody really is going to say anything to you. People talk about it and say things like "I got hammered last night on twenty pints" very openly. On

Mondays, you see the guys coming in and talking about their weekend and they don't see it as a problem. In rural Ireland, what do you do if you're not going to the pub drinking?

'I think, especially, men living alone use the pub for company. What other social outlet do they have? If they're men of a certain age, and they're not into sport or gone beyond it and don't have a partner, where are they going to go to meet people? There aren't very many places. Most of our clientele have no other outlets, I would say. If you are a farmer, for example, and don't have a workplace, or you might be working with one other guy or driving a digger all day, what are you going to do for a social outlet, to meet people?'

That idea of community, which the owner had remarked on earlier, is something fast disappearing in rural Ireland. From declining corner shops to voluntary sports, the individualisation of Irish society is fuelling changing social trends. Perhaps this is why the problem drinker is now more noticeable and a lot less camouflaged by the rest of drinking society. During the Celtic Tiger years especially, not as many people were into hanging about bars all day long when there was a few handy bob to be made. Others were determined to have their Chardonnay on their own decking, no matter how cold it got. They had new kitchens and stereo units to show off, in houses which they were paying through the teeth for.

'One guy who lived in the village, and was in his thirties, used to come out four or five nights a week. The Guards had been putting people off the road all week and I think maybe three people had been stopped at one point. It was a Tuesday night, one of the quietest I ever put down, and there was one guy in the lounge and one in the bar. This local said, "For Christ' sake, I come out to meet people, this is my social outing!" He likes a few drinks but mainly he comes out to meet people. But the other side of that, of course, is that it can be a problem when that becomes a way of life and you are used to meeting people every night.

'For some people, they might have three drinks and come in to meet the lads. The core group of drinkers are like a mini-family—

they don't have any other person to talk to besides themselves. Sometimes the conversation is quite superficial; they're having a laugh or the craic and chatting about their day and that. They're quite connected in a way and there is a friendship there. They would look out for each other. I only see that now and I wouldn't have seen that before I was working. Nighttime drinking is different because couples are out and so on. Any of the daytime guys around at night would be chatting to lots of different people around them and it's a different conversation at nighttimes. The type of person who becomes a problem drinker is hard to classify—I think a lot of the time these people are lacking in self-confidence and it's a crutch rather than enjoyment—it's something they actually need. They need to have about four or five drinks before they're even comfortable in a social situation. That's not the case with everybody but with some of them. I do think a lot of them are very timid at the back of it. They can't actually function socially without the drink.'

I ask the same question I asked the owner—does she feel she is conflicted and fuelling the problems of many of her regulars by supplying them with alcohol?

'There is a conflict there, to be honest with you. My husband would look after a lot of guys. He would cut down on the spirits they were drinking or make sure they get home all right or whatever. But, say the guy we don't serve spirits to, he goes in and gets them in town and then he comes back to us at certain times of the day. People are going to get drink if they want to, no matter where. But you do sometimes feel like saying stuff. Like when guys are telling you their problems. One guy suffers from mental health issues, and you nearly feel like saying, "Can you not see it's the drink?" That's not my job, in a way. My job is to listen to them and they don't want me to tell them that. I can opt out. You can kind of bring up the subject. There was a lady who used to drink in there all day Monday. Her child was in the house having come back from school and would often beg the mother to come home. I used to say to my husband, "How can you stick it?" Having the child in the bar pleading for the mother to come home and she wouldn't budge. As it happens, now she drinks at home all the time. So people will do that regardless. There was another guy who used to come into us and he had quite a drink problem. He was a young married guy. His wife eventually rang the Guards and he was warned not to be around drinking and driving. He just moved on to another village. The sad part of that is that the Guards would have said he was violent to her when he went home and we never would have seen that side of him in the pub. He moved on to another place and didn't solve his problems.

'I remember another guy and his wife rang my husband and said, "Would you do me a favour and just bar him for one month?" He said, "I will." So when he came in as usual my husband said, "Sorry you're barred for one month." He said "Fair enough," and after the month, the wife was my husband's best friend. She said she didn't know where he was or how he was coming home. He still drank, so there's a way of being with people and of handling situations. I would have been quite removed from that when I was working in the office; now I can see the whole story and you do get attached to people. There are very few coming in that I do not like. Most of the people you'd love if they'd sort out their problems, but they're not going to solve them in the pub and I don't think a publican is going to sort their problems either.'

One thing I noticed in my time at the bar was very few under-25s were drinking with the regulars or in their own groups. The normal rites of passage in a rural village, whereby youngsters would be brought into the bar in their late teens for a drink, seemed to be missing. What this meant in effect was that those youngsters in the village drinking were doing so away from adult supervision. Many had told me that drugs were now a feature of village life, and with cheaper drink available in off-licences and supermarkets, the current generation were turning their backs on a traditional night out. Back seats of Honda Civics had become their lounge bars.

'We would have some people in their twenties come in,' said the bar worker, 'but they generally come out at weekends. They might come in for a few drinks and then go to town and go clubbing or whatever. The eighteen to twenty-one age group don't come in, really. They are drinking but they don't come in to us. They're mainly doing drugs. There's only one guy in the village that comes in for a pint from that age group and the rest of them are all doing drugs. They smoke weed and are buying drink in places like Lidl and drink in cars and do whatever drugs they're doing. One of the guys, a father of one of them, was saying, "I wish they would come in because I'd know what they're doing."

'When they do come in, it's all shots and vodka. We notice on long weekends or nights of parties or big nights such as Stephen's Night and that, when they do come in, they go through huge amounts of vodka. It used to be all those alcopops. The way I see them drinking is that they start off pretty okay. They might be having a bottle of Smirnoff Ice or WKD or Bulmers, and then it would come a certain time in the night and it's shots. They would get through a serious amount. Just "One, Two, Three," and go. They'd spend huge amounts. Vodka and Red Bull is the big thing at the end of the night.

'To be honest, girls are more into the shots than the guys. The guys still actually drink pints but at the end of the night they will have a vodka and Red Bull. They might do a few shots but with girls the object of the game is to get as many shots as you can into you if they're going clubbing or whatever. It's a ridiculous way to drink and a lot of the time you pour more stuff down the sink after. What I see now, that I never saw before, is that people will say, "Can I have three vodkas and a Red Bull?" And you return with three glasses and they'll say, "No, can I have a pint glass and throw in the three!" We would never have drank like that. Nobody would even have had a double! The pub experience is central to Irish life, though, and I would like to think it's safe enough for another generation. We hope, anyway!'

——

Following my visits to the bar in Tipperary I was beginning to wonder if we were indeed moving towards a more café-orientated culture than we sometimes give ourselves credit for. It was clear that rural bars have changed significantly in Ireland and some are having to adapt and change with the times. So could another type of social experience take root here? What about a bar without beer, for instance? It would never work, would it? From the outside of the Carrig Rua Hotel in Dunfanaghy, County Donegal, everything seemed normal enough. The site is at the end of the once bustling fishing port, offering commanding views of the surrounding area, including Killahoey Strand, where a US Air Force Flying Fortress landed in 1943 after running out of fuel. Across the bay is Horn Head, a natural heritage area, offering the village protection from the worst of the Atlantic seas. The 23-bed hotel, which had been closed for a number of years, is now expanding in line with the majestic views around. Like many former fishing ports, the town was slow to adapt its business model from trawlers to tourists. While Dunfanaghy has always attracted a certain number of regional tourists, its proximity to Donegal Airport (40 kilometres away) is expected to see the town attract far more foreign visitors and re-ignite commercial activity in the area.

Against this background, Ann Sweeney took over the running of the Carrig Rua Hotel in 2008, having already owned and operated a successful restaurant, bar and shop in the town. Two days into her new venture, though, Gardaí raided the premises and removed all alcoholic stock. Delays in transferring the bar licence from the previous owners to the new management meant that the hotel had been operating without a bar licence since its opening. With 46 employees, mostly local, working at the hotel, and hefty weekly outgoings, things looked bleak for Ann and her staff. Surely a hotel without alcohol would be doomed to failure in a country where the average annual consumption of pure alcohol per person is 13.4 litres, well above the EU average. Or would it?

Ann Sweeney takes up the story: 'We opened up the bar on the understanding that the licence was close to being transferred, and that turned out not to be the case at all.

'On Monday 7 July, at 7.15 p.m., two sergeants and two big vans came and all our alcohol was confiscated from the premises. Many of the staff here had worked for me previously and after the raid I was sitting here thinking, "What am I going to do?"—some of these staff had given up jobs to come and work for me.' After two days' meditation, Ann says she came upon an idea. 'I have a bar nearby, and following government legislation in relation to drink-driving and smoking, the rural pub trade has been decimated. So I thought, why not look at things another way and perhaps there is now a market for an entirely different experience.'

And so, on 17 July 2008 the Carrig Rua Hotel opened its doors as Ireland's first alcohol-free hotel, inviting Kerry Councillor Michael Healy-Rae to do the honours. At the opening, he remarked that there was 'much talk and little real action in Ireland in addressing the problem of alcohol abuse'. The Gardaí, he said, 'have unwittingly provided an opportunity to demonstrate if we are mature enough to be comfortable with the idea of a hotel that provides good quality accommodation and food without having to have an endless supply of booze on tap for its patrons'.

So how does it all work out? Visiting last year, hotel staff were at pains to talk up the positives of working in a dry hotel. Raucous singsongs have been replaced with one-on-one life-coaching sessions, nature walks are being promoted and encouraged, and afternoon salsa classes are growing in numbers, even among staff.

In the bar itself, I found manager Stephen Ferry from Letterkenny training a new staff member on how to make the perfect skinny latte, while a newly installed Slush Puppie machine whirred away in one corner. Herbal teas have replaced high-end whiskeys and smoothies are the new shots. Several alcohol-free beers are on offer, as well as red, white and rosé wines. Ginger beer and homemade lemonade inhabit the fridges. For the non-drinker, it's sort of like going back into the garden and giving Adam a proper heads-up before he bites into the apple. The only problem, though, is that it was 7.40 p.m. on a Tuesday night and the place was empty.

'A pregnant lady was in earlier,' said Mr Ferry. 'She liked the fact that she could come into a bar where she didn't feel under pressure to take a drink. She could sit here with her kids and not see people drinking or falling around the place.' With homemade pastries dotted along the counter, the bar had now rebranded itself as a continental-style café, open from nine in the morning until 10 at night. Diners in the hotel restaurant were allowed to bring wine with them, albeit with a hefty €7.50 corkage fee per bottle. 'The response so far has been very good,' said Ferry. 'Often when people go to a restaurant they are stuck with what [is] on the wine list, but here in this hotel they can bring their own. Of course, we do have some customers who come into the bar and ask for alcohol and there is a look of fright on their faces when I have to say we have none.'

As the evening progressed, locals began to wander into the bar area, attracted by well-known folk singer Roy Arbuckle from Derry, who set up on stage. One couple, Séamus and Betty McQuade, ordered a large pot of tea and sat near the door. Both were teetotallers, and had been coming to the area for over 30 years. 'We never drank or smoked in our lives,' says Séamus, 'and it's enjoyable to come in to a bar like this without the hassle of people knocking glasses against you and being rowdy and noisy. I've nothing against drink, but it can get out of hand. Even though people can bring wine in here, it's not the same as people drinking spirits. That's when things really get out of hand.'

The couple say it's hard to get tea after 9 p.m. in most bars, so the Carrig Rua duly obliges. One local, with a foot in both camps, arrives with a bottle of wine in one hand and a bottle of Ballygowan in another. Others arrive in the bar after dinner, including Charlie and Kate Hill, finishing off their bottle of wine before switching to alcohol-free rosé for the rest of the evening. Once the band starts, the atmosphere is not unlike any other hotel bar, and whilst the staff are not run off their feet, they're not exactly standing around either. By 10 p.m., the bar has filled up, and during a break, the singer Roy Arbuckle remarks that he could get used to playing to a sober crowd. 'It's not that unusual,' he says. 'The great folk tradition of the sixties in New York came out of coffee houses. I suppose in our culture we have grown up over generations thinking that pubs are patrons of the arts, such is the link between traditional music and drink. In terms of atmosphere, I prefer when it is sober—people are more inclined to be attentive to the music rather than drink and themselves.'

Next morning, Ann Sweeney breezed through the lobby, taking names for a music workshop she had organised for that afternoon. There are plans to open children's playrooms and an old-style games room at the back of the hotel and at the time she was also considering hiring more staff; such has been the demand since opening.

'It's amazing, we will have five waiters in the bar today as well as a manager and they will be flat out doing coffees and latte and herbal teas all day,' she says. 'Our takings are roughly the same.' She says she has taken enquiries from AA groups and alcohol treatment centres looking to book in. Three weeks in, and the hotel has yet to take out a single advert. The premises has proven especially popular with young families, who would not normally be allowed have their children on a licensed premises after 9 p.m., while the evolving range of events on offer in the bar helps keep everyone occupied.

She's now not pushed on getting her licence back. If things continue to develop, she may not need it. 'The ironic thing', she says, en route to meet a lady about reiki classes, 'is that over the bank holiday weekend, the café here in the hotel took in double what my licensed premises around the corner took in. So why change a successful business model?' I thought I'd seen the future, folks, and it was looking fizzy.

Two months after my visit, during a local jazz festival, Ann Sweeney learned that her licence had been renewed. That same day she restocked her shelves—the very same day! I called her months later to get an update on how business was going and she informed me. I felt cheated. What about all the AA groups she said were booked in? All the families and non-drinkers delighted with the premises and a chance to socialise without alcohol? Alas, as soon as the authorities gave the official okay, Ireland's first booze-free bar was no more. It hardly stood a chance. While Sweeney may now claim that the 'bar is more of a café with the emphasis on food and music', it is in essence no different to any other hotel bar in Ireland.

So much for new beginnings.

'We were faced with a dilemma when the licence returned. I still believe we would have been able to continue, but perhaps not in the off-season. Now that we have our licence back, next summer I don't intend to take the alcohol out of the bar. It wouldn't make economical sense,' Sweeney said when we spoke. The publicity from being Ireland's first booze-free bar, for a short time at least, will do the hotel no harm in the long run.

For non-drinkers, the revolution, it seems, will not be soberised.

Frances Black, Singer

For me it's the shame and stigma that is attached to addiction in this country is actually the thing that stunts the growth of people recovering. Addiction thrives on secrecy and Ireland is still a secret society. I don't think that's changed in the recent past, and I think the issue of addiction is absolutely huge. You might get more people aware of it, because of the celebrity rehab culture, where celebrities are talking very openly about their experience. This might lead to a little more discussion about addiction issues, but not much.

It's very hard to know, also, with that rehab culture, about how genuine it is. I would say most people are looking for something, and addiction plays a huge role in their lives and it's not for me to judge. I still think in this country the shame and stigma attached to addiction stop people from asking for help. The first step in addiction is awareness and then asking for help, saying, 'Where can I go to sort this out?

I have a huge passion about addiction and addiction in Ireland, to such an extent that I set up a foundation called the RISE foundation, which stands for 'recovery in a safe environment'. Our first project is for family members. In my experience of talking openly about it in an interview or on the radio, I would be inundated with people from families looking for help. So that is why I decided to set up the foundation.

The person in addiction is in a complete haze, and not really present. So the question is, how do you get them to really want to change? In a way, you can educate the family members about how to handle someone in their family who has addiction. For me, that's the first step.

I wouldn't have considered myself an alcoholic. I do know now, but at the time I wouldn't. My drinking wasn't spirits. So my idea of an alcoholic, which would be most people's idea of an alcoholic, was someone sitting in the pub all day or the wino out on the street, or someone who had to have a drink first thing in the morning. That wasn't the way it was for me. My drinking would start with wine about six in the evening and I could have maybe a bottle and a half of wine a night. At the weekend I might go out and drink pints. To me, though, that wasn't alcoholism—I mightn't even have a bottle and a half every night. It might be four nights a week.

My attitude would have been, I'm sitting at home and not hurting anybody or not out in a pub making a show of myself. Whereas in reality, I would have been falling into bed most nights and the effect that would have had on my life was huge. For a start, I would have had a hangover next morning and be grumpy and narky and preoccupied. I wasn't present. I wasn't present to my family. I was getting through the day but dying for six o'clock when I was making the dinner and having my glass of wine. I'd be really looking forward to it and sometimes it could start earlier.

Nobody had any idea. Everyone was shocked when I said I needed to go for help. My husband knew something wasn't quite right as he wasn't a drinker. I do believe there are different stages of alcoholism and I might have been at the middle stage or even before that. People might find that hard to take because if they acknowledge you have a problem, then they have to look at their own drinking and say, 'What does that make me?!'

Or you would get the type of response—'Jaysus, she was no worse than any of the rest of us!'

What changed my life is that I read an article by a journalist. I think it was in the *Irish Times*, some time back in the 1980s. Her pattern was like me except she was into the gin and tonics and then would go and do a day's work. She would come home and have a bottle of wine with dinner and then a little more gin and tonic and go to bed.

She couldn't understand why she couldn't stop and eventually went for help. That was a bit like me. I tried to stop and couldn't and I couldn't understand that. After two weeks of being off it, I nearly lost my mind. I started to sneak it, and these were all things that made me rethink.

When I read the article there was a number at the end, so I thought I'd go and have a chat with them and get assessed. I was completely convinced they would say to me, 'You just need to cut down on your drink.' But then I went to the counsellor, I sat down and was really honest. I would have had blackouts and so on at that time. She said to me, really casually and non-judgmental, 'There is no doubt in my mind that you are an alcoholic and you need to come here.'

It was an outpatient treatment centre and it was for three nights a week, so it was a huge eye-opener for me. When I stopped drinking the career took off. But I was always dabbling in prescription tablets, so really there would be times I was worse than others but I never thought it was a problem. Because it was prescription drugs the doctor gave them to me, so it was all right. It was only in later years, when I had to give up the tablets also, that I realised you could swap over addictions. So I ended up in a treatment centre later on and it was more for the tablets. I would actually say, for me, my primary addiction was prescription tablets because it was harder for me to come off them. It was easy for me to come off the drink. And I still get a longing for the tablets.

They were better than alcohol in many ways because you could function and still have a conversation with people and they wouldn't know. But the side effects destroy your life and the consequences are horrendous. They were a lot worse for me than alcohol and the ups and downs can make you very suicidal.

I wouldn't have had a career if I was drinking. I really do feel my career took off the minute I stopped drinking. Before I went for treatment I had been asked to join a band and I had to go and tell them, 'I have to go for this treatment.' They said they would wait for me and when I came off treatment I joined the band and it went from there. The hardest thing I ever had to do was to walk on stage without a drink.

There is this Irish thing that we can drink and it brings out the creative side within. I don't agree with that, personally. I'm not saying it doesn't work for some people. But I'd love to see those people without drink and see what comes out if they did the right amount of work on themselves and did all the spiritual and soul stuff.

For me I hadn't done much stage work beforehand, and I had great support because it was with my family and there was a great support. It was scary walking on stage, though, as it would be for anybody. I knew I wanted to do it so that's what kept my legs walking on the stage. The fact that I could stop drinking gave me great courage—if I could do that I could do anything.

I think it's scary in this country as we are drowned in addiction. I'm petrified as to the consequences of what is going on, really. That is why I really want to try and do something to look at the shame and stigma attached to addiction. I get up on stage every night and tell my story. I don't have any shame around the fact I'm in recovery; it's not a big deal for me, it's just a disease, and I'm working through it.

So I feel more people need to talk about it, not about the fact that they go into rehab—they need to talk about what it was like and what it felt like. And yes, I will speak openly about it if I feel it can help one person in this country.

If I am successful in setting up a treatment centre it will be an education treatment centre for families about addiction. This is so that anybody who wants to learn about addiction can come and learn that this is what addiction is. It'd about telling people, there is a format that can work and this is how you need to look at it.

The research I have done shows that the cost to the taxpayer of one child in untreated addiction is £800,000 in one addict's lifetime, whether it is alcohol or drugs. So if the government could prevent one child going down that road they will save themselves that money. If they gave someone £1 million to set up a treatment centre they're going to save on things like A&E. I mean fifty-five per cent of people who go into A&E over a weekend is alcohol- or addiction-related.

If you look at Ireland and the way the whole thought process is around alcohol and the minimising of it as a problem. I was doing a conference in Kerry with lots of government representatives and addiction counsellors, and all they were talking about was they were going to come down heavy on drugs. I actually said, hang on a second, addiction is not just drugs, it's alcohol, it's things like prescription tablets and gambling. Yet all you hear is, 'We're going to go down heavy on drug dealers.'

For me, socially, being sober, you are a little more isolated and I do feel isolated. I don't tend to hang around pubs that long. But I have a great life. I have a lovely husband who doesn't drink. I don't think it would work if he was in the pub every night. We go out for meals, we go walking. We go to plays and do all the things that people in other countries do! If you go to New York or San Francisco that's what people do. They don't really go to pubs to hang out. I love going away. I've been in San Francisco and a lot of it is around food and dinner. You might invite people over and they'd have wine, but they might have a bottle of wine and they'd all have a half glass each and some of them mightn't even finish the glass. I'd be amazed at that! They'd be having sips of water and some of them would be more interested in the water. They go to restaurants or go out to [a] theatre. It's just sad for me there's not that many people in Ireland who do that. And that's the reality. So when everyone goes to the pub I get bored and last maybe three quarters of an hour.

Weddings I don't mind because I dance but I wouldn't stay late; I go and have the meal and have a chat but there's a point where it might get a little late and I go. I always have a room in the hotel just in case we need to escape!

I think any country that has been colonised, where your land and home has been taken off you, that type of trauma carries through generations. I went back to college to become an addiction counsellor and one of my assignments was trauma and addiction in post-conflict Northern Ireland. Everybody in the North has been touched by the conflict, as we know, and traumatised by it. What happens in that situation is that the trauma is carried onto another generation, even through the peace process, and manifests itself in a rise in addiction and problem drinkers. This generation is now carrying that trauma. I do feel there is this thing in Ireland where you don't show your emotions and feelings. Secrecy is a huge thing in this country, which was a defence, in that you didn't want anybody to know your business. People are afraid to show their emotions in this country.

If you have twelve in a group receiving treatment, the studies show only about three will make it. So it's scary, and I think, if society was different, that statistics might be higher. It's really hard for a young man to come out of treatment and all his mates are getting pissed every night. This is my experience and I work in the Rutland Centre in Dublin every weekend and do a lot of work around relapse prevention. Everything is lovely for the five weeks people are in treatment and they have great support and a good environment. When they go back into their own environment, in many cases they're on their own. And it's not easy, but that's the country we live in.

Chapter 4
Past Pioneers

It's hard to know what came first, the Irish or the drink. Many travellers in Ireland from the 1600s onwards made comment about the revelry of the drunken Irish. Reference to alcohol, or 'aqua vitae' and 'usquebaugh' as it was called, do not occur in Irish sources until the fourteenth century, although, as Elizabeth Malcolm in her fine study *Ireland Sober Ireland Free* has pointed out, the art of distilling is thought to have been invented as far back as the twelfth century. 'Fermented liquors such as ale and mead had, however, long been staple drinks among Celtic peoples,' Malcolm notes, while adding, 'It is interesting to note that the name of the Celtic goddess, Medhb, literally means, "she who intoxicates"—a clear indication of the significance of drink in Celtic culture.' Or how about this eleventh-century poem to St Bridget: 'I would like to have a great lake of beer for Christ the King/I'd like to be watching the heavenly family drinking it down through all eternity.' It's Irish Christianity, Jim, but not as we know it.

In his introduction to *Inventing Ireland*, Declan Kiberd begins with the probe 'If God invented whiskey to prevent the Irish from ruling the world, then who invented Ireland?' It's a rhetorical rise, sure, but there's a kernel of national truth in there somewhere. By the mid-sixteenth century whiskey had become such a problem in Ireland that the English government felt it necessary to introduce legislative controls. In a preamble to the required legislation, there was notice of how 'Aqua Vitae, a drink nothing profitable to be daily drunken and used, is now universally throughout the realm of

Ireland made'. Stricter decrees were used to limit the making of whiskey in Ireland to peers, gentlemen and borough freemen. By 1571, the manufacture of whiskey was banned in Munster. In 1584 the Lord Deputy received a note for the reform of Ireland. One of the main suggestions was that the previous 'statute for the making of aqua vitae be put in execution, which sets the Irish mad and breeds many mischiefs'. As with today's legislative approach, the series of acts and decrees had little effect on drinking levels.

When we get to the first half of the seventeenth century, excessive drinking and drunkenness were prevalent in most parts of Ireland. And it wasn't just the poorer classes who were at it—it seems most social classes in Ireland had a fondness for the drop. Here is Richard Head's observation of the Irish gentry: 'If you, on a visit to them, do not drink freely then they think they have not made you welcome, so that a man know not how to take a leave until he is unable to stir a foot.'

Writing in the early twentieth century, historian Michael McCarthy noted that the association between alcohol and the Irish had become embedded. His acute observations tell a familiar picture of the social ubiquity of alcohol in Irish society. 'Amongst Irish Catholics, drink is the synonym for hospitality. It stands alone and is not associated with food. Every festive meeting, every social call, every business transaction, must be wet, as they say, with a drink. The man that does not stand a drink is considered a mean man; the man who gives drink freely in his own home and pays for it for others in public houses is a decent fellow. There is a kind of veneration for the man who has spent a fortune or ruined a career by drink; and people expatiate in the great things he might have done were it not for drink.'

The eighteenth- and nineteenth-century story of Irish drinking is one of attempted zero tolerance, beginning with the morally flawed figure of Father Theobald Mathew (1790–1856) and the attempt to form temperance societies in recognition of the growing social problem with alcohol. The Corkonian intoxication with the figure of Father Mathew, founder of the Temperance movement, is well established in both popular song and sentiment Leeside, most famously in the refrain *The smell from Patrick's Bridge is wicked/How do Father Mathew stick it?/Here's up them all says the boys of Fairhill.*

The Father Mathew statue, known locally as 'de statue', has taken on symbolic significance, and is to Cork what Clery's clock is to Dublin—a place where relationships begin and end and friendships are born and broken. The strong connection with the 'Apostle of Temperance' is interesting when viewed alongside nineteenth-century drinking patterns, said to rival our current twenty-first-century ones. Our love of drinking didn't begin today or yesterday, in other words. The Temperance and Pioneer movements were side effects of the guilt and shame associated with Irish drinking. As we'll see in later chapters, that guilt still exists among the Irish problem drinkers in London. It exists, too, in daytime drinkers in rural bars in Tipperary and in those who serve them and facilitate their lifestyles. It exists among adolescents and schoolchildren when they talk about alcohol and their relationship to it. More than likely, I carry some of it around myself. But it's not just guilt that drives the Irish relationship with alcohol, which is one part puritanical to two parts party. As the great addiction writer George Valliant has observed, 'It is consistent with Irish culture to see the use of alcohol in terms of black or white, good or evil, drunkenness or complete abstinence.' In other words, when it comes to Irish drinking, for many it's a case of all or nothing.

———

The story of Fr Mathew encapsulates well this extreme Irish attitude to alcohol. Born in Thomastown Castle, Co. Tipperary, on 10 October 1790, Theobald Mathew felt a lifelong affinity with the poor and distressed and this was evident from an early age. Influenced by local priest Fr Denis O'Donnell, Mathew entered the seminary in Maynooth in 1807, at the age of 17. Not long after, he reportedly threw a party in his room in honour of some kindred spirit, and to save himself the embarrassment of expulsion, the following morning he left the seminary. The Capuchins took a chance on him, and he entered the order in 1810, quickly establishing a name for himself as an engaging and magnetic public speaker.

From a friary at Blackamoor Lane in Cork he captured the affections of the poor and the confidence of the rich, with his treatment of the penitents in the confessional drawing particular attention to his sympathetic nature. As in contemporary society, alcohol abuse was rampant in early-nineteenth-century Ireland. While accounts differ, Mathew himself was known to take a drop, and many argue it was this personal experience that gave him an insight into the alcoholic mindset. I visited the present-day Capuchin order in Cork, where Fr Dermot Lynch lent me his own insights. 'I think the affinity with him by the people came from his own life for the ten years while he was involved in the Temperance movement, he became a Pioneer. Before that he was a moderate drinker. I think his greatness came from the fact that he helped turn the tide of public opinion. It was a very popular thing to drink at the time, yet eventually over three million people took the pledge. The Temperance movement was only the beginning of a large-scale social movement in Ireland, yet it was an important first step.'

There is little doubt that Fr Mathew did a lot of good, particularly for the poor of Cork. Yet he remains a controversial figure, and examining the purported facts surrounding his life means discarding much of the historical hyperbole.

Like all great leaders, he had his demons and was known to be ego-driven, arrogant and prone to serious lapses of judgment. Throughout his life he had financial difficulties and was at odds with the hierarchy of the church. Perhaps there is something in that—in the ambiguous attitude between alcohol and organised religion in Ireland—which Fr Mathew challenged. Says Professor John A. Murphy: 'I think it's fair to say he was at an oblique angle to conventional Catholic thinking in that he was a teetotalling freelance cleric. I don't imagine he was subject to any great discipline by his own order, but then again one of the great themes in the nineteenth century is the tension between diocesan and regular clergy, and he fit into that.'

Prof. Murphy also points to the fact that while on paper the Temperance movement looked impressive, appearances deceive, and the movement had few long-term results in achieving large-scale Irish sobriety. Many of those who took the pledge may not have had full control of their senses. The 'farewell drop', as it became known, often stretched over long periods and reports in newspapers of the time have large crowds arriving in cities such as Cork to take the pledge, already heavily inebriated. The Sub-Inspector for Enniscorthy gave the following account. He 'saw numbers take the pledge in a beastly state of intoxication and hundreds took their farewell drop immediately before receiving it'. He went on to say that many took the pledge and forgot they had done so, only to return again later to take it again!

So even in our giving up, the Irish were giving in.

'All these campaigns lose momentum because of the unnatural demands they place on the individual,' notes Prof Murphy. 'I mean, abstaining from anything is a wholly unnatural position for anybody to take! I think, really, that Fr Mathew was more in line with the Victorian notions of social reform and betterment.' As for the significance of the Corkonian devotion to the statue, Prof. Murphy points out that you can have an attachment to the statue, but that doesn't necessarily mean an attachment to the man.

'Essentially it is a much loved urban landmark and a convenient one as well.

'There was a genuine concern among citizens when the idea to shift the statue was mooted. The idea was frowned upon and rightly so. I think the Father Mathew statue is much more important to Cork people than any corresponding statue in Dublin. I can't think of a Dublin landmark with similar public appeal—perhaps the O'Connell monument—but I don't think it has the same resonance of affection.'

One of those who has sought to capture the Cork association with Father Mathew down through the years is balladeer Jimmy Crowley. As the church's grip on Irish morality loosened, Father

Mathew proved a popular source of sardonic wit in the folk tradition, Crowley explains.

'I suppose he was to Cork what Matt Talbot was to Dublin in a way and he remains popular in the folk tradition at least. Further back you could muster ten good songs about him, from the likes of John Fitzgerald, the bard of the Lee, who wrote an impressive elegy, and several others. They were all very much in the ballad broadside tradition—mostly religious songs—none would have been sardonic at that time. Later on, with the passage of time and a more liberal era, he became a sort of figure of derision to a certain degree.'

Crowley himself joined the ranks in the 1970s at the expense of Finance Minister Richie Ryan, who committed the unforgivable act of raising the price of a pint in excess of the price of a drop of whiskey, thus provoking the ire of Crowley's pen:

'If you go down to Patrick Street you're bound to meet with
    Fr Mathew,
A Temperance man of high degree, sometimes for short he's called
    'de statue',
He tried to keep us off the booze, and on it looked with reprobation
Yet if he had Richie by his side, he'd have success throughout
    the nation.'

'I know people who are complete heathens and are very taken by him,' says Crowley. 'There have been some wonderful clerics in Cork, such as Fr Prout and people like that, who have stepped outside the conventions of clericism. To my mind Father Mathew was part of their story.'

Recently, a play written by Sean McCarthy, who had a 20-year interest in the subject, sought to examine the complexities of Father Mathew, separating the historical figure from the well-known populist folk hero. McCarthy first came in contact with the story of Father Mathew through his grandparents' generation and a few years back he wrote a play based on the life of Mathew. 'There are two extremes in relation to his drinking; one says he hardly drank at all, and certainly not to excess, while others claim he was a drunkard,' says McCarthy. 'Archbishop McHale of Galway, who was a lifelong enemy of his for a lot of diverse political reasons, said that all through the Temperance campaign Father Mathew went up and down the country with a blonde on his hand, and that the profit made on the sale of medals was spent on buying brandy! We know he never made a profit on selling medals because he ended up in prison for debt half way through the campaign, so we can take it that is untrue. In the play we go with fact that he was a heavy drinker, and perhaps an alcoholic embryo, which is precisely what gave him insight into the alcoholic mind.'

McCarthy points to Father Mathew's arrogance as his ultimate downfall. It was while researching the story further in the early 1990s that he came across some documents in a library in Boston which he claims highlight the moral frailty of the man. 'In 1840, Father Mathew and Daniel O'Connell prepared an address to the Irish people in America on the issue of slavery—this became known as the "Abolitionist Charter". It was very strongly worded, and implored all Irish people who called themselves Christians to follow the cause. Eight or nine years later, though, when the question of slavery was more alive and controversial, Father Mathew is brought to America by Governor Lumpkin of Georgia and the Archbishop of Savannah, both of whom are slavers. He lands himself in a very difficult situation, where to my mind he is at his most arrogant and most dishonest. This provides for his downfall, both in life, and also in the play I wrote.'

Despite his reservations, like most Corkonians, McCarthy has deep-rooted admiration for Father Mathew, and sees him in the broader context of Irish social reform.

'He was a man of extraordinary ego to the point of megalomania, and ultimately this arrogance was to be his downfall. He became a figure of fun to people of my generation. But in fact, he was a great social reformer, and also a great liberal thinker. Arguably, he was a liberation theologist long years before the term was even invented. We could do with someone like him now when you look at Irish society and our association with alcohol.'

Writing in 1845, Father Mathew felt in optimistic mood when he predicted the future generations' relationship with alcohol. He wrote that 'all the rising generations are being educated in the strictest habits of temperance; and in a few years, drunkenness will be a thing passed away, never to return'.

Yet by September 1845 twice as many drunkards had been admitted to Cork Bridewell as in the same month in 1844. Faced with mounting evidence that his Temperance movement had not signalled the death knell for Irish drunkenness, Fr Mathew conceded later that year that some drunkenness did exist, but was mostly limited to 'poor sinful females'. Whether or not Fr Mathew would have succeeded in having a long-term impact on the mindset among the Irish in relation to alcohol is debatable. From 1845 onwards, the Famine rendered his work largely secondary. In his fine study, *Father Mathew and the Irish Temperance Movement,* Colm Kerrigan questions whether Mathew achieved his objective of the rejection of drunkenness by mass society. Recent social history would suggest he had little impact. Shortly before his death, in 1856, Mathew said the following:

'We have turned the tide of public opinion; it was once a glory for men to boast what they drank, we have turned that false glory into shame; we have also given to the timid temperance man, to the teetotaller, the protection of his virtue, and a large share of public sympathy for his sacrifice in the cause of the first of virtues, sobriety.'

Today, that passages sounds as it reads, a hopelessly idealistic desire for a better society with a more mature relationship to alcohol, which has yet to materialise. Still, flawed as he may have been as a person, at least he tried.

———

Cut to today and Father Michael Mac Gréil is a man on a mission.

As chairperson of the Irish Pioneer Association, he grew sick and tired of hearing talk that the movement was in terminal decline. A few years back, he decided to visit every Pioneer centre in the country and assess the strength of the movement for himself. When I spoke to him, he had been to over 900 parishes and visited somewhere in the region of 1,100 Pioneer centres. He is currently in the process of compiling a report to present his findings to the Irish Pioneer Movement. He says, contrary to public opinion, the movement is still very much alive: 'It is still there and I think we have to work on it and tend it more. I'm still getting a reaction to my visit and I have a lot of information about the commitment. What people sometimes don't understand is that the Pioneer movement is primarily a spiritual movement and educates by example. Of course we also encourage sobriety.'

He admits there are 'big challenges' within the movement, yet feels that the Irish Pioneer Association still has a role to play in modern Ireland. At one time the Pioneer Total Abstinence Association boasted half a million Irish members, proud to wear the Pioneer pin as a badge of self-sacrificial Catholic devotion. It drew members from every section of society, and could summon over 80,000 people to outdoor rallies as recently as the 1950s. Yet estimates now put membership at less than 150,000, with uncertainty over how many of those are active Pioneers. Within the movement itself, debate is beginning to happen. Many argue that its abolitionist stance has no future in modern Ireland, with some calling for moderate drinkers to be allowed join. Indeed, on its website as part of its 2009 Lent campaign, the slogan was 'Why not abstain or reduce your alcohol intake this Lent?' It's a very big 'or', showing that the movement perhaps realises the strict abstinence game is up. There seems to be a new consensus emerging within the movement that abstaining from alcohol completely should be encouraged among under-18s, while moderation should be the ideal for those aged over 18.

Fr Mac Gréil says that it is impossible to accurately comment on the strength of the Pioneers in Ireland, given that they are a largely unseen organisation. 'We have always been a discreet group and have never gone for publicity. We are a spiritual movement who offer up abstinence for the sins of intemperance.' The image of a teetotalling membership, sternly anti-drink, is somewhat misleading, he says, pointing out that being in favour of abstention doesn't necessarily mean being anti-alcohol.

'Our mission is sobriety in society, sure, but we're not anti-drink. We may have had that image in the past, but we encourage people to drink in moderation. I mean, I am strongly in support of well-run pubs and would hate to see anything happen to the rural pub in Ireland. It is a very important social institution, and in many senses a well-run pub is also an institution for moderate drinking.'

Yet with alcohol such a pervasive facet of Irish life, the Pioneers are finding it increasingly difficult to get their message across. There are mitigating factors, argues Fr Mac Gréil. 'I am totally opposed to the identification of sport and alcohol. I say to workers in Guinness, sure, support our national games, but do it anonymously if you believe in it so much. But what they're doing is using sport to promote their products, and that's not promotion, that's advertising a mood-changing substance in an area identified with youth. It's a disaster in this country.'

Fr Mac Gréil believes that the availability of alcohol in recent years in more outlets has fuelled our increasing dependence. 'I think you have to study the false propaganda of the alcohol industry, the manner in which they promote the subtle and psychological way to sexual satisfaction and athletic prowess through the use of their products. I think a lot of it is a big lie. The big scandal at [the] moment is off-licence[s] and the supermarkets using alcohol as loss-makers to encourage people in [to] buy more. When you go into a supermarket now, alcohol is there like a stack of turf.'

Historian Diarmaid Ferriter sees the decline of the Pioneer Association in Ireland within the broader context of social and religious change and points out the inherent contradictions in a movement which promotes silent self-sacrifice on the one hand while simultaneously calling mass rallies and large-scale publicity events.

'It's interesting how it operates. It was meant to be a personal thing yet it thrives on mass participation through its structure and rallies and all that. I mean, personally I can remember being taken out of school to take part in these mass gatherings. I'm sure people, too, will recall borrowing Pioneer pins when going for job interviews in order to make an impression. It sounds pretty surreal now!' Ferriter agrees that the movement has witnessed a gradual decline since the 1960s, and offers little hope of resurgence.

'There's little doubt that it's been in decline for decades, much the same way as young people going to church has declined. I think there is a pressure on a whole generation nowadays that would make it very difficult for them to be part of a movement like the Pioneers.'

While the Irish Pioneer Association admits hardship in attracting members in the 30 to 50 age group, it does claim something of a resurgence among those under 25. A rebranding of the youth wing in the 1980s had a positive effect, with the emphasis now more on social outings than sacrificial penitence. Twenty-six-year-old Su-zann Scott, chairperson of the Young Pioneers, says that over 25,000 young people have joined the movement in recent years, and claims the association is having little difficulty attracting younger devotees. (The Irish Pioneer Movement is currently updating their database but feels membership may be closer to 18,000 currently).

'For me being a Pioneer is not just about not drinking, it is a huge social outlet, with so many competitions and events organised every week. There is a real sense of belonging and it works like having an extended family. That's why I choose to be a Pioneer—I now have friends in every corner of Ireland.' Scott says that modern Ireland is in need of the Pioneers now more than ever and feels proud to be part of a movement focused on changing society for the better. 'There is sacrifice and prayer involved, but we just want to try and promote peace and harmony in the home and in general society. Ireland has the highest rate of binge-drinking in Europe, so the Pioneers have a huge role to play. I'm always proud of my Pioneer badge. The way I look at it, I know if I never shame it, then it'll never shame me.'

Visitors to Ireland such as Dunton Fynes Morrison, Sir William Petty and Arthur Young all give us descriptions of the drinking and drunkenness in the seventeenth and eighteenth centuries, which read like 250-year-old equivalents of Prime Time specials. From those accounts, the image and idea of the 'Drunken Paddy' emerged and went overseas. That image has been hard to shake off, and in any event we haven't tried too hard, culminating in everything from cartoons in the British press in the nineteenth century to modern-day US shows such as 'The Simpsons', which rarely has reference to Ireland without the booze. Those stereotypes exist because those social connections to alcohol in Ireland exist over many centuries.

Long before glitzy advertising campaigns, drinking patterns in Ireland were abnormal. Our ancestors drank to take themselves out of the daily misery of eighteenth- and nineteenth-century life. Yet before that, they drank because of a lack of self-control and a romantic and sometimes religious attachment to mood altering. And yet we're not always a weak-willed race—the abstinence movements of the nineteenth and twentieth centuries are evidence of a sobering of thought and maturing of attitude in Ireland towards excessive drinking and drunkenness. Today, those movements struggle to hold onto their messages, and are looking for ways to adapt to the society they operate in, rather than vice versa. Moderation and reduction are the new buzzwords of the Pioneer Movement, where activities and sober social outings are promoted above pious abstinence. But what chance had they? Every abstinence movement in Ireland has been destined to failure, doomed by virtue of society's longstanding relationship to alcohol. The makers of modern Ireland were as much barmen and brewers as they were poets and politicians. But our relationship to alcohol through the last few hundred years is a complex one. Undoubtedly there have been long periods when consumption levels have been excessive, such as the eighteenth and early nineteenth centuries and early twenty-first century. But per capita consumption fails to take fully into account the numbers who abstained during those periods. Even today, 150,000 members of the Pioneer Movement is still an impressive figure, given the decline of the Church and religious movements in the past decades. As Elizabeth Malcolm points out, 'Much attention, both serious and frivolous, has been devoted to the drunken "Paddy", beloved of the popular press and music hall. But the drunken "Paddy" is only one side of the coin; the other side is the teetotal "Paddy".'

Moderate Paddy, though, has yet to reveal him- or herself.

Mary Coughlan, Singer

n hindsight, the first time I ever got drunk I was about fourteen and drinking Babychams and I don't remember a thing after the night. I do remember getting a few Babychams into me but I don't remember an awful lot after that. The next time I started drinking I was about nineteen, when I had my first daughter, Aoife. I had the next child when I was twenty-one. I had three children by the time I was twenty-four, and didn't drink during those years because I was really into my whole foods and natural childbirth and breastfeeding. I think I had a bottle of Guinness once and a few glasses of wine, but it was okay to do that in those days.

My social drinking started when I was about twenty-six or twenty-seven. I started going out for pints when the kids were a little bit older and I started singing at the same time. There was a lot of socialising around that. My worst drinking was the two years before I gave it up. Claire, my daughter who is seventeen now, was born. I hadn't drunk for the pregnancy because I had been in St John Of God Hospital before I got pregnant. I actually got pregnant on a weekend out from St John Of God Hospital. I thought I was completely cured because I had been off it eight or nine months by the time I had my daughter. When she was six weeks old, I went up to Quinnsworth, as it was called at the time, and bought a bottle of vodka. Every single day, then, for two years I drank an average of three bottles of vodka. I was hospitalised thirty-two times in those two years and ended up with a condition called metabolic acidosis. It landed me in intensive care in the Mater during St Patrick's weekend. I was critically ill with absolutely hours left to live and all I was thinking about was drinking again and how long would I be there for. At that stage I had already had a miscarriage.

Drink with me was pints at that time. There are lots of photographs of me including a really famous one on the cover of a particular album with a pint of Guinness in front of me. The second album also. I would sing with a pint of Guinness on stage, but really it was only pints at that stage. That was totally the image I was projecting. The first time I had a gin and tonic I was thirty. I hung with people who were well known for it already in the trade, like the Pogues and Nick Cave and stuff like that. I remember once being interviewed for the New Musical Express (NME) in England and the publicist or manager knew I had been drinking champagne the night before, so he asked if I had any champagne left. He suggested it would be a great idea if I walked down with it in the morning. I said, 'Ah ya no problem,' and I did it. One of the other pictures they asked me to do was to lie down outside in the street with my head in the double yellow lines in the road. What the fuck! I did it. I was a wild fucking woman with a vocabulary like the backside of a loo door and a voice like bleeding cherries. So I became known for the boozy image.

I didn't realise until the later years, and going into the Rutland Centre, how much damage I had done to my kids. Everybody I knew, all the mothers, at that time all drank at weekends. I remember going to a bar called the Summit, when I lived in Howth, nineteen or twenty years ago. I'd [go] for a few pints in the evening after school, maybe a pint of lager or two, and let the kids run around. Go home then and do the homework and then the dinner. And these are in normal times, now, and maybe later at night you'd walk down for a few more pints. It wasn't until I started buying drink for my house that I knew it was a problem, which I had never done up a certain period of my life. This was in the 1980s—maybe 1989.

I was abused horribly when I was a child and I done an awful lot of work in that area. It wasn't until I accepted it that things began to ease. Looking back on my drinking, I think there was no other way I could have coped. I used drink to hurt myself and it wasn't until I realised how much I was hurting other people that I stopped, when I had some sort of decency left in me. I was hurting myself because I was a bad, bad person.

That abuse had left me with an intrinsic self-hate. I used to say I was lower than lino, that I was a worm. I had felt like that since I was about seven. I had felt depressed, and had attempted suicide. I was locked up in a nuthouse when I was sixteen. There was a fact there I hadn't acknowledged. I'm not saying it was the reason I drank, but there was this feeling of being worthless. It wasn't until I addressed that that I could actually say goodbye to drink.

Now, I haven't had a drink for about fifteen years. I had been to several treatment centres but the Rutland Centre was my salvation. I don't know if it was the time or circumstance; I was thirty-seven when I started there. I was so bad that I couldn't go there from the hospital, and I wasn't allowed home either. Nobody wanted me home. It was really the end of the road, and it worked because even though I did initially think about 'Will I ever be able to drink again?' when I was laying on that hospital bed on my own. What prevented it was the fucking shame of it and what I had done to my daughter Claire. I spent her second Christmas in an Accident and Emergency ward and they all came in to see me on Christmas Day. Her second birthday I was down in a nuthouse and let out for the afternoon. The inability to connect with her was probably the most painful experience of my life.

I was listening to my three eldest children in the Rutland Centre every Wednesday when they had to come in and I never knew they felt so bad about me drinking socially. When they were little, Eóin, my son, was saying how lonely he felt. Eóin is twenty-eight now. How lonely he felt when myself and the mothers I used to hang around with would throw them a mineral and a bag of crisps and let them run around the car park up at the pub. He really felt lonely and felt scared. One time I drove home and he thought I was going to get them killed in the car. I had to sit there and listen to that. And listen, also, to my daughter tell how she used to listen outside the bedroom. Because I used to drink in a spare room and I had a mattress on the floor there and she used to listen out to see if I was alive. I slapped my daughter once, because she was pouring my last bottle of vodka down the sink. I got really angry with her and hit her a belt. When you're in treatment, and if you look at that shit every single week for six weeks and you have to listen to them saying it over and over again. I had a wonderful therapist there. She was the greatest bitch on two feet and I hated her but she sorted me out! After the first family day in the Rutland, she asked me the next morning, 'How do you feel?' I said, 'Oh, grand.' And in front of everyone she started screaming at me. 'How could you feel grand, because I listened to your kids yesterday.' That's when it started. They were making me look at what I had done and it clicked with me. Yet I came out of the Rutland Centre and I went home and drank. I don't remember what I drank but I do remember that my partner found me passed out on the kitchen floor. I don't remember how I got the vodka, or going for it. I phoned the Rutland Centre and went back out there straight away and did one-to-one counselling, which lasted for a long, long time.

It was only then I started to address all the things I hadn't told them in there, about me and what happened to me as a kid and how I had felt all my life. I was dealing, really, with being ashamed for my kids when I was in there, and I hadn't dealt with the shame of me.

I haven't had any drink all my life since then.

When I came out, I hated everyone with drink. I hated them because I couldn't drink with them. I was left babysitting a lot of the time while everyone went to the pub because I couldn't stand going to the pubs. I was very good friends with people who had children and we always had a social dinner on a Sunday and I began to resent people for drinking the first year I was out. About three years on I was driving through Dalkey. In my past, I used to drink in the car an awful lot. I would buy drink and drink it in the car. A few times I drove into Dublin to the early house near Pearse Station. I used to go and get drink also in the Spar in the morning. They would open at seven o'clock and a guy in there did me a favour and I'd buy a bottle of port and down it before I called the kids for school in the morning. Nobody would know. My favourite tipple in the car was a bottle of rosé. I would put a straw into it and drink it. So one day, I rang the Rutland Centre from a particular harbour which was one of my favourite drinking sites, and I pulled in the car. The car filled up with gin and tonic. I could smell Gordon's Gin. I could see the bottle, I could smell the ice and smell the lemon and smell the tonic water. I rang the Rutland and I said to my counsellor, Maura, 'I'm never going to drink again.' I said to her, 'Can I say that?' She said, 'You can, if you really want to.' So I said, 'I'm never going to drink again, never ever.' And that was it.

So I'm at peace with it now. I was in a very nice part of Italy doing a gig a few years ago and the promoter said to me, 'This is where that great rosé wine comes from,' and I brought two special bottles home for Christmas dinner for the family. So I was comfortable doing that. I have only gotten respect from people since giving up. I think because from very early on I was upfront and public and my drinking. I did huge interviews with the *Irish Times* and with Mike Murphy on the radio. That was probably one of the best interviews I have ever done in my life—it was an hour long and I did the whole show with him about drinking. I felt it was that shame of being a mother and alcoholic and I had met so many from treatment. You feel like such a scumbag . . . [A] lot of the men in AA also, I felt, looked down at women. They were just the men having pints on the way home. All my drinking was done at home. I rarely went out to the pub in my last two years of drinking. I drank constantly at home and I think I did the publicity to get rid of the awful shame of it and to say, 'Well, this is it, and it is a disease.' And the only thing you don't have to do is to drink to cure it and deal with it. All that time I was dealing with it in all those interviews I did. I was very, very public about it and it was a kind of a deterrent also. But I felt I have enjoyed every moment since and everything I have learned about who I am and the relationship with the family changes and the co-dependents come out of the wall. They find it harder to live with it than I did. I think that's why I had to leave my husband. He would have drunk every single day for all of the years I lived with him while I was sober, which was about ten years.

I cried on occasions when he was opening really expensive bottles of wine. The guy I live with now is from New Zealand—a great outdoors type—and never drank. He had a few beers with the family at sixteen or seventeen and that was it and it's no big deal. It's great to have a relationship with someone where drink doesn't enter their lives. Because in the past it was a nightly dinner thing. I had often cooked dinner for fifteen people on a Sunday afternoon and woke up on a Monday morning and had to clear the table after all the drink and cigarettes. So that was not going to last.

The pain and isolation that people are feeling, that's why they drink, I think. Carl Jung wrote the twelve steps of Alcoholics Anonymous and I read him a lot. I did a ten-week course and was going to go on and do addiction counselling but I didn't have time; the career started off again. He speaks of it as being a disease, which means ill at ease with your psyche. He talks about alcohol and drug addiction and depression as being various stages of being ill at ease with your spirituality and your physicality, your emotions. It's about being split off from things, and that's where I was, right smack bang in the middle of that. My children would have inherited that so by the time they were ten, I was emotionally unavailable to them.

I don't think it helped my career, the fact I was sober. But I think that for the first time in my life since I stopped drinking I am only now realising what it's like to be really sober in my head. I have a new manager, Jools Holland's manager, and am playing the Sydney Opera House in August. I have the greatest records I've ever made out. I have broken every connection with the past, including my husband. I might not be up there in lights, but everywhere I go I still have a career. It's much smaller than it was and much more manageable and much more fulfilling than it was. Now I go into clubs with three hundred or four hundred people and love every minute of it. I'm glad I'm an alcoholic because I might never have gotten to this level of understanding of myself and the rest of humanity or the humanity within my sphere of living. And I certainly have compassion for people out there that I never would have had beforehand.

If you're asking me what I think of Ireland, I think this country is fucked and it has been for a very long time. And whether it is TV or computer games or the pub, Ireland has gone through this huge identity crisis. It came when we joined the EEC, and we had to shake off the Church and we had to shake off all the shame and we had to acknowledge it.

They say there was seven hundred years of oppression by the Brits but the real oppression was done by our own. I do feel that there is a collective unconscious and I do feel the country hurts.

There was abuse in my family, abuse in my parents' family, and I do believe I have called time on it now because I have confronted all my demons.

It's always better to talk it out. So many people are in denial in Ireland. I know personally people who have tried to stop coroners' reports. There are an awful lot of deaths that are drink-related and not reported. Lot of heart attacks, brain injuries, and [a] lot of it is alcohol abuse. I don't think the government can do anything about Ireland's way of drinking. It's a cultural thing. I know when you're seventeen, and there's drinking in your family and you're emotionally fragile. I don't think anybody can do anything about it. I don't think banning drink or putting up the price does anything. Kids have to find their own way. Addiction, as far as I'm concerned, is a huge personal pain people have and what they do to bury pain is to use, food, alcohol, and drugs. Anything that removes you from reality and become overused and keeps you from thinking about your life.

My kids know and I've talked to them about it and my fears. I suppose I'm very excited about Cian. I was sober for three years before he was born and he is twelve now and he's going into secondary school in September. To be quite honest, I'm looking forward to it as much as he is, because I'm going to be there physically, mentally and emotionally all the way this time. I have worried about my kids feeling lonely and abandoned. I drank on that for years and felt guilty about that and remained fucked up about it. A fella said to me one night in the Rutland Centre in an aftercare group, having been there for two years—'Get off the fucking cross, Mary.' His point was, whatever I had done was over with and I had to get on with now.

I swear to Jesus I have a life beyond my wildest dreams and I don't go to AA. I discovered scuba diving when I was forty-eight. Horse-riding. There's a new man in my life. I have grandchildren. Looking forward to building a house, looking at a site. All that stuff.

The first time I went on holidays I remember it was a little difficult and the last holiday I had with my husband was particularly difficult because I knew we were going to split up. I'll never forget him drinking wine on our holidays and that was really difficult. I work really hard at things now. But it's only in the last four or five years that I have been able to reap the rewards.

The at-home drinking in the last few years has been huge. I know people who have built bars in their houses. And they are now staying home more and they say it's because of the recession and so on. I think it's because people are hurting. There is going to be a huge thing of drinking at home, and women have always drank at home anyway.

I remember growing up, even, there were two women who were absolutely stunning on our road. We were never let into their houses, and I found out when I was in my twenties that it was because they were alcoholics. Lovely-looking women and very well kept, and I had no idea. I remember when I was living in Howth and I had a few women friends and we used to drink and the question did come up an odd time, 'Do you think we're fucking alcoholics?' We did drink a lot, very rare an evening would go by and you didn't have three pints. And where that wasn't going to rip anyone apart, it was the beginning of it. And you get progressively worse. I remember not sleeping one night because of the jitters and getting into the car and driving in to the early house. So that's where it leads you.

With the AA meetings I had planned to do everything I was told to do, so ninety meetings in ninety days. If you had told me to jump off a house I would have done it. Some days I went to two meetings and really felt the need for them. It was just for the connection, and I loved the aftercare group. Anything to do with pain and grit and real soul-searching I loved. I'm not knocking AA. If this is what people need to get over their addiction then that's fine. I just didn't want to stay sober, I wanted to find out why I drank in the first place and find out what would keep me away from it for the rest of my life without saying this bullshit of 'One day at a time and I'm Mary and I'm an alcoholic and so on'. I didn't believe that. I had a public forum, though, and I did engage with that and it was cathartic for me and I did it. I did go to AA for a long, long time at lunch and in the evenings. I still go because of the social element. A lot of the women I know in New Zealand I have met through AA. There's a huge difference going to AA in other countries. In Sydney, the AA there is like counselling sessions; it's not just surface stuff. But it's easier not to drink there too. I think the scene in Ireland now is really, really bad drinking, more so than ever. I saw a girl one night, when I was coming up through Temple Bar, and she was on a bollard and she had a skirt on up her arse and every bastard that passed her out on the street was having a feel off her. She was puking her guts out. I went over and asked her if she was okay and she told me to fuck off. It was so depressing. I was doing a show in the Olympia and had to walk back through Temple Bar six nights a week. Monday night not so bad, Tuesday night okay too. Thursday, Friday, Saturday—give me a fucking break. Vomit everywhere and that was in the height of the Celtic Tiger in 2002.

I know a lot of artists talk about needing drink after shows. I remember once finding it hard to sleep and sharing it at an AA meeting in Bray. The reply was 'No one ever died from lack of sleep!' And it's true. I never worried about the effect not drinking would have on my creativity. The only person who worried about it was my ex-husband.

He felt I wouldn't be any craic any more. But I'm the best craic now; I have just finished a tour and got an email back from the band saying they really enjoyed every minute of it.

They were all having a drink and I was buying them a drink after the show. They could have one drink before the gig and none on stage and they are my rules. They all know now, as well, the difference between a drunken musician and a sober one is a huge benefit.

I don't buy the drunk artist thing. Shane MacGowan's thing is the most depressing and disgusting scene. I hate all the people around him for doing what they're doing and I know most of them. Shane MacGowan and myself and Nick Cave used to do it to the best of our ability in dressing rooms after gigs. Huge bags of cocaine and huge bottles of drink and pills. Shane is the only one carrying on that lifestyle. People have died in his company, some very young. I was singing in the church at one funeral and in the middle of the thing in came Shane and slithered to the back of the church. I have no time for anybody like that. I have compassion but I have no time for the people who he hangs around with. I did a huge tour with the Pogues and sang every night Kirsty McColl couldn't do. I did the most frightening gig of my life at Brixton Academy and all those people jumping up and down completely out of their minds. It was fucking horrible. I sang with him at the Point and at the Olympia. And I thought, what the fuck are you doing here, Mary, do you really need this kind of shit in your life? It was all this give him a bottle, give him this give him that, get him on stage, wipe up his vomit. Maybe it's just too close to the bone, but I can't stand the people who were around him. What the fuck has he done? The people around him, as far as I'm concerned, are like the people who used to hang around me when I was drinking, fucking leeches and hangers-on, just there for the session. At the height of my fame I was doing seven nights a week in the Mean Fiddler in London and two nights at the Palladium, all in the same month.

I always talk about my story every time I'm asked, because I think it's so important to talk about the reasons people drink rather than the drink and the curse of the drink and all that. I rarely met an alcoholic or drug addict that hasn't been through some awful sort of emotional pain. I think a lot of kids nowadays suffer from emotional abandonment. Their parents may have been slaves to the work and acquiring money and houses and careers, and I am so happy I was okay when rearing my first three children in that I spent time with them at home. I do think that had some sort of good effect for what was to come.

I would say with my generation, eighty per cent of the children in my class were beaten either at school or home. And I think it's for different reasons people drink now. I don't think anyone has any core beliefs now any more. It's hard to find it. I have five children from the age of thirty-three to twelve so I have an array of teenage experience in my life. The ones now have fuck-all. I think kids are left a lot to their own devices. I don't think there's any guidance and I know I didn't do it with my children. I didn't know what it was to be a mother and a parent. I didn't know good parenting. I learnt parenting skills, though, and really took responsibility, and my life has changed completely because of it.

Chapter 5
The Forgotten Irish

'Now the summer is fine, but the winter's a fridge
Wrapped up in old cardboard under Charing Cross Bridge
And I'll never go home it's because of the shame
Of a misfit's reflection in a shop window pane.

So all you young people take an advice
Before crossing an ocean you'd better think twice
'Cause you can't live without love, without love alone
Here's the proof round the West End in the nobody zone.'

Missing You—JIMMY MACCARTHY

I first started thinking about Irish emigrants and their association with alcohol following a cup of coffee with RTÉ journalist and author Paddy O'Gorman. For the last 20 years, Paddy has been documenting the plight of Irish emigrants in England. With a mother from London and a father from Cobh, from where so many emigrated, Paddy's observational eye has always been well in tune with the state of the ex-pat and how it can manifest itself adversely. Or, as he explains himself, 'The pub is hugely important to the story of emigration.' Paddy's own father worked in London, all the while managing to sidestep stereotype. 'My own dad never drank and I came to understand that's why he married an Englishwoman, he married outside the culture of the other Irish men. He had a visible distaste for the heavy drinking culture and an aversion to it. He never had any time for what he called the "rubbish of pub talk".'

Perhaps it was this personal remove that allowed Paddy to document the extent to which alcohol dominated the emigrant story. Issues of loneliness, of cultural inadequacy, of sentimentality and of a certain amount of personal freedom from being in another place all played their part in allowing addiction and abuse to run riot. I knew it from my own limited experience in the bars of Cape Cod, where hordes of Irish on J1 Visa programmes crammed as much drinking into a three-month stay as possible. Hey, I was one of them!

O'Gorman, though, doesn't see emigration per se as the issue— more how we Irish act out during the transition to another environment. 'The emigration thing in the 1980s was a hell of a lot better than being unemployed back home. Yeah, they were paying a fortune on their flats, same as we did in Rathmines in the 1970s. I think every male negative thing tends to be accentuated in the migrant worker. The Irish in Germany, in the 1990s, when the Berlin Wall came down, helped create a very ugly drinking scene. There was an awful lot of mad behaviour on drink and little villages with "No Irish" signs up. These German towns were not allowing Irish in pubs any more because of young men who behaved in an absolutely disgraceful fashion.'

In moral terms, though, not everything was black and white. 'In the eyes of many, it was a double-edged sword. While drink may have been bad, it was nowhere near as bad as sex. Drink was nearly a kind of substitute for sexual joy. Associated with merrymaking, in Ireland the morose atmosphere of the male drinking group is different to many other countries. It's an odd thing.' While others in this book have come to see the strict moral rule of the Church as manifesting itself in an unhealthy reliance on alcohol, O'Gorman sees it slightly differently. 'It might not be a popular thing to say but we would have sank without the church, and without its influence on men abroad. I am told stories about Fr Eamon Casey and his ability to go onto dance floors in Kilburn or Cricklewood and say, "Men, men, for God's sake stop". It would have an effect on guys mad with drink. These were men who would have ended up in prison and many of them did. People like Fr Casey had a huge positive effect on Irish culture abroad.'

The Irish abroad, like many emigrants, are lacking wider

societal structure, however lax, to ensure drinking patterns don't get out of control. For example, horizontal policing by peers, where older brothers or members of a family might tell individuals to go easy, is less apparent. 'Ah sure, there is none of us married, we're all separated, and that's the work' is a phrase often heard among emigrants, be it in Berlin or Boston. But, perhaps there is something in the nature of the men themselves that makes them become migrant workers. A feeling of being out of sync from an early age, of not quite fitting in. Add alcohol to those feelings, and you're in for a whole lot of self-destructive behaviour.

'It's a sad life,' says O'Gorman of the emigrant problem drinker. 'I was working in London in 1978 with a lot of Irish guys. One day some of them were remarking that "Jack Doyle has died." I'd never hear of Jack Doyle, even though he was from Cobh. I rang my dad and he said he was an awful man who used to steal our chickens as kids!

'My dad went on to say he was a terrible drinker. And over the last twenty years, I met all these old guys who said, "Ah sure I had a drink with Jack Doyle." I thought, "They can't all be telling the truth." But at this stage of my life I actually think they really did all drink with him. In the later stages he would pour his life out for a drink. There is nothing romantic [or] glorious about it and there were many Jack Doyles in bars all over London.'

Prof. Brian Girvin, Professor of Comparative Politics at the University of Glasgow and a noted historian, describes arriving in London in the 1970s and seeing police vans lined up in the street to deal with public order offences at closing time. 'That was my direct experience of the Irish emigrants and alcohol, with fights left and right of me! Historically, I think the evidence we have from the 1940s and 1950s shows the amount of money the Irish emigrants were spending on alcohol.'

Probed on whether he felt the colonial legacy was to blame for Ireland's reliance on alcohol, Prof. Girvin reserved judgment. 'I'm always slightly reserved when the colonial thing is put forward to explain all the negatives and none of the positives of the Irish experience. I think a lot of peasant societies drink heavily. One of the things about emigrants arriving in Britain was that it was a much freer society compared to Ireland. I think that people from rural backgrounds arriving there must have found it quite challenging. An awful lot of single males fell between the cracks, with no sister or mother to look after them. The Church was really the only focus for many of them. And the Church was never overly anti-drink. Many of these males were displaced with more money than they were used to and more freedom and many lost control as a result. I'm inclined to think when the Irish left Ireland, as other communities have done, they took a public aspect of their culture with them. Italians took the restaurant, the Irish took the pub.'

More recently, a study carried out by Dr Mary Tilki, Principal Lecturer in MA Health and Social Care at Middlesex University, examined the social contexts of drinking among Irish men in London. Mainly focused on men who left Ireland in the 1960s and 1970s, the study explored the 'possibility that tolerant attitudes to alcohol in Ireland persist on migration to Britain and are then confounded by a culture of binge drinking among young people in general'. One of the sources for the study was the 1999 Health Survey for England, which included first- and second-generation Irish for the first time and found they were more likely to consume alcohol to excess than other ethnic groups and the general population. For the last three decades, in fact, repeated studies have pointed to higher alcohol-related mortality rates in England and Wales among Irish-born people than among other ethnic groups. Others point to higher rates of suicide, admission to psychiatric hospitals and general medical complaints among the Irish in Britain.

The men who left Ireland from the 1950s for the UK were mainly employed by building contractors on a casual basis and the Irish pub was central to their economy. It's where many were picked up, dropped off and often paid their wages for a day's work. It was, in many ways, a 'home from home'. Society in Ireland at the time was a strange mix of teetotalism and alcohol abuse. Alcohol was at once embraced and condemned, as it still is. The focus on abstention, though, in previous decades, with children being required to 'take the pledge' at Confirmation time, meant that many young Irish adults never had the opportunity to learn how to drink sensibly or in an ordered manner. Alcoholism operating within that culture, then, was often regarded as a 'good man's fault' as opposed to a disease or illness which needed treatment or any concerted therapeutic action.

As Dr Tilki points out, 'Although the pub had an important economic function for Irish men in Britain, its wider social functions cannot be underestimated. It afforded an escape from overcrowded and inhospitable digs, shared with strangers and where visitors were not allowed.' Discrimination against the Irish, particularly during the period of the Troubles in Northern Ireland, meant the pub offered a safe haven from societal hostility. The pub also served as a rite of passage for many young men, just off the boat and drinking and working with adults for the first time. Men who were admired and respected in the Irish enclaves had names like Mule Kennedy, Bull Gallagher, Big Mick or Elephant John, with stories of their drinking exploits continuing to the present.

The public drinking place has, as Dr Tilki notes, a 'key function in facilitating sociability and alcohol promotes relaxation and conviviality. In most cultures, rules around drinking stipulate that alcohol is consumed in a sharing social context with goodwill and bonhomie.' What the pub did was allow Irish men from different parts of Ireland and many working under different employers to socialise with friends and build up their list of contacts. This was particularly evident with men from Gaeltacht areas who had limited English. 'In addition to the alcohol, music, cards and games whiled away the hours for Irish men, with no "home" to go to, kept them in touch with their culture, and protected them from homesickness, loneliness and isolation.'

Dr Tilki's report offered a bleak assessment of the plight of the Irish in Britain, unless urgent action is not taken. 'Given the unequivocal poor physical and mental health, high levels of suicide and concerns about dangerous patterns of consumption among Irish men (and women) in Britain, urgent action is needed at national and local policy level,' she noted.

I travelled to Cricklewood, hoping to meet what is left of the Irish emigrant drinking culture. Leaving the Willesden Green Tube station and walking towards Cricklewood Broadway, the Irishness of this part of London has become somewhat muted. Polish, Latvian, Greek, Pakistani and Indian faces now populate the Broadway, and even some of the Irish bars have Polish signs outside advertising drinks promotions. Many of the Irish in this area left to chase the Tiger in the noughties and haven't returned. Those who made their mark left the area, finding in areas such as Surrey and Richmond a more salubrious neighbourhood. Houses in the area still have a rented feel, though, with glass bottles outside doorways and unkempt lawns a feature. First port of call was the recently opened Cricklewood Homeless Centre, run by Danny Maher, which is dealing with the many aging Irish with alcohol and other problems.

The new building opened in 2008, with financial assistance, somewhat ironically, from Irish building contractors. The charity itself has been in operation since 1983, when locals noticed a rise in the number of Irish on the streets following the building crash of the 1980s. 'You might know the story, most of our lads lived in one room, worked on the buildings and the rest of the lads were in the pub. When the working lads got off the sites, they went straight to the pub and drank most nights. They went home then to their little room, and when they lost their job, they lost everything. So that's the reason they set up a soup kitchen in a local church from 1983 up to the present.'

Over time the centre changed from a soup kitchen for the homeless to what is now a community centre assisting vulnerable persons in a wide variety of circumstances from mental health issues to addiction, housing and job assistance. 'Most of the work is still around homelessness,' says Danny Maher. 'Irish are the second biggest group—the first largest ethnic grouping we deal with being African refugees. A major trend these days is for us to be working with many from Eastern Europe, mainly Polish. We call them the new Irish, they are very similar backgrounds in ways, Catholic countries with major drink problems.'

The centre is built to reflect Maslow's triangle of needs, with the clients taking a journey from the ground floor to the top, where they will leave with a capacity to look after themselves. 'There are Irish people here who have problems going back thirty years,' says Danny Maher. 'So their journey will take a long time and it's doubtful they will ever fully reach their destination. Our plan for them is to improve their lifestyles. Young fellas will come in, though, and we would have more hope. There is a young Irish fella now from Limerick, came in a few weeks ago and he is homeless and young. So we will be looking to get him back into work and accommodation as soon as possible so he doesn't fall into the lifestyle.'

From the Diarmuid-Gavin-designed gardens to the IT suites and medical facilities, the building caters for those marginalised either by society or their own habits in a state-of-the-art environment. When I ask Danny why it is that alcohol plays such a role in the lives of Irish emigrants, he points to loneliness and loss as major factors. 'I came over here myself thirty years ago as a young fella and didn't have any family here so I have some understanding of what it is like. Fellas came over here at fourteen and fifteen and went straight onto the building site and they only had the pub. I think they got into bad habits at a very early stage. I suppose this country and their employers exploited them as well. When they think about Ireland now, everything is loss. For example the Galtymore is gone, a major dance hall and icon of Irish community. The National Dance Hall in Kilburn, major meeting point for the Irish, is gone. These streets, up to two years ago, [you] wouldn't have been able to walk along the footpaths with the amount of Irish men waiting for the pickup for buildings. That has been going on for twenty to thirty years. Now not one of them, the demographic has changed. The Irish emigrants are losing everything.'

————

The traditional Irish 'session'. (*Christy McNamara*)

Comedian Des Bishop (see page 42). (*The Irish Times*)

Saturday night in Ennis, Co. Clare.

Outside the Carrig Rua Hotel in Dunfanaghy, Co. Donegal: Ireland's first booze-free bar. (*Declan Doherty*)

Barman Stephen Ferry serves up a pint from the 'Slush Puppy' machine, installed behind the bar at the Carrig Rua Hotel. (*Declan Doherty*)

Singer Frances Black (see page 74). (*Andrea Smith*)

Representations of the drunken 'Paddy'. (*The National Library of Ireland*)

The Father Mathew
statue on Cork's
Patrick Street, in
honour of the
nineteenth-century
Temperance
Movement leader.
(*Wikimedia Commons*)

Singer Mary Coughlan (see page 93). (*The Irish Times*)

John Leahy, ex Tipperary hurler and now drug education officer (see page 124). (*Sportsfile*)

Dr Chris Luke in the
Mercy Hospital, Cork.
(*Dr Chris Luke*)

Ennis writer and actor, Mark
O'Halloran (see page 153).
(*Getty Images*)

The outside of the Guinness Storehouse, one of Ireland's most visited tourist sites.
(*Guinness Archive/Diageo Ireland*)

Guinness Storehouse cooperage exhibition, showing the close association between Ireland and Guinness down through the ages. (*Guinness Archive/Diageo Ireland*)

One of our great natural resources

Guinness: One of our great natural resources? (*Guinness Archive/Diageo Ireland*)

(Left and above) Workers in Guinness availing of their daily beer allowance. (*Guinness Archive/ Diageo Ireland*)

Night Raven volunteers tend to a young city reveller in Copenhagen. (*Ulrik Jantzen/DAS BÜRO*)

Actor and long-time teetotaller Niall Toibin (see page 184). (*Niall Toibin*)

Taking part in the national day of Irishness: Temple Bar on St Patrick's Day. (*Photocall*)

A homeless man in Temple Bar. (*Photocall*)

A pint of plain is your only man? Eamon Morrissey in *The Brother*. (RTÉ *Stills Library*)

Ian Woosnam holds aloft a pint of Guinness during the Ryder Cup celebrations in Ireland. (*Press Association Images Ltd*)

Irish singer and well-known boozer, Shane MacGowan. (*Press Association Images Ltd*)

'We're in danger of drinking ourselves into a national stupor.' Brian O'Connell in Temple Bar, 2008. (*Matt Kavanagh/The Irish Times*)

On the third floor, where hourly therapy sessions and meetings take place, I met with Gerry, a 47-year-old former labourer from Mayo, who first came to the UK in 1978. He was 16½ years old at the time, and got work on the building sites.

Most of his family were in London, and him being the youngest, it was inevitable he would follow suit. Before he came to London he experimented with alcohol only a handful of times. But things quickly changed. He's now sober six months, the longest period in his adult life without drinking.

'The carryon was lunchtime, around one o'clock, everyone go to the pub and have a couple of pints, especially in hot weather. The safety regulation that time was more common sense, not the type of regulations you have today. So everyone, even the foreman, would go for a couple of pints at lunchtime, depending on whatever you get in over half an hour. Some people might have four or five pints, especially if it's a day of ninety degrees. Some might only have two.

'If you were travelling out of town, you'd go straight to the pub after work. And again, some people might only have three or four pints or some would stay until closing time.

'For me, it progressed as the years went on until the point where drink takes hold. For the last few years, drink was virtually my god. I got so dependent on it.

'You'd never be out of work, really. You had the contacts if you were here for years and would get to know nearly every Irish person. Sometimes you'd get sick of work and go on a binge, maybe for two weeks. The binge would last until the money would last. You end up starting from scratch again, a vicious circle.

'I was living around the area. The pubs them days, in the nineteen-eighties up until the late nineteen-nineties, when the work was good and the money was there, were great. On a Monday night in a pub, the place would be packed after the weekend. In for the cure and for some people the cure would lead to the session again. If you had too much Monday, you had to go another night and then the weekend would be nearly on top of you and it would be the full blast again.

'Some jobs would be only five days. So you would get up Saturday morning and have a shower or bath and you'd be bored. So the first thing you'd do is go to the pub and your mates would be in there. Even if me working mates weren't there, there would be someone there you would know, because you're around the area for so long, it's like a big, big family. Even in Kilburn you'd know people, no matter which pub you'd go to.

'I never really sat down and thought about the drink. You start to realise you have a problem when you start missing time over work. That's the first sign, I think. Missing Monday started first. In them days in Biddy Mulligan's in Kilburn you'd get more in it Monday that you would get in it Saturday or Sunday night. The pubs used to close at half two or three o'clock in the afternoon but Biddy Mulligan's would stay open. If you were in, you were locked in. So if you did the full monty on Monday, you'd end up missing Tuesday, and if you missed Tuesday you'd have a full week in it. It would creep up on you gradually. Eventually over the years.

'In my heyday I could drink fifteen, sixteen or seventeen pints. I remember a cousin of mine said to me one night years ago, do you know how many pints you drank? He didn't drink and kept count. He said I drank eighteen. I was twenty-one at the time.

'I tried to stop. God only knows how many times I tried. Locked myself away in the room for three or four days in torture. The minute I hit outside again the temptation was too easy and straight at it again. I drank everything and anything. In the morning it would be a few pints of cider to cure myself. It's easily drank. Maybe a few brandy and ports. You'd go by what you'd hear what the best thing for the cure was. Which is nonsense; the best cure in the long run is no cure. You'd try anything. If you drink a few of them anything would cure you. I decided to return to Dublin at the end of the nineteen-nineties to help me slow down the drinking. I knew it was getting the better of me so I thought a change of scenery, a change of faces would help. But it didn't. It was the same carryon in Dublin.

'No matter where you are, if you're out in the Sahara Desert you'll get it if you are that desperate for it. It had a grip got on me very badly. The last few years in Dublin I used to get up an hour earlier in the morning. I had to leave the house at six-thirty a.m. for work so I'd get up at five-thirty a.m. to have a few cans to settle my stomach to go to work. I knew then I really had a problem. But I needed that hour of drinking to stop the shakes in the morning, to stop the dry retching, the vomiting. I'd have maybe two, three, four cans. Then I'd be sound and head off to work.

'That would keep me going until breakfast time, ten o'clock, when I'd go to the off-licence instead of the café. I'd have my other top-up then, which would keep me going until lunchtime. Two or three pints then. Maybe four pints. I was living on drink. Come in then in the evening I'd go to the pub. For a couple of years I was living on takeaways at eleven o'clock at night—that was the only bit of food I had.

'Down through the years I was in a few relationships, but I was married to drink already, put it bluntly. One relationship I was in for four years and she was a good woman. She eventually said to me, "Me or the drink". It was like being hit with a fourteen-pound hammer. Without hesitating I said to her, "I can't give it up." That was the end of that relationship after four years. There was no competition between her and the drink. I did love her but there you go.

'I don't think a dependence on the drink is down to your family. My father always had a few pints, he still does to this day and he's nearly ninety years of age. I started at an early age and the work situation I was in, it was all drinking. But then I had a choice. I know people who had their few drinks and didn't make a pig of themselves. I realise now it creeps up without you knowing it. At the time you don't realise you're doing damage to yourself.

'In 2000, I went back to Ireland, and it was the same. I knew a few fellas from here and started using a pub all the time. You get to know people in the pub and unfortunately there are people there that have the same problem you have. You click with them people. You won't click with the person that's only in for one or two pints.

'I was ten years away from Cricklewood, and when I came back last year a lot had changed. Lot of faces missing. I heard a lot of them died and a few of them moved to Ireland when work was good. A few of the old faces are still around.

'The two main ballrooms had closed. I mean in the 1980s many a time we left one of the ballrooms, The Galtymore, at two in the morning and get a taxi to a twenty-four-hour shop and fill the boot with drink. Then up to some flat and keep drinking until you fell asleep. Wake up in the morning and, anything left over, cure yourself and off to the pub again. I know for a fact there's fellas doing the same thing I started doing with them in the early eighties.

'I knew, though, I was at the end of my road. I hadn't been eating properly for years. I used to be average fifteen stone in my heyday and the weight fell off me. Which it would fall off anyone when you have cider for six o'clock in the morning and cider for ten o'clock in the morning. I was down to eleven stone when I went into detox.

'I was weak. Only for the detox and the medication and all that, it helped me a lot. It helped the horrors, the shakes. I was on ten tablets a day for two weeks to help keep the rats away. It was my last call out for help. This centre here, only for it. I came out and they put me into a fine house where all the people in the house are absent from drink. We're having therapy now five days a week. My family at home know I'm not drinking, but I haven't really gone into detail with what I've done to stop. It's not a thing you like to advertise, that you were in drying out.

'When I was growing up there wasn't such thing as an "alcoholic", there was such a thing as a "heavy drinker". Or "he likes his drink". There was no such thing that time as "he had a problem with drink".

'I wouldn't be able to settle back in Ireland now because I'm too far gone. A year and a half before I came back to England, I was in Mayo because through drink I had four or five broken ribs. Then I broke my shoulder through drink so I went home for a bit.

'There's a local pub there over the road and you see married couples in their early fifties and they come into the pub at eleven o'clock at night and I can't understand that.

'I would be pie-eyed that time, only ready to fall into bed. They would come out for an hour, maybe, which I would never be able to do. Not if I lived for a hundred years. They go out at eleven o'clock at night, I go out at eleven o'clock in the morning. That's the difference.

'For example, down through the years I often found myself in early houses. I remember one job in particular where the early house was between the Tube station and the job site, which was a disaster. You'd get off the Tube and have to pass the pub. If I felt rough at all I'd go in and have one, maybe two quick ones. A couple of mornings I'd go in and there would be someone from the job in the pub before me!

'This is the longest now I have been off it. If you had told me this time last year I would be six months off it I'd say you were crazy. The first few months were hard, I was still nervous. Even after a month off it if some car hooted a horn, I would jump. My nervous system was completely destroyed by thirty years drinking. I was spitting up blood in the end and my liver was not too good. If I kept going I wouldn't have seen fifty, in other words.

'It's hard to say but it's the truth. As time goes by things are getting better.

'My main objective is to stay off the drink. It's a cliché, but I'm taking it one day at a time.'

———

The Shannon was one of the bars Paddy O'Gorman mentioned where I might still find Irish daytime drinkers. When I got there, just after lunch, I counted maybe 10–15 Irish guys drinking at the bar. In clichéd fashion, the Pogues were on the sound system. Men hunched over the bar drinking lager with whiskey chasers, popping out every few minutes to check betting slips or smoke. We met a man called John Derry who seemed to know the lie of the land in Cricklewood. With him was a smaller man with a lined faced who spoke with an English accent but, from what I gathered, was of

Irish descent. John didn't want to speak on tape initially, asking that we first chat among ourselves about the scene in Cricklewood and the Irish drinking habits. He kept referring to the others at the bar as 'serious drinkers', not placing himself in that category by virtue of the fact that he worked from time to time. The supposed hierarchy among daytime drinkers never ceased to amaze me!

Off tape, John told me about close relations dying due to alcohol, about how much the area had changed, and about how little those who remained had in common with the Ireland that has emerged in their absence. It was a depressing scene, almost uniquely male and aged 50+. Later, three young Irish guys in workers' clothes called in, having finished something of a day's work. They downed shots and pints in equal measure—Red Bull and vodka followed by pints of Carling. A few of them clashed with one of the older lads in the bar and I couldn't help but feel that neither generation had learned much from the other.

Many of the Irish guys I spoke to complained about a new wave of Eastern European workers, who were now lining the Broadway each morning hoping for the pickup. There was a latent racism and wide stereotyping in many comments, and this from a class of Irish who faced English hostility when they first came to London in the 1960s and 1970s. How quickly we forget. Several others were invited to join our conversation but refused to speak on tape and demanded it be turned off, somewhat obsessively. It was as if they wanted to still be in conflict mode, to still have to watch their step and to mistrust everyone new to the group.

One told me, 'We're all right when you get to know us, but we're a very shy people. Myself, I was in prison for a couple of years because of my beliefs. It doesn't matter really at the end of the day what area you're in, you got to get away from certain influences.' It came to a discussion about the Irish homeless. One of the guys at the table took exception. 'Now, hang on, there ain't no Paddies sleeping on the streets here. Fuck Off. We have a homeless centre for them. We look after our own.'

But I saw several older Irish hanging around the Tube station or sitting in shop doorways with their hands out. Pride keeps some of them from seeking assistance. Some of the guy won't even ask for a cup of tea in the Homeless Centre because of pride. One of the men we met told me about his brother, who ended up on the streets following a failed relationship. Everyone tried to help him; in the end, though, he wanted out. Others in the bar bought him drink, even though they were asked not to. 'What else could we do?' they asked. 'If someone don't want help, they don't want help.'

The men told me about bars in the area open at 6 o'clock in the morning where the cleaners served the drink to customers. They told me about the ballrooms, where 'a lot of mismatches took place!', and volunteered how in their prime they had no trouble with women. 'We can still turn on the charm if we want to,' said one, through cigarette stench and shaking hand.

It was difficult to talk as the tape recorder was making other customers paranoid. I got the feeling many here had been 'active' during the Troubles and were wary of having their names recorded. One of the homeless staff told me afterwards that during the 1980s, informers used to sit in on Alcoholics Anonymous meetings in the area in order to get information.

John offered up some insights: 'We're like fish out of water, away from your own country and come over here for a bit of work. Things maybe haven't worked out for some properly. The older people living in bedsits have no real quality of life, paying from eighty pounds a week up, living on top of each other. It's not like back home, where people live in proper accommodation and stuff. I think it is more close knit back in Ireland as well. People don't give a shite over here. If someone dies here, it's "such-and-such-died" and next day carry on as normal. People back home would be more concerned. I think it has all to do with family and caring in the community. They pull together back home. A big factor is the Eastern Europeans undercutting workers. A Polish man will work for maybe twenty to thirty pounds a day. Lot of people in there on the dole and might get a wee bit of work here and there. Everybody bonds with each other and looks after each other. I think people are nowhere as bad in drinking in Ireland to what it is over here. They say the Irish drink more away and I'd agree with that.'

John's friend, the ex-Irish with a strong English accent, interrupted by outlining the place the pub held in emigrant culture: 'All the environment around us since we came here has been pub orientated. If you wanted something you had to go to the pub to get it. They cashed our cheques and took some money off us. They organised accommodation. Everything was the pub. Still is and all.'

Around the corner from Cricklewood Broadway, I noticed labyrinths of bedsits and multi-occupancy houses, where the last generation of forgotten Irish emigrants live out their days before dying, mostly prematurely. I was brought to meet Séamus, a 55-year-old former tradesman, also from Mayo, who has lived for 12 years in one room. The year previous I had been in Africa reporting on developing world stories several times, hearing about appalling human rights abuses in displaced camps in eastern Congo, documenting the aftermath of post-election violence in Kenya and the effects of climate change on the families living along the Zambezi River in Mozambique. Nothing, though, had prepared me for the shock of seeing a fellow Irishman, in 2009, in central London, living in the most deplorable and squalid conditions. In truth, it was heartbreaking, shocking, and I was totally unprepared for the deep impression it left. Perhaps because this is what full-term alcoholism looks like. His room contained his worldly possessions—among them two battered and stained radios, a TV and DVD player, two tennis rackets, some videos, books, a ragged duvet, a stepladder, one chest of drawers, a poster shrine to Celtic Football Club, Kerry footballer Colm 'The Gooch' Cooper and ABBA. Empty cans, cheap brandy bottles, drained naggins, flagons of cider and bottles of wine littered the floor, as well as ash, cigarette ends, leftover Cup-a-Soups, empty pots, a ready made meal and a book of Joseph Conrad short stories. For every Shane MacGowan, there are a hundred Séamuses, albeit without hefty royalty payments or a blindly supporting public to fall back on.

Séamus wore a pair of black cords one size too small, blackened white socks and a v-neck diamond-patterned jumper pulled over his gaunt frame. He'd had a hard night, little sleep. In the previous two years his three best buddies had all died, all living in the rooms next to and above his. Drink took them all, and now Séamus was even more isolated, rarely leaving his room because of the embarrassment of been seen drunk and deteriorating.

Over the remnants of a half-cup of Strongbow cider, Séamus told me his story:

'When I came here I didn't know the ropes. 'Twasn't to Cricklewood at all I came first and later, then, I even went to Scotland and Australia. Most of all I love Scotland. Look at that wall there behind you, that says it all. Celtic, Celtic, Celtic. They are two points clear of Rangers now and playing them on Sunday. Today's Saturday, isn't it? It's Friday? Oh yeah. Well, they're playing anyway Sunday week in Celtic Park. With a bit of luck I might be up there myself. I used to go to see them all the time. I love them.

'The area has changed for the worse. One time even this very house was full of characters. There was poor auld Patsy, Billy Simpson—who I had great time for altogether—and Eoin Kilbane. They're all gone. Dead. Drink had a lot to do with it and all, like.

'I'm here nearly twelve years. Another great mate of mine who lived here got a council flat in St Paul's Avenue. He drank forty-three cans in the one day. Now, Jesus, if I done that I'd be stone dead. No bother at all to him. He's a big man.

'Over the years, with regards work, we were all labouring. The last few years I've gone a bit downhill. Me back is knackered. I worked on a golf course in my hometown when I was about fifteen and I was trying to keep up with the big lads. They were big strong men and that is where I done in me back. There was an older man on the job, who was about sixty, and "Slow it down," he said to me. "You're trying to keep up with us." Big rocks. Doing up Westport Golf Course. Jaysus it's a fine golf course now. We lifted rocks onto trailers and I done in me back.

'There was plenty work when I came over here. Now there is no work. Half of them are dead anyway. Few pints after work. I would say it's much worse now. In Ireland it's bad too—I listen to Radio Éireann and ten percent unemployment in Ireland.

'There's a *céad míle fáilte* there for me any time I want but I cannot go back to nothing. My sister is there and she has the home place and that. Great girl but she wants me back. But what would I go back to? Back to nothing, like. And I would be a waste of space to her. Jesus, it would be all right if things were right, like. Oh, she wants me back, alright. She's not worried about money or nothing. She doesn't care about nothing. But sure I'm after spending all me life in England and to go back with nothing, just empty pockets. Wouldn't I look great? So everybody has their own little thing.

'Leaving the drink aside? It's impossible almost. When you live in a room on your own. I palled around with a lovely girl. She got fed up of me. She is a nurse. She done everything she possibly could to put me on the straight and narrow. She brought me back to Killarney. And I hope they lift the All-Ireland for that reason.

'Great girl. Brought me back and done everything for me. I was off drink then and it would only take something, like Rangers to beat Celtic or something like that.

'They're playing Sunday week now, Celtic and Rangers. I might make it yet. Jesus, we might all go. We might all go.

'I was here when I was off the drink. I used to go to Celtic Park every few weeks. At the same time all me mates were all heavy drinkers. Jesus—they're all dead now. Tom is the only survivor. Some of them would knock on the door at two or three o'clock in the morning. And sure I'd answer the door straight away for them, no problem at all. Jesus, they're dead now. The man other side that wall there. Billy Simpson. He was sixty-eight. And Patsy was in the room across, he was sixty-nine. And Eoin in the back room was from Achill Island. But Jesus, we were all the one gang, a crazy gang. All great mates. Nobody would see each other wrong. It's a different ball game now. It's beating me now and all, I know it is. At the same time I'm fighting a good aul' battle, as best I can.

'I'm in love with a lovely girl, but sure it's drink again. She was going to marry me and everything if I gave it up. Didn't happen, like. But sure a man cannot be an altar boy all his life, can he? When you weigh it up, like. Great girl, love her to bits.

'The landlord is not up to much, hasn't got much time for me. He was around a while ago, could still be here. All he thinks about is money, money, money. Like ABBA, you remember the song,

"Money, money, money, it's a rich man's world"? Well, he can have his fucking money. That's the way I look at it. He'll only wait for somebody to die and he does up the room straight away and moves someone else in. There's more to life than money. Do you know what he should do now? He should go out to Stockholm in Sweden and meet that girl there in the poster, Agnetha, look at her. She could sing that song to him. A week in Stockholm would do him good. It's my life ambition to meet her, and please God I will some day. I have her number in that drawer there somewhere. I used to write to her and everything but she didn't write back to me, though.

'I usually go to a café. There is a kitchen here in the building but it's dog rough, very seldom I eat here.

'All my mates are dead. I have no company here at all. I'm not really happy here. The move is on. Only a matter of time. I don't know where, though, as close as possible to Celtic Park would suit me, that's for sure.

'I'll give you one bit of advice, the next time you go on holiday, don't go out to France, or Japan or anywhere like that. Go to Celtic Park. That's where you'll find atmosphere. All Irish.

'I was home about two years ago, and I do phone home regular. 'Twas John Glynn and the people from the hall here that brought me back last time. 'Twas sort of embarrassing, like, everybody has their pride and everything else. I went back and I had nothing. The family gave me money and everything and it was embarrassing, like.

'My family hadn't much money, my father might sell an auld cow or a bullock or a sheep or that type of thing to pay the rates. He struggled to bring up the family. There was eight of us and two died. He went drinking a Fair day, a few bottles of stout maybe. He wouldn't drink then until the next Fair day, until he sold something else. He came up the hard way.

'I was awful young when I had a drink. I was only going to school, like. There was a Horse Fair in Westport, show-jumping and all that. The auld fella was in one part of the tent and I was at another. I was only about ten or eleven. He didn't see me. Me mates were buying me drink. He couldn't afford a drink.

'I went flat out with the drinking then as a teenager. I shouldn't be alive at all, you know. I don't deserve to be alive. Flat out altogether. Fourteen, fifteen, everything. The swinging sixties. Drink, women and gambling. Gambling came first, still does and all.

'Kato Star—look at the picture of him up there behind you and the crucifix underneath him. I had four hundred pounds on him Saint Stephen's Day. He sailed in and I told the whole town, days and days before this. I even told Julie to put her last set of knickers on him. She didn't back him at all. I put everything I had on him, hadn't a bob left for Christmas. Three pounds.

'He won at 5-4 and I got nine hundred pounds back and I painted the town red. I went stone mad.

'I don't go the pub much any more, Jaysus, it's too dear, over three pounds a pint. I'm drinking cans of cider now. Three of me mates are dead and the best mate I had has gone. He got a flat. I don't have his phone number; I have a mobile there and don't know how to use it.

'I get the papers every morning down the road there. I get the *Mayo News* and all, like.

'Nice to keep in touch, like. I can see an All-Ireland in that team yet.

'The house and woman I had all went simultaneously—do you like that word? It means together at the one time! I was engaged to her and all that. I had a house in Westport, built it myself with these two paws. Built it meself, roofed it meself and plastered it meself. Anyway, things didn't work out. We're the best of friends. She got married since and she has four daughters now. And look at me here in this room. I have nothing here. Even the mouse pulled out. There was a mouse here one time but he pulled out. He got fed up.

'I love the gambling. I'm good at it, though. Oh Jesus, I'm well ahead of the bookie. Honest to Jesus. Well ahead of them. There's a man up there in Ladbrokes, he hates to see me coming. Hates the sight of me. I done it again the weekend. Man United they were 4-2, didn't collect for a week. I do it all the time.

'There's a great kick out of it. Even poor auld Julie. She never bet in her life and she loves her football. Now she would think nothing about putting a few hundred pound on a football team! Talking about the future, there's a lad from Northern Ireland—McIlroy. Oh Jaysus, there's money to be made on him yet. He's going to go places in a big way.

'Another Tiger Woods.

'If I got me aul' head together I could take the bookie. I could leave William Hill in the park. Every morning when I get out of that bed I think, what can I get William Hill for? That's my life's ambition, to leave William Hill in the park. Oh, leave him begging for cigarette butts. In the park. Me life's ambition.'

John Leahy, Former Tipperary Hurler

My first drink was a flagon of Linden Village Cider, bought in a pub before a local disco in Mullinahone, County Tipperary. I was about twelve and a half or thirteen years of age. There were trees about five hundred yards from my house and we went there drinking before the disco. There used to be discos every second week, and a few months after that I was served in a pub for the first time. I was thirteen years of age and ended up with lads fifteen or sixteen. I remember I went with them and had a few pints of ale. I would have been a fairly quiet and calm type of person and very shy, but I changed that night. I went to the disco and had great craic and the whole lot. At the time I was working and had a few bob in my pocket. Two weeks later, I got really drunk and sick in the toilet, got into an argument with lads I was drinking with. Looking back, that tells me drink didn't suit me—day one. From that drink to my last drink, there was periods of mayhem and trouble in my life and it all came and revolved around drink.

From the age of fifteen or sixteen, I was drinking more regular, often hanging around with older guys. In—two pubs in the village I couldn't get served in. But at fifteen, I was drinking in one of them regularly and there was no issue out of it. We won the junior south final in 1985, when I was fifteen, and I was drinking in the pub after it, and there was no issue. But yet I couldn't get served in the pub across the road until I was seventeen. In the early 1990s, I went to a sixteenth birthday party up there, and the place was serving sixteen-year-olds now. The culture had changed and there was acceptance there that hadn't been there a decade earlier.

At sixteen or seventeen, I stopped drinking for a period. I got it into my mind to make the Tipperary minor hurling team. I remember Christmas 1986 and drinking hard. I was doing stuff like robbing drink in the bar and having the craic around the town—really drinking heavily. Waking up in the bed after Stephen's Morning, I remember saying, 'I'm not drinking any more.' I had to be carried home the night before and don't remember getting into the bed. I had probably wet the bed also and I said to myself, 'That's it now, I'm going training and making the Tipperary team.'

That year I drank two pints of ale shandy after the Munster final and I drank a few pints on the Sunday night of the All-Ireland and that was it. I didn't drink for the rest of that year. I suppose the pattern changed when I went working. I got into the Tipperary senior hurling team at this point and started working with a beer company. I got into a routine where I would have a few pints on the weekend and that. Maybe after dinner on a Sunday I would have a few drinks and go into the disco in Clonmel. I would have had a car at the time and would have thought nothing about having three or four drinks before driving into town. Then we'd drink all night and drive home. We used to go out the back roads and I know that for loads of lads that was the pattern. Sunday night was the night to go out. In my time drinking that changed to Thursday nights and now it would seem to be Saturday night.

When I played with Tipperary I got a great start in 1989 and again in 1991, when we were in the All-Ireland. There was a great drinking culture around the matches at that time and the sport was different. I remember two or three of our guys before the All-Ireland in 1989 had a few pints on the Saturday night. We were staying in the Burlington and they went across the road to the lounge and had their two pints. That was a regular thing for a few of the players, through the championship. They'd have a few pints on the Saturday night. The first few years of the championship, when it was over, there was a great session after the last match. It could last for three or four days and the panel would stay together. Then we'd break up and mightn't see each other until we went back training.

We might have a few pints after training on an odd night, and the last league match we'd have a session, then take a break and then back training.

I did that for maybe four years. Looking back, when I used to stop in January and train it was fine. But I suppose when I was twenty-two or twenty-three I found that it went to February when I stopped drinking and then it went to March and then to April. The last year of my drinking, playing with Tipperary, was 1996. I would have drank two weeks before we played in the championship. Now, if you told me that six or seven years previously, there is no way I would have believed you. What happened is that it gathered momentum. I remember after the All-Ireland in 1991, I put on ferocious weight for the championship in 1992. We played Cork and one of the selectors told me not to run with the ball, just to hit it when I got it because I wasn't fit enough. That was all drink related.

I never drank at home. I suppose with the hurling, people liked to be in my company and with Tipperary on the crest of a wave they were getting information that would be linked directly to the camp. It was normal rural life. I would have went into pubs a lot of the time saying I would only have a cup of tea and [a] sandwich, and I'd nearly be waiting for someone to offer me a drink.

They might say, 'Will you have a pint?' and I'd say, 'Ah, no, no.' The pressure would come on and I'd have one and then maybe two and then that was it.

Down through the years I would have missed appointments and presentations of medals. With the drinking you are afraid if you leave you'll miss something and yet it is the same thing every week.

From the age of thirteen no one ever really pulled me aside and said anything to me about the drinking. I remember a Guard saying something to me one night. He had twin sons my age and I was very drunk the night before and he spotted me walking down the street. He called me and said, 'If I see you drinking again, I'll kick the arse off you. Don't let me catch you again.' That was the only warning I got. The parents would have been onto me at home, because with the car and everything. But I didn't see any danger with it.

With my job as a sales representative for Finches I was in pubs every day of the week and I would have prided myself on the fact that I didn't drink. Yet I found I would get up in the morning and rush through my day's work. I wouldn't give customers time and would be watching the clock to try and get finished by four or half four so I could get back to my local. That was regular practice, particularly on a Monday. We had some great days' drinking as well with good craic and banter. I could get to the pub some days at half four on a Monday and mightn't leave that pub until Wednesday morning.

We'd drink all day Tuesday—be in the bar at half ten in the morning. I was always meant to be working that day but I had it set up so that the Tuesday run hadn't to be in until Wednesday evening. I could double up with work on a Wednesday by ringing a few people. I wasn't doing my job properly. Wednesday night I'd go up to a pub in Mullinahone and have three or four pints and then I'd come home. I was always last leaving the pub. On Thursdays I'd come into Clonmel into the nightclub and go drinking. God knows where I'd stay Thursday night, and I'd get up and do a bit of work Friday—it wouldn't have been a busy day for the job. I'd probably go in and meet some lad for lunch and go off drinking for the day then. That would stay going until Sunday.

That was the pattern for the last nine to ten months of my drinking. I would have lost relationships with girls through my drinking. You wouldn't give it time and would always be in the pub. I would have been caught two-timing and all that.

At that time, the mindset would have been that's normal.

The last nine months, a friend had given up the drink himself and I would meet him once every month or every six weeks, and he'd often say, 'John, do you think you're drinking too much?'

'Jaysus I'm not,' I'd say, 'no more than my friends.'

I never realised I was drinking every day of the week. I woke up loads of times dying, and saying, 'I'm not drinking any more.' I never blamed the drink, though, I blamed my system. I would be lying there with the head fried off me and I'd often have DTS and be thinking there were things under the bed and be afraid to get out of the bed and all that kind of stuff. But I never blamed the drink; I always thought there was something else wrong with me.

The crux in my drinking came when a few friends organised a trip to Manchester. It was an opportunity for a session after Christmas, which wouldn't have been a good time with work, but I was going anyway and never told them at work I was going. We were going to see a match, heading over on a Friday night for the match Saturday. I never told work I was taking Friday off—I just rang in the order and took off.

Vodka and soda was my drink of choice and I was really, really drinking them. I remember the Friday night in Manchester we went out and had good craic. I was knocking these things down—two of the guys wouldn't drink with me. On Saturday we went to the match, Aston Villa v Man United, and it ended up nil-all. We all went on the piss after and arrived back to the hotel after the night's drinking. There were a couple of lads around the counter. Two of us went to the hotel bar for a drink and we started talking about the match with the lads at the bar. I said I would have loved to see a goal scored at Old Trafford. One of the guys couldn't comprehend it, as I was a Liverpool supporter. I was saying, 'What difference does it make?' It stirred in me and I was drinking a glass of vodka and I flipped. With the glass in my hand, I punched the guy into the face. I thought, 'What the fuck am I after doing?' I remember I had to go out of the hotel and the next thing the police came and I was brought away and put in a cell that night. In the cell, it was the first real time I examined what had gone wrong with my life. When I looked back, there were two previous incidents when that aggression and anger was there. I remember another night at a work do when one word led to another and I lashed out again. I was reprimanded at work; I think that was five years previously. Maybe two or three years before that again, at a disco, I met a girl and her brother didn't take it kindly and I lost it with the brother. Each incident ended up being more harmful to each person involved. That night in the cell I prayed and asked for help.

It was the first time it had sunk in that when I looked back at my life, every night I was in trouble I had drink taken. Lo and behold, the first man at my door was the friend who had been asking me about my drinking. I had to go to court first thing on a Monday morning and got bailed into a hostel.

He booked into a hotel and I was allowed to leave the hostel at seven in the morning and be back in for eleven at night. On the Wednesday I got bailed back to Ireland.

I had it in my mind I was going to get back to Ireland and head off to America. I remember deep down I had a lot of realities to face coming home, including my family, because the incident made national news in the papers. I had to ring my employer because I didn't turn up for work. The employer wanted meet to me on a Tuesday and given that five years previously there had been an incident, this was not new to them. I thought I was going to be out of a job, and met the two directors of the company. They asked me what happened and asked was I going to do anything about it. By this time I had organised to go in for treatment so I told them I needed a month off. I remember I got a good bollicking and they went outside the door and said, 'Your job will be there and we'll suspend you without pay.' That was the first break I got.

I had to meet the county board in Tipperary, which wasn't nice either. They were fully supportive, though, once they saw I was doing something. So I did the month in treatment, and didn't look back, really.

It's thirteen years this year since I stopped drinking and it's no coincidence that I haven't been in trouble and I haven't been locked up or in rows in that time. That shite hasn't gone on in my life since I stopped drinking. It was a big readjustment. In 1996, I went back playing for Tipperary and back into work. I was as nervous going to my first call out as my first day in school, because I was out in the public domain again and people would have known about my story. I would have got a bit of grief from people in the street and so on. I got it on the pitch also—lads would have been throwing it at me about the incident in Manchester. They were all quite hurtful, and I used often say to myself, 'Is it really worth putting myself in these positions?' I contemplated not playing any more and some days I found it hard to get up and go training or to go to work.

I remember one chap in a rural village and he was only about twelve years of age. I came out of a shop and he threw this thing at me about Manchester and it shook me. I said to myself, 'This will never leave me.' I can still get it at times today. When I do go out or go to a drinking scene now, I have to be fairly vigilant and careful who I mix with and where I go. It can still be brought up. Even this year at an occasion I was at, it was brought up.

Usually, the person will be drunk and they may not mean it, but it's still there and that is part of it. All I can do is not follow that behaviour today.

The fact that it was in the national media meant everyone in my locality and throughout Ireland knew I was in treatment for drink. I would have gotten a lot of support on how to handle things. My employers, as well, were a great help to me and I valued it. For my final court case, one of the company directors had broken his leg a few weeks previously and he travelled over to give a reference in court. I got a two-year suspended sentence and paid a fine of nine thousand pounds or thereabouts. The reference from my employer made a big difference.

A lot of my friends never considered me [as] having a drink problem, because I drank with them. A lot of them would have drank as much as me or more than me. Now, for me to give up drink I'm questioning their drinking. If you look at denial in Ireland people have an acceptance of the amount they drink and that level is very high.

For anyone trying to stop drinking or taking drugs, it is a lonely spot. I never touched it since and I have to say, coming out of treatment, the aftercare programme was a big help to me. The group were very caring and kind and I got a bit of mothering and that helped me a lot. I was twenty-six when I stopped drinking. The hurling helped and I would have been well known, so I had nothing to hide—it was all out there. I know for a lot of people there is a stigma for people having to tell their story. For me, there is nothing to find out about!

I currently work as an addiction counsellor at a treatment centre and see many changes in the way addiction is today. You no longer see the guy coming in with drink issues alone. It's drink and drugs now and that culture has crept in in the last number of years.

In my time drinking, we hadn't as many different types of drinks to choose from, either. There was either Smithwicks or bottles of Guinness or maybe a pint of ale. In terms of spirits you might have drank a vodka or brandy. Now you have all those alcopops and flavoured drinks, making them easier to drink and a lot higher in content. Drinks sponsorship has come into sport and as a nation we are painting the picture that drink is okay. The advertising culture is a bit manipulative and they have these small 'drink sensibly' logos. That's all okay for the person who can drink normally, but for the person who can't it's a problem. I often hear people say they don't have the same problems in France with the drinking with young people, who can drink wine and so on. Yet the law in France means there's no alcohol advertising allowed. Liverpool played a few weeks ago and had to wear black on their jerseys because they are sponsored by Carlsberg. The Heineken Cup in rugby is called the H Cup. As a culture, there is panache in their policy and they are trying to combat it. In Ireland we're quite the opposite.

Chapter 6
Guinness and Late Nights

Accounting for one in every three draught drinks bought in every pub in Ireland, it's virtually impossible to explore the theme of drink in Ireland without taking account of the Guinness phenomenon. Symbolically, the logo of the harp, used by Guinness since 1862, was adopted by the Irish government in the 1920s, with the Guinness Harp facing left while the official government version, perhaps ironically, faced the other way. According to practically every travel guide to Ireland, no visit to the country is complete without sampling a pint of the black stuff or taking a visit to the Guinness Storehouse. And where better to hear firsthand about Ireland's drinking culture than inside the gates of our most renowned brewery? The hallowed home of Guinness for the last 250 years is one of Ireland's most frequented tourist sites, hosting an average of one million visitors per year—and all this just to see the past and present life of a working brewery! For many drinkers, it is, in essence, the equivalent of Charlie and his impoverished relations getting all-areas access to the Wonka factory. Visitors are often required to book their tickets days and weeks in advance to avoid the lengthy queues at the St James's Gate site. Like Scotland and haggis, Guinness has become somewhat embedded in the imaging of Ireland, Inc., over the past 100 years and more. Lonely Planet guides can't get enough of it, with instructions on Guinness etiquette and separate 'fact boxes' advising of the medicinal nature of Guinness, and telling would-be visitors that 'one way to test the quality of a pint of Guinness is by examining the size of the rings of foam left inside your glass (the bigger and thicker the better). Remember: if it's a good pint, order another one.' What ever happened to four green fields and *céad míle fáiltes*?

I'd never been to the site, or even had a particular taste for Guinness during the good old bad old days of my drinking. Living in Cork, if stout was to be drunk it was more Beamish and Murphy's, like. When I visited the Guinness Storehouse, on a rainy Thursday in February, stewards marshalled the lines of tourists waiting to be shown inside. What never ceases to amaze me is the sheer scale of the Guinness brewery, its absolutely pivotal place in the heart of the capital city. I'd only seen it from the outside, passing by having arrived in Dublin many times by train at Heuston Station. When Guinness owners Diageo tentatively approached a review of the Guinness operation at the site during the property boom (55 acres in the heart of Dublin was a tempting offload), the plans drew a furious public backlash, ensuring the site remains part of the brewing operation. For now, at least.

Plans are afoot to divide up the operation, with a new brewery being built in Leixlip, where Guinness heir Desmond Guinness, who still lives in the fairytale-gothic Leixlip Castle, has provided lands. (I was there to interview him once, as Marianne Faithful appeared ghostlike on the landing and Guinness himself whizzed about preparing for the visit of Jerry Hall that evening, unloading crates of wine from the boot of his car!) The Guinness family is rightly proud of their heritage and association with the emergence of the modern Irish state, having set up the Iveagh Trust, an initiative for homeless housing in Dublin, and been, for centuries, the largest taxpayers on the island. The family have also, particularly in the case of Desmond Guinness, been responsible for the re-appreciation of seventeenth- and eighteenth-century Irish history and architecture, underlining the cultural and economic contribution Guinness has made to Ireland. The St James's site itself has been turned into a sophisticated tourist experience, with interactive tours, archives, snazzy restaurants and bars, offering visitors panoramic views of the city while enjoying their complimentary pint. Previous to the present facility, the Guinness Hop Store catered for tourists, but by the year 2000, roughly 340,000 visitors per year were coming through its doors. The current tourist centre was a former derelict building which had blown up in 1987. In 1999, the company put £30 million (sterling) into the building, to act as a showcase site for their brand heritage. Here, the folklore of Ireland and its most synonymous alcoholic drink can be packaged, digitised, and delivered over the course of an afternoon. The majority of visitors come from the UK, Italy, the US and France, with the centre catering for up to 6,000 visitors a day during peak season.

As an ex-drinker, I'd be lying if I said the prospect of a complimentary pint at the end of the tour wasn't a tempting offer. It's times like that when alcohol can often catch you unawares. You might go weeks, months, a year even without thinking of the booze and its seductive qualities. Then BANG! While minding your own business, it comes calling again. In this case, the fact that everyone on the tour was given a glass of Guinness to enjoy underlined the apparent normality of taking a drink. It's easy to be fooled into thinking that having a sup along with everyone else wouldn't do any harm. In fact, it would be rude not to. The pint takes on the guise of a seductive woman, letting her dress slip off her shoulder, pursing her lips, and whispering enticingly, 'Come, brush your lips against my rim, don't worry, it'll be our little secret.' I usually answer the calling with thoughts of when I did drink and how distinctly unglamorous the whole thing was and how much of an eejit I made of myself. Like being unable to walk into a shop because of paranoia, or getting into a habit of taking my clothes off and running around gardens naked, while dinner guests looked on utterly bemused. That usually does the trick and helps put any cravings to bed. Counsellors call it rewinding or fast-forwarding the tape—I can't remember which. All I know is that it works for me.

I took lunch at the Guinness Storehouse restaurant with two staff from the Corporate Relations team in an effort to find out how the company was performing, what drinking patterns had emerged over the past decade, and what the downturn held in store for the dark stuff. Corporate relations executive Rhonda Evans told me that in 2001, according to Diageo's figures, 70 per cent of all alcohol in Ireland was sold in pubs. By 2008, that figure was down to 45 per cent, with 55 per cent sold in the off trade, representing a remarkable shift in Irish drinking patterns in a relatively short period of time. Several factors have been identified in accounting for this shift, including the simple fact that people were commuting longer hours to homes many of them had spent big on. Naturally, they want to showcase, enjoy and entertain in their plasma-screened palaces.

In the 1980s, the culture of going to the pub in the evening after work and before dinner was pretty well established in many urban centres. Now, with longer commutes, it can often be seven or eight in the evening before workers get home to dinner, leaving little time for a sociable drink in between.

Aside from the setting, people have also increased their repertoire of drinks, so they're having wine with meals, as well as beer in the bar. The era of males drinking beer and beer alone disappeared, and now they are as likely to sip champagne, cider or gin and tonic. The rise in wine sales over the past decade has also been indicative of how quickly the Irish have taken to the supping in their own domestic environments.

Rising prices in bars didn't help either. Of course, ask any publican, and they will tell you it was the smoking ban and drink-driving clampdown wot dunnit.

'During the Celtic Tiger,' says Rhonda Evans, 'people were going on more holidays and experiencing different things so the pub wasn't the sole entertainment experience. Restaurants became hugely popular, and still are. The move to home consumption was hugely dramatic and lots of people in the industry are still taking time to adjust to that.'

Not so in Diageo, though, whose brands include spirits, draught lagers, beers and stout. Rather than rue the demise of the public house, Diageo was quick to adapt to people's changing social environments. So, they have bottles of beer, cans of beer, 12-packs, 6-packs, buy three and get a free glass, increased branding in supermarkets, instore promotions, mini-fridges, hats, scarves and headbands . . . the list goes on.

'We put as much effort now into selling our brands in the off trade as we do in pubs,' says Rhonda Evans. 'Once we realised the shift in where people were consuming and buying, we moved too. You can't make people go to the pub if they don't want to choose.'

Undoubtedly the growth of the nightclub culture had an impact, with shots and bottles becoming the late-night beverage of choice. There was a period in Ireland in the early 1990s when sales took a dip, especially among younger drinkers. Towards the end of that decade, Ireland was topping binge-drinking leagues in Europe, with the trend peaking in 2001. For now, though, Guinness is back in vogue (and having a huge upsurge in business in Asia and Africa). It has had to adapt quickly and Guinness spent a lot of time and money getting the Guinness can product right, so that the pour quality at home would be the same as in the pub. It's worked, with over 60 per cent of people drinking Guinness in the pub now buying cans to drink at home also. Those with increasingly hectic work lives, who couldn't afford to wake up mid-week with a hangover, were also catered for. Guinness mid-strength has been on trial for the past two years. Instead of 4.2 per cent ABV (alcohol by volume), it has a low of 2.8 per cent. The company calls it a 'slow burner', but with the government indicating it will give lower duty rates for the product, it looks here to stay.

Alcohol consumption in Ireland per capita has been declining by between 10 per cent and 20 per cent since 2001. This was a period of almost full employment, of large inward migration and of a general atmosphere of immediacy and excess.

During the last 12 months of 2008, excise duty on alcohol was down 10 per cent, although due to lower VAT levels, cross-border purchases have risen dramatically. Industry insiders point to the fact that one in six households went up to the North between September and December 2008, with the off trade in Northern Ireland increasing by 23 per cent. Most problem drinking in Ireland is now more concentrated during the Thursday-to-Saturday period and it remains to be seen how the downturn will affect drinkers and drinking patterns in the coming decade.

If there is one thing Guinness is good at (besides brewing), it's marketing and advertising. Bar Coca-Cola, the company was one of the first major drinks companies in the 1920s to launch mass advertising campaigns. In recent years, the company has taken flak for its sponsorship campaigns and for launching a 'drink responsibly' campaign only after binge-drinking figures had peaked. Many felt that Diageo, like other members of the drinks industry, were only too willing to add to the corporate till in the decades previous and failed to fully engage with the issue of problem drinking in Ireland.

While the company has always been aware of its citizenship role, from sponsoring charities to good causes, in recent years it has developed more and more its corporate social responsibility role, in response perhaps to a wider understanding of Ireland's relationship with alcohol. From a Diageo Ireland point of view, this policy has been gathering a huge amount of momentum in the last 10 years, and Diageo point to the fact that they were the first drinks company in Ireland to communicate to consumers the benefits of responsible drinking. So, for example, they launched the 'Don't see a Good Night Wasted' advertising campaign in 2002, followed by the 'Wake Up Call' campaign, which saw a guy going through the horrors of the night before while waking up next morning.

Eventually, perhaps recognising that self-regulation is better than imposed rule, the industry set up an organisation called MEAS, which is an independent charity working to engage in the area of consumer communications through brands such as Drink Aware. 'The ultimate aim is to change behaviours and attitudes also,' says spokesperson Jean Doyle. 'At the moment as an industry we are in the midst of a five-year plan delivering a twenty-million [euro] fund dedicate[d] to the area of awareness and education. Everybody appreciated that the industry needed to focus on this area. There were issues around how certain brands and certain types of things were being promoted. We believe that self-regulation and co-regulation is the best way forward.'

It's noticeable that in recent campaigns by MEAS, the focus has shifted from the individual drinker, regretting his/her actions on a night out, to looking at the impact that person has on their direct environment. So the A&E nurse, the shopkeeper and the taxi driver all relay the impact problem drinking is having on their lives. It's an effort, then, for a collective response by society to a problem which reaches every sector.

As Jean Doyle notes: 'At times the industry can be the whipping boy. We should of course be around the table when people are talking about alcohol misuse, but there are other areas of responsibility, be it government policing and enforcement of existing legislation, or parents or the individual. Ultimately there is a strong need for individuals to take responsibility for their own behaviour, and that's one thing very relevant in the Irish context. If there is a cultural acceptance of getting drunk, and how much you drink and all that macho stuff around it continues to be acceptable, then it is very difficult.'

Despite their endeavours, suspicion remains in some quarters that the drinks industry's efforts in relation to responsible drinking are mere public relations exercises designed to soften legislation. Advertising continues to be a bugbear of critics of the industry, and certain quarters call for a complete ban on alcohol advertising in Ireland, much like the French model. 'In relation to advertising we have the most strictly regulated advertising and sponsorship activity,' says Jean Doyle. 'The French model hasn't proven a link between the reduction in misuse and the ban on advertising. However, we are already very highly taxed and [governed] by stringent legislation.'

New controls mean that drinks companies are not allowed to advertise in any medium where less than 75 per cent of the audience are over 18 (most European norms are 70 per cent).

But does the use of stringent controls make it right that national sports, such as hurling and Gaelic football, are so heavily identified with brands such as Guinness?

'If you take the GAA, Guinness came in behind hurling at a time when it wasn't as popular. Everything that was done was considered appropriate by the GAA. We [see] that things like filling sports cups with alcohol is not on, that signage in the stadium is less than twenty-five per cent of any advertising that's there. The whole thing has been stripped back. As far as we are concerned it is absolutely appropriate if it is done right.'

Yet the drinks industry spends roughly €70 million in Ireland on advertising each year. Guinness is at the heart of several high-profile sports campaigns, including sponsorship of GAA and rugby.

Recently, the *Observer* Sports Magazine, when profiling Croke Park, had the following to say: 'Guinness is the somewhat predictable sponsor of the Irish rugby union team. Technically, "the black stuff" isn't actually black, but a dark ruby red colour due to some of the malted barley being roasted. Ten million pints are bought worldwide every day; a recent survey found that 70 per cent of Irish respondents "felt closer to Guinness" as a result of their sponsorship of the team. Heartwarming.'

In terms of general drinking patterns, Diageo, like most drinks companies, are at pains to point out that problem drinking does nothing for their business model and that advertising is aimed at moderate drinkers.

'It is in none of our interest[s] to see people being drunk, it damages our reputation and the environment in which we can legitimately operate,' says Jean Doyle. 'From a business point of view, the responsible drinking agenda within Diageo is about investing in longer-term consumers of our brands—people who do themselves damage do other people damage also. We don't want to be trite, but Guinness is two hundred and fifty years old, and it's not in our interest for people to abuse it and for it to become associated with the problem.'

———

Established in 1998, the Guinness archive makes Diageo the only corporate body in Dublin to host their own public archives. With two staff, the facility is a mine of social and economic history. But, to be perfectly honest and juvenile about it, I really only wanted to know two things—how many free drinks did workers get down through the years, and is Guinness really good for you? Since its opening the staff have been gathering and amalgamating documents spread out over the site. Underneath the offices were 3,000 linear metres of paper records, containing 10,000 images, a few hundred cans of film and all sorts of signage, instruments and oddities related to the brewing operation, including the original lease Arthur Guinness signed on the St James's Gate site in 1759 as well as brewing recipes from the 1790s. About one third of the collection has been catalogued to date, and aside from throwing light on Irish drinking patterns, it also gives an insight into Irish economic and social history, with somewhere in the region of 14,000–16,000 employee files.

Prior to WWI, the workforce was almost 5,000 strong (mostly males), undertaking what was tough physical labour, and being paid 10–20 per cent higher than the average industrial wage in Dublin at the time. Pensions were introduced in the 1880s, at least 30 years before the first National Pension Act came into being. A medical centre was also established in the late nineteenth century for employees and their families. Dublin has always had a housing crisis of sorts, and recognising this, Guinness first started building accommodation for employees in the 1880s with the Rialto Flats and nearby Thomas Court scheme. The company was, in many respects, akin to a mini-Statelet.

Or, as archivist Eibhlin Roche notes, 'Guinness has been an all-inclusive company and such an integral part of the Irish story. We estimate that by about 1930, one in ten people in Dublin were dependent on Guinness for their livelihood.'

When workers went into pubs to unwind after a day's graft, their choice of beverage was slightly less complicated than it is today—there was whiskey or there was Guinness. That lack of choice pretty much stayed that way until the 1950s and 1960s, when lager arrived in Ireland. Although thirsty Guinness workers didn't need to stray all that far for the sup. Three taps were located on site for workers, and instead of a tea break, they could opt for 'time at the taps'. Men who lined up with their tankards were allowed fill once. For every hour of overtime worked, the entitlement increased (each four hours' overtime resulted in an extra beer—it would cripple the public service!). The taps closed down some time in the 1970s and the policy changed to take-home beer, such as cans and bottles, a policy that remains to the present day.

Despite allegations from medical professionals that higher volume beers helped fuel today's binge-drinking culture, the alcohol by volume (ABV) in the present-day pint of Guinness hasn't changed all that much since its inception. One product, foreign extra stout bottles, which is on sale in Africa and Asia, would have been brewed in the 1800s with a very high ABV rate to enable it to withstand long sea journeys. This was done by adding extra hops into the beer, thereby increasing its longevity. It is still on sale today at 7.5 per cent ABV. But the foreign stuff is the exception; today's pint of Guinness is the baby of the family, only 50 years old and remaining at 4.2–4.3 per cent ABV since its launch. The general trend for Guinness has been for a fall in ABV since WWI, when additional taxes were placed on barley for beer use. After the war, the ABV never quite reached its pre-First World War years.

Pretty much since the beginning, Guinness was considered good for you. So much so, in fact, that mothers who had just given birth were given a glass of Guinness in maternity wards all over the country as a matter of course. Is there a more insightful example of a country's relationship with alcohol? 'It was pretty much widespread for any woman who had given birth, because of iron levels, to be given Guinness,' says archivist Eibhlin Roche. 'I mean, up until pretty recently, if you gave blood with any of the blood banks, you were given either a cup of tea or a half pint of Guinness. The company would have provided stock to the Blood Bank and also the maternity hospitals free of charge.'

The association between Guinness and good health, or in other words between alcohol and vitality and robustness, has even deeper roots. The word 'porter' derived from the 1700s, when this new dark beer was being produced for the first time and became very popular very quickly with market porters in places like Covent Garden. It had perceived strengthening qualities. The adoption of the name of the beer, then, in the 1700s linked it to this idea that the beer had strength-giving qualities. When Guinness first advertised in 1929, the advertising agency went around to bars in London, asking punters why they were drinking Guinness. Nine out of 10 said because it was good for them. Guinness wasn't alone at the time, with products like Bovril and smelling salts also advertising their supposed strength-giving dimension, yet somehow with Guinness the tag stuck.

From the early 1930s up until the outbreak of WWII, the company actively encouraged doctors to advocate Guinness for their patients. The archive has hundreds of letters of correspondence from GPs across the UK and Ireland lauding the medicinal properties of the beer and telling how it transformed the lives and ailments of their patients. This kind of begs the question: if that was the attitude of the medical professionals, what chance had wider society to keep tabs on its drinking?

Or maybe it's perfectly normal for alcohol to be prescribed as medicine and Guinness really is good for you? Dr Chris Luke, consultant in emergency medicine at the Mercy Hospital in Cork, takes a benign view of Guinness. 'I liken it to Rowntree's or Quaker Oats, to be honest. I think Guinness have a long and very noble philanthropic tradition, in terms of the Iveagh Trust and providing accommodation for workers and so on. My understanding also is that one of their first medical officers travelled to Germany at the turn of the nineteenth century and visited their systems, bringing a lot of the efficiency there back with him. In addition to that Guinness also had a huge reputation in areas like training in first aid and safety and [in] funding the St John's Ambulance service.'

When asked, though, whether the product itself was good for you and whether it would still be appropriate in Ireland of 2009 to offer it to patients, Dr Luke said:

'I would like to think that in 2009 we are beginning to leave behind powdered vitamins and distilled chemicals. I am firmly of the belief that foods can be much better than medicine and Guinness is a foodstuff. It comes down to this, really—how would you prefer to get your iron, vitamin[s] and needed calories into a patient? By pill or injection or by a pint of the black stuff? The bottom line, same when prescribing any medicine, is that if you stick to the right dose, then a patient will get the required iron and vitamins. In the early nineteen-eighties, I remember when I was an intern in St Vincent's Hospital in County Wexford and we prescribed whiskey and brandy at night to patients. I think it was a very valuable tradition. For example, if your seventy-five-year-old grandmother is used to a sherry at night before admittance, then in my experience it's much better to continue with that small glass in hospital than to give a Valium. Many people have learned the hard way that chemical substitutes can be a lot more addictive than a glass of sherry. I'm not encouraging or recommending a free-for-all, but if you're asking me if a glass of Guinness can be medicinally useful, then I think yes, it can.'

———

Following the conversation by phone with Dr Luke, I was interested in the wider role alcohol plays in society, and how alcohol and health impact on a day-to-day basis in one of Ireland's hospitals. So I arranged to meet Dr Luke at the Mercy Hospital. When I got there, at 11 a.m. on a Tuesday morning, he began our meeting by taking me through a labyrinth of corridors, past makeshift waiting rooms, canteens turned into consulting areas, overstretched staff and impatient patients. While he wanted to set in context his thoughts on drink, Irish society and its implications on health, he also wanted to show what the second A&E unit in Ireland's second city looks like at what should be a relatively quiet time. He says whatever past impression there may have been of the medicinal properties of specific brews, 55 per cent of all patients who pass through the Accident and Emergency doors are there because of alcohol-related illnesses or incidents. Having said that, he's not fully discarding the general medicinal properties of alcohol and its benefits for society.

'About ninety per cent of us drink,' he says. 'We love to drink and regard it quite rightly as a divine gift and I have a lot of sympathy for that idea. I'm interested in toxicology. I'm interested in herbal medication and drugs, both clinical and illegal, because they have such an impact on my work in lectures to parents. So you have cocoa leaf in the Andes and you have cannabis in Afghanistan. Wherever you go, particularly where the landscape is hostile, you often get tucked away in the undergrowth a divine emollient, which eases the grim predicament of existence, to quote Beckett. I've absolutely no problem with the fact there are natural entities that have a God-given purpose to be there. If you are a native Andean Indian struggling in the low-oxygen height of rugged terrain in the Andes, lifting granite blocks to build Aztec temples—why not chew cocoa leaf?'

While the Guinness brewing operation stretches back 250 years, Dr Luke points to the fact that the Irish have always had a relationship with mind- and mood-altering substances long before the Guinness family got in on the act.

'Our remedies seem to be mushrooms and alcohol and those are the truly ancient intoxicants. I often joke that the reason we have such fabulous Celtic mythology is because of fabulous Celtic mushrooms! That's partly humorous, but I'm certain psychadelia has a role to play in Celtic mythology and Celtic culture and designs and much of that has come from mushrooms. Similarly with alcohol, we have had alcohol since the dawn of time, with mead and beer and cider, so I mean it's utterly natural.'

The difference nowadays, he says, is in concentration of alcohol in products and in the range available. 'Fast forward the last five hundred to one thousand years of globalisation, which really means the conquistadors and the taking over of the American wilderness and the taking over of Australia. In tandem with that has been the taking back of exotic fruits and drugs. By the time we get to [the] year 2000, at the peak of the Celtic Tiger, the population who are well used to mushrooms and drink suddenly have access to all this exotic range of intoxicants and also have the money to afford it. What we have is the native natural alcohol consumption suddenly multiplied by increasing concentration of the alcohol. In addition to that, you have the consumption of other drugs that are relatively new to our culture.'

In terms of concentration, while Guinness may buck the trend by offering lower-strength ranges, the general trend over the last two decades has been for higher concentrations of alcohol in the majority of products. 'What happened is that in the last twenty years we have seen an increase in the concentration—a doubling, effectively. It's very difficult now to go into any shop and to get less than fourteen per cent alcohol in a bottle of wine, for example. That's a fact, so in a sense, drugs fuelled drink consumption and drink fuels drug consumption and that's what's new. So you have both a diversity and scale which is new and that's where I come in. The impact on the Emergency department is really [astonishing] if you look at it very carefully. My own feeling is that the majority of attendances to A&E departments are fuelled by drink and drugs. Nearly one third of the population of Ireland attend an A&E department every year, which is good reason for investing in them, and we're talking in excess of 1.25 million people. I'm convinced that more than fifty per cent come to hospital urgently, suddenly, unexpectedly, because of drink- or drug-fuelled mishap or ailment. I'm also including tobacco. I'm talking about shots of alcohol, which are extraordinarily strong compared to what they were twenty or thirty years ago. I'm talking about drink-fuelled consumption of cocaine. I'm talking about the misuse of marginally legal drugs from head shops. I'm talking about the misuse of over-the-counter drugs, inappropriate prescriptions of drugs by doctors. If you put it all together, I'm certain that it adds up to the majority of our patients. So it's quite an extraordinary figure and the bottom line is that this all results from, in my view, an increase in concentration of alcohol, not the volume.'

Dr Luke points out that alcohol consumption levels have been moving upwards since the late 1950 or 1960s, as the Irish economy has gone through economic and social changes and improvements. 'In the last fifteen years, we have seen a normalisation of intoxication of both . . . genders,' he says. 'Women are now beginning to overtake men in terms of binge-drinking and liver failure and young girls are beginning to overtake teenage boys in terms of premature presentations.' He notes that companies like Diageo have been saying consumption has stabilised and says he's 'optimistic our dwindling prosperity will bring some kind of dip in the overall volume consumed'. He seems to be agreeing with the drinks industry—that a comprehensive, multifaceted approach to the issue of problem drinking in Ireland is what is needed. 'My main concern is the numbers, rather than the style or morality or philosophical issues. Ultimately, it's figures we need to think about, and my own feeling is that we should really try to define or describe the scale of the problem numerically. I really think that police should screen for alcohol or cannabis or cocaine in anybody that has been arrested for violence or disorder. I really think we have to measure alcohol measures in almost every patient for a period of time until we get some sort of idea.'

In terms of our drinking habits, the industry has a huge role to play in lowering the ABV levels. 'I don't think we should worry about volume; I think we should stop concentrating. What I mean by that is that the shots culture is the embodiment of catastrophic concentration. So you're moving from Babycham, light ales, Indian ales and little sherries of the 1970s and 1960s, to these high concentrations of alcohol with forty per cent and fifty per cent which are actually lethal.'

Dr Luke says his ambition over the next 20 years would be to see wine dropping back towards 7 per cent and 8 per cent ABV and beer dropping back towards 3 per cent and 4 per cent.

'That means that we can return to the ancient order of pub culture, which worked so well for so many years in Ireland. Paradoxically I think that pubs have a lot to offer in terms of stabilising our culture. Going to the pub in Ireland in the 1970s it was perfectly possible to go to a snug and sit chatting for hours and hours and hours while nursing just half a pint of beer. Because that's all you could afford. There is nothing inherently impossible about nursing half a pint of shandy, even, for hours at a time. The atmosphere in the pubs has been so altered by the Celtic Tiger, particularly, that the atmosphere is often hostile or menacing and not conducive to conversation. I yearn for the days when we can revive our oral tradition, because that is what was great about Ireland in the 1970s and 1980s. It was about conversation and comedy and creativity and that, to me, is what craic was. It was obviously lubricated to some extent by libation, but it was fundamentally about conversation.'

———

The decline of the bar trade is therefore a cause for concern, not just for the drinks industry and health professionals, but also for wider society. Diageo company representatives had pointed out that off-trade or at-home drinking is not regulated in any regard, while 'on-premise' consumption is very highly regulated. The move from pub to at-home drinking has also had repercussions for another sector of the drinks industry, often seen as the whipping boys for the ills of Ireland's association with alcohol. I'm talking, of course, about nightclubs.

The clubbing scene gathered pace in the 1970s and 1980s, but really came into its own commercially in the 1990s, with the rise of the dance scene and new drugs such as Ecstasy. In the days before late-night bar licences, a proper night out wasn't complete without a visit to a club. Dr Luke has studied the club culture, and firmly links the alcohol epidemic to the rise of the drug scene and vice versa. 'You can't have one without the other; one of the reasons we have such increasing concentration of alcohol consumed, in my opinion, is because of the advent of Ecstasy in the late 1980s. The acid house culture meant that the drinks industry were suddenly threatened by a collapse in their profits and they retaliated, as it were, by employing the designers who had brought the music and clubs and fashion and so forth, to the deployment of vehicles of drink. They also increased the strength of drink from the 1970s to the 1990s. So you end up with psychedelic drinks, coloured, blue, green, any kind of neon, and delivered in very trendy sexy vehicles that were very sweet and very tasty, particularly to young women.'

Dr Luke has a point, and for anyone who experienced the clubbing mecca of Sir Henry's nightclub in Cork or any other thriving nightclub in the 1990s and 2000s, there weren't many pints of the black stuff being poured! In earlier chapters, I referred to the allure with which nightclubs in small towns, such as the Queens in Ennis, were viewed in local folklore. They were sites of almost limitless possibility, where dreams were made, and many a nightmare began well before the chip van had pulled away. In the first few years of sobriety, I went to a few clubs, but for me, sobriety and late-night clubbing just don't gel. Some clubs, where the focus is more on music and ambience, can be tolerated, but generally the drinking den/cattle-mart variety holds little appeal for the non-drinker. Many of the clubs I frequented in the 1990s and 2000s are gone now (Sir Henry's was knocked down a few years back), although the Queens in Ennis is still going strong. In the bar of the Harcourt Street Hotel, in the heart of Dublin's nightclub sector, I met with Barry O'Sullivan, the Chief Executive of the Irish Nightclub Association (INA), who told me about the decline of the sector and how the industry is calling for extended opening hours and how changing drinking patterns have impacted on his members. By the year 2000, the association estimates that there were 530 nightclubs in Ireland—in 2007 this figure had shrunk to 330. 'The rise of nightclub culture grew from the late 1970s and 1980s. The biggest change that happened for nightclubs since that growth was in 2000, when government removed the requirement for nightclubs to serve meal[s]. That gave birth to what we all know now as late bars,' explains Barry O'Sullivan.

The nightclub sector has noticed fundamental shifts in drinking patterns over the last decade. Whilst typically, clubs are now aimed at the 18–35 age group, many have installed so called 'VIP' rooms to cater for those of an older age. Late bars have prospered among this age group, with brighter lighting, lower music and a more relaxed environment, and less emphasis on dancing and more on continuing drinking. It is estimated that up to 3,000 late bar licences now exist nationally.

'In the 1990s, if you wanted do go anywhere past pub hours, you had to go to a nightclub and there were queues in every nightclub as a consequence. To be honest, businesses didn't have to put a whole lot of imagination into their product; they really just had to open the doors. If you look at the average club now, they are promoting their business hard, from websites where in some cases each actual night of the club will have its own Bebo page.'

Having run a club in Temple Bar for eight years, O'Sullivan said the notion that everyone rushes to the counter for the last hour of drinking time, loading up on high volumes of shots, is simply not the case. He also says that the nightclub sector is often blamed unfairly for fuelling the binge drinking culture and points to other factors, such as the tendency for clubbers and pubgoers to begin the night at home with a few drinks.

'In terms of drinking habits, it's one of the misconceptions out there I have to deal with, especially from politicians when they talk about binge-drinking. As a sector, we know that sixty per cent of young clubbers will have one to three drinks at home before they leave. They will visit three or four bars on a night out, and have one or two drinks in each venue. We know also that the average consumer in a nightclub will have 2.7 drinks over the course of a night. So the nightclub is at the end of the course of the night's drinking, and thirty per cent of it is done before they ever leave the house. That's what is happening in Ireland today.'

To back up his claims of how society scapegoats the nightclub sector, O'Sullivan makes reference to the Heaven nightclub in Blanchardstown. In 2007, security staff turned away 29,000 customers, mostly on Saturday nights, for being intoxicated. Many clubs in Temple Bar will turn away 200–300 people during the course of a night, which highlights the sheer scale of alcohol abuse being carried out, if nothing else. 'Look, there is no value to us in letting customers into our venue who are intoxicated. All it takes is for someone who has had too much bump into someone and injure them and [it] could cost us thirty thousand euro.'

The point the nightclub industry consistently hammers home is that the majority of drinkers are now fuelling up before leaving the house. This is borne out also by the experience of well known bar and club owner Paul Montgomery in Cork. Montgomery is the owner of one of the busiest nightclubs in Cork, Reardons, as well as several other late bar venues. He also owns a block of student accommodation, which he opened with a bar on the ground floor. Several months in, the bar was replaced with an off-licence. 'He then sees this migration of young people from their apartments, bypassing the five bars he owns and going into nightclubs for a dance,' says Barry O'Sullivan, 'I think the nightclub offering will hold up better than the pub offering as we go deeper into recession. The pub offering can be reproduced in the home environment, where cheap drink can save money. You can get friends over and put on some good music and watch sports or whatever on plasma-style televisions. So the pub, now, can come to the punter in their sitting room. The downside to drinking at home, of course, is that you're looking at the same faces all the time, and people still want to go out! And that's where nightclubs will come in.'

The sector is lobbying hard for closing times to be extended from the current 2.30 a.m. limit to 4 a.m. in Dublin, the reason being that the volume of nightclubs in Dublin is greater than anywhere else in the country. For instance, in Harcourt Street within 200 yards of each other are four prominent nightclubs— Copperface Jacks, D/Two, Krystle and Tripod. Between them they can churn 8,000 punters onto the street at the same time.

The whole city of Cork has nightclub licences for 16,000 persons, showing the high density of clubbers catered for in Dublin. Also the sector is looking for government to introduce permits which would recognise the difference between normal bars and nightclubs—currently no such legislation exists. 'The Guards have come to realise that restricted trading hours don't lead to an improvement in public order,' says O'Sullivan. 'Our thinking is that putting everyone on the streets at the one time creates problems.'

One gets the feeling, though, those problems exist regardless.

———

A more recent development in terms of Ireland's drinking history has been the high number of pub closures over the past decade. Reports estimate that somewhere in the region of 1,500 pubs have closed over the last six years, or almost 10 bars a week. The drinks industry expect a further 9,000 jobs to be lost in the industry in 2009, which could represent a 20 per cent reduction when taken along with 2008 figures.

What trends are showing is that alcohol is leaving the main street and crossroads and becoming more and more an acceptable part of the home environment. The days when alcohol in the home consisted of a dusty bottle of sherry, taken out once a year when Aunt Vera arrived, seem a distant memory, oral fragments of another time. Now, weekly shopping baskets are as likely to have a six-pack of beer or shoulder bottle of spirits thrown in. A casual visit by a next-door neighbour, or a night in watching a movie, is enough to prompt the opening of a bottle of wine. In many ways we're returning to a more medieval style of drinking, less evocative of the nineteenth- and twentieth-century forms. The changing nature of community has seen the closure of corner shops and post offices—not just in Ireland. With the erosion of community spirit, there is an increasing sense of loneliness and isolation in rural communities and anonymity in our urban ones.

With alcohol, those feelings can be muted. The difficulty, too, in Ireland is one of perception. If Guinness really is good for you, and red wine proposed as the cure for a host of ailments, then what's the big deal?

Ireland, Inc., continues to hold Guinness dear as one of its flagship and defining brands, like the Cliffs of Moher or Kerrygold.

Some of that is down to the pioneering efforts of that company over the last 250 years to provide for its workers and their families. Like Fr Mathew in Cork, benevolent deeds live long in the folk culture.

Yet the fixation on Guinness in Ireland, the pride in the pint, and the closeness of branding between Ireland and a pint of the black stuff, suggest a deeper forging of identity between the people and its pint.

The fact that the brewery remains our largest tourist attraction—not the areas of breathtaking scenery or the historical monuments, but a working brewery—says much about perceptions of Ireland abroad. Yet they are perceptions we have not denied. From American presidents to Ryder Cup captains, the thing to do in Ireland is to have a pint; only then can the visitor go truly native. Yet as trends change over the next decade, those perceptions will be challenged. The cost of the craic, both financially and socially to the state, may place pressure on the branding of Ireland, Inc.

When the Ryder Cup was won on Irish soil in 2006, captains and players celebrated by downing pints of the black stuff in one gulp, to a TV audience of millions, all the while egged on by thousands of cheering spectators. Is that the epitome, the sum total, of what defines the national spirit?

We think nothing of having a drinks company sponsor our national sports. Road traffic accidents on weekends and late nights spiral, accident and emergency wards struggle to cope with the casualties of alcohol abuse, and our few alcohol treatment centres are starved of funding. Still, though, the national image continues unabated and unaltered.

As Bono might say, I don't mean to bug you.

Mark O'Halloran, Writer and Actor

For me, drinking has become related to my creative impulses. If I am writing, I would probably go out every night and have two or three glasses of wine in my local bar and then take notes on the walk home. I would be afraid if I gave that up! I know writers who have been in trouble with drink and gave it up and found it difficult to find a new creative way after.

Also, drinking allows for random association in your head. I'm not talking about drunkenness, just a few glasses. If I was to look through my notebooks, a lot of stuff there I have come up with after having a few glasses of wine. I don't know if those thoughts would have been there otherwise, which is interesting.

Beryl Bainbridge talks about cigarettes doing that for her. I mean, she drinks also, but when she gave up cigarettes she stopped writing for ages.

As a young teenager, drink was talked about as being a maturity thing. I got served in pubs at fifteen, but I had been drinking flagons of cider from about the age of fourteen onwards. We did lots of outdoors drinking down the tracks in Ennis or over where the Bishop's field used to be near the river. If we couldn't get drink we talked about how we were going to get drink. It was a massive part of our lives and being able to hold your drink was really important. There was never a thought that you wouldn't drink. It was always something you would do when you grew older.

If you think about it, how many pubs are there in Ennis? I mean, there are a lot of them and drinking is a huge part of the social scene in rural Ireland. It's massive. It's there for christenings and weddings and funerals and every day during the week also for a lot of people.

I don't know whether it's something to do with the fact that Irish people aren't very direct with each other. When you are trying to understand what Irish people are talking about you have to go through lots of different routes, whereas with drink, it cuts all that out. I think there is also a shame element in it. Irish people like the shame of the morning after in some perverse way.

When we were younger, if you were found surrounded in a pool of your own vomit somewhere in a field or near the tracks it would be seen as a disgrace. However, at seventeen you were brought into a bar with your father and bought your first pint. The lads would buy you three or four pints and you would be a bit locked and go home.

It is so ingrained in our social lives that we don't know any other way to interact with each other. Also we're not a great theatre- or opera-going population. I mean, in the west of Ireland there isn't a lot to do. Men went to the pubs to get away from the women and children. I know that sounds very sexist, but I think it was a great way for men to communicate with each other.

Drink in theatre is constant as a theme. McPherson goes through it in every single play and it is also a constant in Tom Murphy's plays. In fact, I think drink is mentioned in every Irish play there is! There are wonderful descriptions of the wake in Playboy of the Western World, when the characters are dry retching on the holy stones at the funeral and so on.

I'd love to know are Irish people actually drinking more than they did before.

I think men always drank in the way they do.

In Dublin, those addicted to drugs and homeless are seen as a terrible shame. For the most part, people are able to keep it together with drink and still function. We tend to forgive a problem drinker a lot more than we would another addiction. I think that's because in most Irish families there is always someone with a drink problem.

I think there is a huge emotional catastrophe involved with drink—it really does wreck families.

A friend of my father's was known as an alcoholic. The reason he was known as an alcoholic was that he drank so many pints and got himself into such a state that he was brought to hospital. And that was an alcoholic. My mother had the opinion if you only drank beer and didn't drink spirits, you couldn't be an alcoholic, which I kind of subscribed to. I never drink spirits now in case I become an alcoholic!

Irish people are very slow to use the word 'alcoholic'. I know people who would have been friends of mine who would have gone through treatment because of drink. Others would say to me, 'I never saw them drunk!'

There is a huge fear around people who don't drink. There is a fear they are watching you. They're counting how many drinks you're having.

Also, generally speaking, Irish people are very good with drink. It is great fun! It becomes oppressive after a while. I mean, you have to be careful of it, because it's so massively accessible and such a part of our social and family lives. No matter if you never had it in your family you have to be careful with yourself around drink. If you're drinking heavily in your late twenties it can develop quickly into something rather painful for everybody.

Secondary school is the place to start talking about the issue— when I think back, there was no education whatsoever. I would say a majority of schoolchildren drink so there should be open discussion.

I remember from my own school days, people who didn't drink were stupid or squares. It's as simple as that—they were holy Joes who needed Pioneers badges. I got hooked by all the rock 'n' roll myths. You know, the Jack Daniels and cigarettes, annihilation and all that!

I have a number of friends who are alcoholic and to a greater or lesser extent in denial about it. There are people who, when I was a kid, from the moment they drank I knew they were insane with drink. I certainly would know the damage it does and it makes people, especially around children, emotionally promiscuous with their children. With drink on, it's friendly, it's great and so on. With no drink it's standoffish and prudish.

The not knowing what is coming back at you screws kids.

It's a big thing with Irish weddings as well—there's a thought that you shouldn't bring kids because we'll all be getting drunk. That's a uniquely Irish thing.

Firstly, I find I could drink every day, and when I'm doing a play I do drink every day. I would have two glasses of wine. At the weekends I'd have more. By some people's definition that's a lot. It doesn't create a problem for me. I live alone and I don't have children so it's all about maintaining my own sanity. If I drank heavily I would lose my mind. Other people can do it quite easily. I do appreciate the creative impulses that it unleashes, though. When I'm not writing I mightn't drink at all.

For a year I gave up drink. For it to work, I think you have to stop judging people and get into a totally different headspace. I felt sorry for a lot of people. You also just have very little tolerance for spending five hours in a pub. You go in for an hour and leave. Going into clubs, you have to leave about 12.45, when it all goes nuts. Walking home, the town is just like *28 Days Later*—zombies, freaks and vomit—it's very strange. It was a good year for me. I got extremely healthy and found I had so much time.

I decided to go back to drink because I like drinking. I like pubs. My local I love. It's a part of my life. My friends all drink. I felt I was being very isolated without it. We could all do Bikram yoga four times a week, but reality is a different matter!

The local I go to is interesting in that you can go there and you know the people vaguely, but they wouldn't know anything about what their family lives are like. Your friends call in and the bar staff you know really well. There is something light in the place and detached from the heaviness of your work and there is a breathing space there. I think a really good bar gives that to its clientele.

In general, the Irish are not the type of people who visit each other's houses. We never had visitors growing up, maybe on a Sunday afternoon, perhaps. We meet outside the house.

When I came to write and act in *Adam and Paul* I spent a lot of time studying addicts. Those boys and girls I looked at on the street, first off I was interested in them physically. I saw both characters as two classic clown characters, because the drink has always been a staple of comedy. So I wanted to shift it on to drugs. I always said the character Tom Murphy played, the reasons he became an addict and all that was because no one held him as a child. Without that stability, what else is there except to cover it all up with whatever drug you can find? I think alcohol does that for a lot of people as well.

It was—the first thing I noticed when I came to Dublin was the heroin problem, and I thought it was shocking. It's interesting that those lads comes from places where families are in great difficulty and where there is no stability—without stability you can't stand up on your own two feet, really.

I'm interested in the subject as a writer but I don't want to write about alcoholism, just like *Adam and Paul* was never about drug addiction. I'm interested in what it does. I'm writing a family story at the moment and I think drink is going to be a major part of it. It's hard to write an Irish family story without it.

I feel like I'm in the middle of a drinking culture so to comment on it is really strange.

The acting community has always been hard drinkers. You know the Donal McCanns and all of that. The Abbey was famous for the drink. These days there is so much more of a lid on it. If someone came in with drink on their breath there would be serious trouble from the other actors. Nobody wants it any more and everybody is much more professional.

When you look at what happens to an actor going on stage—it's the same amount of adrenalin you get from a car crash. It gives you [a] huge high and you can't go home with that coursing through your veins. You won't sleep—I've tried it. For my year off drink I was doing a few plays and it would be six a.m. when I'd fall asleep. Whereas two glasses of wine can take the edge off things. I talked to an older actor once and I said something about another actor being an alcoholic in the nineteeen-seventies.

His reply was that 'Ah, we were all alcoholics in the seventies. You got over it!'

Chapter 7
Teenage Kicks and Night Raving

Copenhagen, the city of the Little Mermaid and Tivoli Gardens, has on the surface a carefree attitude, with locals and tourists taking advantage of the pedestrian streets and public parks that inhabit the city centre. Yet hang around a while and a different scene emerges, with the city's open spaces colonised by hordes of drunken youths, making them no-go areas for locals after dark. Despite its affluence and relatively low levels of social inequality, Denmark is facing an alcohol abuse crisis, with its young, to borrow a phrase, 'probably' some of the worst alcohol abusers on the continent.

According to an EU survey some years back, among 15-year-old Danish boys and girls, 70 per cent had been drunk at least twice in the past year, while 89 per cent of 16-year-olds had been inebriated. Latest government health studies (2007) show that alcohol consumption in Denmark results in approximately 3,000 deaths annually—or 5 per cent of all mortality. The majority of these alcohol-related deaths occur at a relatively young age. Over the past few years, sales statistics are fairly constant, but high consumption of alcohol remains, averaging 11.4 litres of pure alcohol annually for Danes over the age 14, which is lower than Ireland, yet above European average. Since 1994, national health interview surveys have shown that a growing proportion are exceeding the sensible drinking limits (14 units of alcohol for women and 21 for men), that more men than women are exceeding these limits, and that the young and the middle-aged in particular have very high weekly consumption. Studies also show that alcohol consumption is unevenly distributed socially, with consumption increasing as the number of years' education increases.

When viewed from an international perspective, Danish young people rank top in Europe in terms of frequent intoxication. Out of 15 EU countries and Norway, only four countries have a less restrictive alcohol policy than Denmark. As a government report noted, 'In Denmark, decisions concerning border trading and taxes seem to have gone in one direction while efforts to tackle (e.g. age limits) seem to have gone in another. With a view to lowering total consumption in a population, particularly good effect has been achieved by regulating prices and tax.'

Sounds depressingly familiar? Not unlike Ireland, Denmark has tangible issues surrounding alcohol misuse, fuelled in part by a minimum purchasing age of 16 in shops and off-licences (up from 15 some years back) and 18 in bars and nightclubs, low beer and liquor taxes (beer costs just 67 cents a bottle), and liberal advertising laws. 'We are the country of Tuborg and Carlsberg, and images of these products are everywhere,' said Dr Pernille Due, a researcher at the University of Copenhagen. 'I went to see *Harry Potter*—the audience was mostly children—and there was advertising for Smirnoff and Tuborg. Denmark stands out when it comes to problem drinking, but there is not a strong will on the part of government to handle this problem.'

———

Much like the Guinness St James's Gate site in Dublin, the Carlsberg brewery occupies a large chunk of central Copenhagen. While the brewing operation has been moved off site in recent years, administration and head offices remain on site, as well as a museum and visitor centre. I'm in the staff canteen, having lunch with Knud Hedeager Nielsen, Public Affairs Manager for Carlsberg Breweries and an influential member of the European drinks lobby.

Staff are allowed have beer with their daily meals, and a large fridge area carries an assortment of Carlsberg products, from specialist brews to regular beer. Of the 30 staff having lunch, perhaps one third are drinking alcohol. For any of them who get too dependent on liquid lunches, the company has a comprehensive alcohol treatment programme available to employees, which is 100 per cent funded. The free availability of alcohol in the workplace highlighted for me how, despite our shared problems, different cultural attitudes exist across Europe towards the role alcohol plays in society. How would it work for an Irish brewery if drinks were allowed at lunchtime? Would it work in Woking, for instance? Judging by the packed bar in the Rovers Return in *Coronation Street* every lunchtime, it's highly unlikely.

In recent years, Carlsberg has had to take a leading role in Danish society in tackling issues of alcohol misuse. The manner in which they have done this, and their efforts to lead the way, are interesting when held alongside efforts by the Irish drinks industry to do the same. 'I think it became evident to us almost a decade ago that we also needed to play a role in the efforts to help reduce misuse,' says Knud Hedeager Nielsen. 'In 2000 we defined our position in relation to these matters. There is a lot more acceptance now of companies being involved in corporate social-responsibility-related issues. There is an expectation among public and politicians that companies should take [a] greater role on social issues. We are on the brink of launching a new strategy on all this and on responsible drinking. But for the past seven or eight years, we have increased our activities both here and throughout the world.'

The manner in which Carlsberg tackles the issue of abuse is to focus on targeted activities. The company funds specific programmes, and say they are wary of getting involved in cosmetic projects which have little impact on the ground. They are wary also of political manoeuvring for public relations purposes, often used across Europe, they say, by various different political parties. 'We see and we believe, unfortunately, that to tackle misuse politicians tend to go for the easy option in the public eye,' adds Mr Nielsen.

'We think that is unfortunate, because too much of that is without any behavioural impact and does not really address the issue of reducing harm caused by misuse. For example, there is a lot of good legislation already, but the enforcement of this legislation is, we believe, inadequate. You can always add further restrictions, you can add higher age limits, you can introduce bans on advertising, and it's what I would call signal policies. But, unfortunately, these have very little impact.'

Again, as with many in the Irish drinks sector, the industry in Denmark is keen to return responsibility for alcohol education to the home. By way of illustrating this Nielsen tells me about his own experiences with his teenage children. On the children entering their early teens, all the parents of his son's school met and formed a strategy for getting their offspring through adolescence. So, for example, it was decided that mobile phones would not be given to any of the children until they were a certain age, and a joint policy among the parents was also evolved for introducing the children to alcohol. One positive of this type of joint approach in a small community is that it removes peer pressure, which might exist if some children were allowed drink at home or at a younger age than others. With a united approach, parents too can better ensure children do not play one set of parents against the other or give false information as to where they are staying. The school facilitates the meeting of parents once or twice a year, and it benefits from having universal policies and greater parent participation through what can be difficult adolescent years. It's the type of community-led approach that could work very well in Ireland, where, for the most part, school and home life are separate worlds, rarely colliding.

Carlsberg, like Diageo, does not believe that health warnings and advertising restrictions have an impact on problem drinkers. This is a further issue with exporters like Carlsberg, who say pan-European trade is affected by having to apply different health warnings in different regions. 'In terms of health warnings,' says Mr Nielsen, 'the health lobby was very keen to introduce these with the blessing of many governments. However the same NGOs pushing for this include cancer associations who admit that it has had no impact on smokers and their behaviour towards smoking. Why, then, do it with alcohol? Why not spend resources in terms of targeting the audience where the problem exists? I speak about targeting the youth that goes out at night and help[ing] them in a positive way and help[ing] with guidance. We need to make sure parents are equipped to have the critical talk with kids when they enter the teenage years. We have lots [of] example[s] of parents saying, "I don't know what to do." Being a father myself, we and everybody in the business cares about our kids. So it['s] not because we are there to get the most profits. No, we're here to sell beer to adults. It's a very clear position. We [are] here to produce beer for adults and not young people.'

One of Mr Nielsen's big bugbears is being forced to place warning labels on products for specific types of drinkers, and he picks up a bottle with a label to illustrate his point. He highlights the area of women drinking while pregnant, and says that the focus should be on involving frontline medical staff in educating about the dangers.

'The targeted approach is for us the most effective. Take the issue of pregnant women and drinking. Now, when you look at the label and legislators decide to put a pregnant woman with a cross over to indicate, "If you're pregnant don't drink this." Do people really believe this has an impact? Again, research has produced ample evidence it has no behavioural impact. The excuse from the anti-alcohol lobby and politicians is that, yeah, maybe, but it raises awareness. But again, there is no long-term impact of such measures. What it does have is a tremendous cost impact for the industry to add these warnings to their product. It makes it difficult for cross-border trading and so on. If it worked, then fine, but it doesn't work, so why bother industry and our cost base with these initiatives?'

One of the ways in which Carlsberg and the public health lobby in Denmark work together is for the drinks company to provide information packs directly to medical staff, so that those on the frontline of the health service can speak with authority to patients.

'So, for instance, instead of a drinks company telling . . . pregnant women the best way to drink, it's the doctor or midwife.' This type of approach works when it is a complementary support to already established protocols, but if it gets to the stage where the stakeholders in the health sector are reliant on the drinks industry to inform patients, then moderate society might as well throw in the towel. In Ireland a collaborative approach between the drink industry and the public health lobby seems a distance away.

Carlsberg say that as far back as 1997 they got involved in the area of corporate social responsibility to do with alcohol abuse, but, much like in Ireland, it took until 2001 for concrete programmes and initiatives to be launched. The response currently is a united one from the drinks industry in Denmark, yet that approach is showing signs of strain, with beer and spirits companies destined to adopt different approaches and work independently of each other, thereby undermining the argument for self-regulation.

It is an admittance, in effect, that certain types of alcohol are promoted in different ways and that a united industry response to the problem of alcohol abuse is not entirely satisfactory. When I put this point to Fionnuala Sheehan of MEAS, the body funded by the Irish drinks industry to promote 'responsible drinking', she denied this was likely to happen in Ireland also. 'We don't differentiate between different types of drinks. To us alcohol is alcohol is alcohol. The industry is united on that point,' she insisted.

The split in Denmark between on-premise drinking and off trade works out at roughly 75 per cent at home and 25 per cent in bars and restaurants, which is different to Ireland, although we're certainly moving in that direction. Alcohol advertising was very tightly controlled on Danish airwaves until a decade ago, when laws were relaxed. Carlsberg argue that drinking levels have remained unchanged since then. They also feel the EU is fixated on introducing tougher measures which are unjustifiable. 'This is now a huge debate within the EU,' says Mr Nielsen. 'They will come out with a report shortly looking into alcohol's impact on consumption and misuse. Unfortunately it is not a balanced report;

we have seen some of the conclusions already. It is influenced by a political agenda. It is saying, yes, there is a strong indication that advertising has a huge impact on behaviour. We don't see it this way.' This is a typical drinks industry response to the advertising debate. But if advertising doesn't have a large impact on behaviour, then it sort of begs the question of why Carlsberg had a £10.5 million advertisement budget for the last World Cup alone?

———

In another area of Carlsberg's European headquarters at Valby, Eric Thorsted is helping to ease the brewing giant's social conscience. Eric adopted the 'Night Raven' programme in Copenhagen to help cope with the numbers of youths drinking on the city's streets. Sponsored by Carlsberg and many other leading corporations, including McDonalds, the programme involves hundreds of adult volunteers patrolling the streets at night in distinctive yellow jackets and offering advice and support to teenagers in need. They offer taxis home, point out the dangers of excess drinking and help intervene if teenagers are in danger. In 2006, over 50,000 volunteers gave their time to the programme in Denmark, and about 45 per cent of the overall budget is provided directly by Carlsberg. 'We generally try to avoid government funding,' says Thorsted. 'As well as the nighttime work we also work primarily in disadvantaged areas with families, where we help with parenting skills. Implementing anti-bullying projects. Companies giving up to two hours free per month for employees to do social work with families in need.'

Thorsted began the project over 10 years ago, when he left his job as CEO of a major insurance company. Night Ravens had already been successfully up and running in 400 cities in Sweden and 500 cities in Norway. Last year 50,000 volunteered in Denmark, with just three reported assaults on volunteers.

'If you're there at night because you feel it is right to be there, then that gives you an advantage,' says Thorsted. 'You can then create an atmosphere of safety in the area you are in and help prevent violence, misuse and so on. We wear very recognisable luminous jackets so normally children come to us—we don't have to go to them. We're seen as a source of authority, sure, but as a source of positive authority.'

The Night Ravens are present primarily to protect children who have already decided to misuse alcohol, not to address the reason why that abuse occurs in the first place. Or perhaps, in more cynical terms, they are a very visible marketing presence for Carlsberg in the fight against public disorder and drunkenness.

'I don't really accept that argument,' says Thorsted. 'We are made up of average adults—there are no Rambos or saviours in the programme. The oldest member is 88. We give each volunteer an ID card which allows them [to] use buses and trains free of charge when they are on duty. We can also provide insurance and all mobile phones are provided by the Lions Club.' During his decade in charge, Thorsted has noticed changes in the demographic of alcohol abusers. 'We used to focus on the sixteen to twenty age groups, but for past four years the focus is on ten to eighteen-year-olds. That is worrying.' So, the question is, could the initiative work in Ireland and how much of it is for PR purposes?

It's Friday night in central Copenhagen, and I'm standing outside a teenage disco. On the ground near me is a 14-year-old girl who is vomiting repeatedly. She is wearing high heels and a pair of hot-pants. It's -2°C. Her hand is bleeding following a fall, and two of her friends hold her hair back from her face. Several drunk and loudmouthed teenage boys, like crows pecking at a milk bottle, gather round. From the basement disco, other teenagers are led outside to get air and sober up. Inside, roughly half the teenagers present are drunk, despite the fact that the club sells 1 per cent alcohol in an attempt to promote low-alcoholic alternatives. Up until two years ago, there was no age limit on buying alcohol in off-licence premises in Denmark. Many of these teenagers will bring a change of clothes with them, changing in public toilets near the La Scala entertainment venue, exposing as much bare flesh as possible without their parents ever knowing. 'We tell our parents we go outside to a house with our friends,' one youth tells me.

I've tagged along with a Night Ravens group of three volunteers, who remain outside. One of them has called the intoxicated 14-year-old girl's stepmother, and the group waits until someone arrives to take her home. 'I guess she had some vodka,' a 15-year-old friend says. 'The club starts about ten o'clock and goes on until late. I wouldn't like to be at her stepmom's house at breakfast tomorrow!' All the kids seem to have respect for the Night Raven workers, cemented, of course, by the free sweets and condoms the workers hand out. It definitely wouldn't work in Ireland, then!

Mainly the volunteers themselves are middle-aged parents who are concerned with the way their city is turning out and who have a strong sense of social responsibility. The youngest volunteer tells me he is training to be a social worker, and ironically enough, when he's not doing a good deed, he's a bouncer in nightclubs. 'The problem is that they [the kids] are starting earlier. When I was young we were not drinking until about sixteen or eighteen. Today, the kids start at twelve or thirteen and stay out all night. The parents don't seem to care. It's easy for young people to get drinks in bars—if you have the looks and the money, then sure.'

As we wait, young kids continue to limp, stumble and crawl out of the teenage disco, all bare-chested bravado, smudged mascara and torn tights, as friends try to sober them up in anticipation of the return home. The volunteer says the majority of the blame should rest on parents and not on the children themselves. 'When I am wearing the yellow jacket it is a whole different world. It's a good reaction. Most of the kids need a grown-up to talk with. For many of the young people the parents don't care. If the parents did care then they wouldn't allow their kids to run around the streets drinking and yelling and wearing short skirts.' I wonder how the volunteers react when someone they come across is in a distressed state and requires medical assistance. 'We try to get in contact with their family. If they are drunk we call the police or ambulance. When they know we are calling then they come,' said one of the Night Ravens.

Other kids I talk to say there is not much pressure on children to drink at a young age in Copenhagen. Most do, but crucially, those that don't say they can go to parties and drink minerals and not feel left out. The volunteers take me to see shop windows where alcopops and minerals are sold side by side and point out that it's these types of premises that are allowing children easy access to alcohol with few restrictions in place.

The Night Ravens are, if nothing else, a novel way of patrolling the problem, although finding adults with time to volunteer is their biggest challenge. How many Irish parents would be willing to give up their Friday or Saturday nights in order to hold the hands and hair of drunken teens in Temple Bar?

Although it's not like they're queuing up to volunteer in Copenhagen either. 'We have only about twenty-five volunteers in the whole city of Copenhagen,' one of the older volunteers told me. 'We have a lot of parents in the block where I live and I mentioned this to them, and said, "Why not come and join us and try it?" The answers are "We don't have time" or "I have to be home with the kids" and all that. So it's very hard getting volunteers in a city. Some of the ones we have are coming from thirty kilometres away. I think I am one of the only ones who live in the city centre who also volunteer. I do it to make a difference. I like to go in town and drink beer sometime but I see a lot of people fighting and causing trouble. I don't want to see that.'

Closer to 1 a.m., in another part of the city centre, we meet 16-year-old Sinit and a friend, out for the night. I asked them what young people's attitudes towards drinking were. 'Some people don't control themselves and drink a lot. But I know a lot of young people who can control themselves so I think it's okay. I think it's okay to drink at sixteen. The Night Ravens' attitude is kind of respected. It's very easy to get drink here. At fifteen, I went to a club where you had to be twenty-one. There were a lot of guys buying me drink, as well as the bar staff! In shops, if they are old ladies, they might not let you buy drink, but anywhere else there is no problem. At a party, though, there's not really pressure to drink if you're in the right company. Everyone knows about the free sweets and condoms. Maybe it's different in Ireland?'

———

In a secondary school in County Clare, I arranged to spend time with a group of Leaving Certificate children. The principal and some of the staff organised my visit on condition I didn't divulge the name of the school, which I agreed to. At the school itself, I was keen to hear how attitudes had changed since my adolescent days in the same region, a decade or more earlier, and to compare notes with the Danish adolescent experience. What I was struck by was the fact that seemingly little discussion takes place in secondary schools around alcohol issues in Ireland. The children I met, mostly 16–18-year-olds, told me my visit was one of only a handful of times they had ever discussed alcohol in a school setting.

It's not something, in retrospect, that surprised me all that much. I remember in my own school days the only real discussion on addiction was when we were all herded into the computer room early one morning, without warning, where a hardened Dublin heroin addict told us his story. Now, for secondary school students in the west of Ireland, a hardened Dublin heroin addict was about as far outside our cultural reference points as an Islamic shoe bomber would be to a class of trainee Texas Rangers. So, aside from the initial shock value of hearing about needles on skin and so on, it had little meaningful effect. At least with the movie *Trainspotting*, there was a soundtrack we could relate to. Of far more symbolic significance were the nights out with teachers towards the end of Leaving Certificate, such as the Graduation Mass, when students and teachers mingled in a bar afterwards. One teacher drank beer out of a cup that had been won by the one of the school sports teams. We egged him on as he took an extra-long sup of the stagnant lager, and afterwards students and some teachers all made their way to the local disco together. But this was in the early 1990s, when only a fraction of the statistical research into alcohol abuse existed. Teachers and students alike could be partly admonished for not knowing any better—yet nowadays there seems little excuse.

The first question I asked was, at what age did the students feel it was okay to start drinking? In the majority of cases, the answer was 15, and often with parental consent.

'My parents would know where I was and so on. I would come home sober usually. It wasn't a problem,' said one girl. In terms of getting access to alcohol in the local town, the general feedback was that there was little trouble. 'You might be stopped for ID or that but there's always some ways to get around that,' said another girl. One of the lads in the class commented, 'There's never really that much of a problem getting drink from whatever age you want to get it.'

Of the class of 19, I asked for a show of hands as to who went out regularly, and all but five put their hands up (two in the class abstained from alcohol completely). Four in the class said they were allowed drink at home. 'When we are sixteen or seventeen our parents have no problem with us drinking. I was fifteen when I started,' said another girl.

One girl, prompted by the others, gave an account of her drinking life, which often occurred at home with parental consent: 'I drink at home. I started when I was fourteen or that way and it was only small bits, but now it's getting more. Now I'm sixteen. I drink cans no bother at home. I might have about six or seven cans and that would be no problem with my parents. I go to pubs also. They don't want me out in fields.' When I asked if the school had promoted debate around alcohol-related issues, one of the guys said, 'In school there is no awareness around the issues. All we had is a questionnaire asking do we drink. But what can be done? Most of us drink and with it so cheap now—can get three cans for a fiver—there's not much school can do or say about it.'

Later, I handed out a survey to all Leaving Certificate students in the school, and asked them to fill it out overnight. It contained 11 questions, asking about drinking patterns both within the adolescent group and their wider family, how much money was spent weekly on alcohol among the group and whether or not Ireland was becoming a more café-orientated society.

Of the 66 students who filled in the questionnaire, 40 per cent felt there is peer pressure on them and their peers to drink alcohol, while 60 per cent felt it is up to the individual. Of those who answered the question 'Could you envisage not drinking alcohol as an adult?' 38 per cent said they could, while 62 per cent felt they would drink alcohol when older.

When asked, finally, if alcohol had ever affected the students or their families adversely, 40 per cent said it had, while 59 per cent said it had no effect. From those who said it had a negative effect the comments included 'My parents divorced because my mother became an alcoholic and couldn't raise the family' and 'My uncle likes to take a few too many drinks, and it upsets my Granny which upsets me.' Another said, 'I have an uncle that has problems with alcohol, and after seeing him it turned me off binge drinking' while another said, 'One of my Grandfathers died from liver failure due to alcohol and also my uncle is a recovering alcoholic.' Asked whether or not the students thought Irish people drink too much, one answered, 'Yes, nightlife in Ireland is famous worldwide and we are developing too much of a bad reputation.' On a lighter note, one respondee said, 'No, I don't think the Irish drink too much. We are widely perceived as alcoholics by the Americans, but what do they know? I mean, most of them think we have leprechauns.'

———

The Aislinn Drug and Alcohol Rehabilitation Centre in Ballyragget, County Kilkenny, is the only place in Ireland where youngsters under 21 can receive residential treatment for addiction. It has a total of 14 beds, and that has to cater for a wide range of addictions, from eating disorders to drug and drink issues and also gambling. Some of those beds are taken up by the HSE, and others by the probation services, which leaves only a handful of beds for the wider population. Last October, 91 children were on waiting lists to get into the centre for treatment in an attempt to get their lives back on track. The centre struggles for funding and has been trying for years to get government assistance. Thus far its efforts have fallen on deaf ears. The Alcohol Taskforce Report had made recommendations that some of the considerable excise gained from alcohol sales in Ireland should be put towards treatment services such as the Aislinn Centre, but this recommendation was not taken up. (Public health officials have said privately that the Department of Finance didn't like the idea of other government sectors dictating how excise was spent.) When I asked the Minister of State with responsibility for health promotion within the Department of Health, Mary Wallace, about the centre and its lack of beds and funding, she said, 'I'm not familiar about what happens in Kilkenny, I can only talk about my own community.' The public health lobby will say her reply could be interpreted as indicative of wider government ambivalence towards the need for comprehensive treatment services for young people in Ireland. Or perhaps the question should be this: given the wealth of statistical information showing how binge-drinking and rising alcohol-related harm have impacted on Ireland's young people, is it good enough that the government minister with responsibility for health promotion within the Department of Health only knows about her own community?

The day I visited the centre, clinical manager Geraldine Hartnett said that alcohol remains the number one drug problem for adolescents who come into their care, although increasingly in recent years clients have more than one addiction. The centre provides a wide-ranging response to the emotional and psychological needs of the young adults and children who are admitted to its six-week programme. Daily counselling sessions are combined with arts and crafts, personal development and other therapeutic approaches, and the children are drawn from a wide cross section of society.

Hartnett wouldn't be drawn on the percentage success rate for those who are treated at the centre, yet international statistics suggest as few as one in three will beat their addiction following treatment. Hartnett takes a wider view and believes every youngster who passes through a treatment process benefits, but the programme doesn't come cheap, costing in the region of €350 per day. Despite the best efforts of the staff, the social environment clients come from and return to is what makes breaking the cycle of addiction at a young age so difficult. Yet, again, the message from the centre's staff is that Irish parents need to take more responsibility. 'The culture of alcohol in Ireland almost encourages relapse. In terms of rates of addiction reoccurring, or relapse, I wouldn't like to put a percentage on it. I think, though, parents' own drinking has a lot to play with the kids ending up in here,' says Hartnett.

While the centre is not directly funded by government, it does receive income from providing beds to the probation services and the HSE. With studies in Northern Ireland showing that an untreated addict can cost society upwards of £500,000 during his/her lifetime, it's difficult to understand why government places such lack of emphasis on residential treatment funding for young addicts. 'We don't actually get any funding from government,' says Geraldine Hartnett. 'It's very expensive to keep someone in prison. But if money is invested in services such as ours, and people are worked with therapeutically, then that gives them a greater chance of becoming effective members of society.'

In recent years, like many others on the frontline tackling Ireland's addiction issues, Hartnett has seen an increase in the number of youngsters presenting with multiple addictions. 'A few years back alcohol was the main drug in Ireland and there wasn't a lot of disposable income knocking around. Five or seven years ago, the trends began to change. The sheer volume of drugs and the number of drugs being taken and that was very noticeable to us. There is this whole subculture emerging and everyone knows who is dealing and how to get in touch with the dealers. Most of the youngsters who come in here ended up dealing to fund their own habit. This creates a culture of violence. There is a sub culture in Ireland where drugs are freely available and there is no need to control use and people don't have to work to get large sums of money.'

Defining problem drinkers, though, is still an issue in Ireland, says Hartnett, who also believes many youngsters don't seek treatment because the terms 'alcoholic' and 'drug addict' have quite severe social definitions placed on them. 'I don't know if you can define someone under eighteen or twenty-one as alcoholic. Perhaps they are not psychologically developed enough to know alcohol is a problem. But I do know in my heart if someone is a true addict. Often, it is someone who suffered or is suffering from something such as sexual abuse, and to live with that pain they have to drink or use. They often don't have coping skills to live with the pain. Sometimes, alcohol and drugs keep someone alive until the pain is too much.' Again, Hartnett points the finger at the society these youngsters come from: 'In Ireland drinking alcohol is normal even when it is causing problems. There's a delusion around the effects of drink. Even if is someone is holding a business together, often alcohol is robbing their family of their presence, be it due to too much time spent at the golf club or the GAA club and so on.' The solution, she feels, lies in greater parental responsibility. But it's not easy.

'People always talk about school playing a role, but it needs to be parents. Everything we do in life reflects how we are in our own family. Parents need to be educated around alcohol and abuse and use. Another thing which has had a huge effect on our culture is suicide. Parents have been emotionally disabled in a way and now have huge fears for their children. Some of them will say it is okay for them to behave any way they want, as long as they are alive. It's hard not to despair sometimes. I mean, having ninety-one youths on a waiting list to get in here is really saying something about our society and how seriously we are taking this problem.'

————

Three of the youths at the Aislinn Treatment Centre agreed to speak with me on condition that I didn't name them. These are their stories.

'Mary' was a 21-year-old from the south of Ireland who had developed an enormous capacity for drink and drug use from a very young age. This was her second time attempting to get sober. I started drinking when I was twelve. There would be a lot of alcoholics in my family. My dad is in recovery twenty-five years and it is in both sides of the family—both my mam and my dad's. The thing is I would have been aware of it all my life but you don't accept it when it is happening to you. I would have really seen myself at sixteen or seventeen as just having a good time and having drinks and doing what all my other friends were doing.

I grew up in a rural town in Kilkenny and would have moved to Callan and then on to college in Waterford. From the age of twelve to fifteen, it would have been just naggins of vodka or stuff before a disco maybe once a month. Then the time intervals got smaller and when I got into college it was four or five days a week. Drink was so widely available and so cheap and everybody was drinking. That was the thing to do in college. Then when I went to work full time I had a week's wages, so was coming out with six hundred euro or seven hundred euro a week. I would spend my days off sitting in the pub from half nine in the morning until closing time that night. That's what I did on my days off. Obviously it became a problem as my life just became too unmanageable. I wasn't able to get into work. My friends were slipping away and I was in with different crowds. The drugs came with the drinking. It blew up from there. March last year I went for treatment and it lasted for three months and I relapsed after that.

You have to give up a major part of your life and start a new life. I have to give up all my friends this time and my meetings are going to be my social life from now on. When I got out of treatment the first time I stayed with it. Someone gave me an example, saying that addicts and alcoholics are so used to these massive highs that normal life seems boring.

I would have been away from home a lot so most of my drinking and using would have been hidden. My dad would have known the signs. I got in trouble before I came into treatment last time and my back was against the wall. I went into treatment not having a choice. This time I decided I wanted to go in for myself. I was drinking in pubs very young, from the age of fourteen upwards. You don't know when you go in what you're going to like, so I would have started on alcopops and vodka. Then it progressed to cider when I was around sixteen. I'm now twenty-one years old and if I went into a pub now I could drink twenty-five plus bottles of beer along with ten tequilas and a half bottle of wine on top of all that. I have a massive tolerance. I could be sitting beside a man of forty or fifty years of age and sit at the bar beside him all day and have drink for drink with what he was drinking.

I knew one of the counsellors here and talked to him about two weeks before I came in. He knew I had problems with drugs and alcohol and so he pulled a few strings for me and got me in. I was ready to leave Ireland before I came into treatment. I wanted an easy way out and now that I'm here, it's making me stay. My dad was in recovery when I was born and my mam and my two sisters don't drink, so none of my extended family drink.

But anywhere I would have gone or lived I would have looked for drink or drugs. It was there in front of you and all around you. Even walking down the streets, there was heroin addicts on the road and people smoking joints. If you know what to look for you can find it so easily. But to avoid it and live in Ireland? You can't avoid it because it is all around you and that's why it is so hard to abstain. I think we are bad here. For instance, on holidays I have brought drugs through the US and Spain and when I get there, it seems the same; there are drugs widely available there. Drink is everywhere too. It's part of other countries' cultures but the likes of Spain and the US and that don't seem to abuse it as much as we do.

I think the government should be ashamed of the fact that this is one of the only adolescent treatment centres. It's a disgrace to any government in any country. The problem is right there in front of them, they can see it. It's getting bigger and bigger and if there's no help for people they have no hope. It's very hard just to stop from going to AA meetings or NA or whatever. You need special treatment and somewhere to go. A lot of people coming in would be in trouble with the law, maybe, and this opens their eyes. The first time it opened my eyes to everything and you accept it. It's not something that you can get in your environment naturally. I think the stigma has gone away now too, because people realise that drink and drugs problems ruin people's lives and this is a positive way to deal with it. I'm three weeks and three days here and I'm off drink three weeks and six days. Before I came in, I had lost my job and life was a total disaster. I broke up with my boyfriend. My parents weren't talking to me and I was just totally isolated.

I drank for about three days before I came in. My advice to parents is that I tell them not to be fooled, because we are all very deceptive. I lied for years and it comes off the tip of the tongue. If parents were worried I would suggest a consultation with their children or get someone in AA to go and talk to them. Pressure from parents isn't necessarily good and they can go about it a different way instead of pressuring their son or daughter.

There's plenty ways to do it.

When I come out this time I'm going to stay away from pubs. Because that's what happened to me the last time. My first time back in a pub after treatment. The first time I went in. I went in to meet a friend and he asked me what did I want and I said an orange juice. The barman came to the bar and he asked me what I wanted and I said, 'A Miller, please.' Just like that and I had it half drank before I consciously knew what I was doing.

I don't really have any true friends left. The true friends I had are lost and the ones I am left with are the ones that are using. They're pub friends.

People find that when they are in my kind of situation that there are very few people that will be there for them apart from family and one or two close friends and that's the reality of it. When I was going into treatment the first time, people said to me, 'Jesus you don't have a problem,' or that. But they just don't see it. Lot of people would have said, 'Sure this is crazy, your dad is only sending you in there because blah blah blah' or 'You're only nineteen or twenty and growing up like anyone else.' The fact of the matter is, though, I know that I have ruined my life.'

'Seán' is originally from the UK and now living in Munster. This is his third time attempting to get clean and sober. He is 16 years old.

I was born in Manchester and lived there for twelve years before moving over here. I hadn't drunk once when I lived in the UK. Since I came over here, the drink has taken over. I didn't know anyone over here, but after I went to school I got to know people.

First thing I drank was a naggin of vodka and I just threw it down my neck. The feeling I got walking around and not knowing what was happening got me straight away. Everything was a laugh. My dad is an alcoholic and my mum drinks every now and again. My dad used to be around the house every day drunk. He used to be pissed off his head every day and wouldn't go a day without drinking. I don't know if he still drinks or not; I haven't seen him in about ten years.

I only got drunk once every now and again when I was twelve. But soon as I turned fourteen, I started going to parties and raves and discos. I started drinking more and more and dossing school every day and going drinking. I moved on to Ecstasy then and buying litre bottles of vodka for myself. I would go crazy after vodka, go fighting and smashing up the place. I was sent to a detention centre for criminal damage. I smashed up my principal's house when I was drunk. His wife and kids were in the house at the time. I drank two naggins of vodka and five or six cans of Carlsberg before I did it.

The amount I drank depends on how much money I had. Usually I'd just go buy a super naggin or a shoulder of drink with a few cans. I stopped drinking vodka for ages, because I went over to Spain on holidays and I nearly got sent out of the country for fighting.

I was drinking in pubs. Most of my mates would drink but not as much as me. They might drink four or five cans and they'd be fucked.

I got the money from going to Youthreach, which I got paid a hundred and twenty euro a week for. If you have been kicked out of mainstream school, you can get your education there and they pay you. I did my Junior Cert and got on okay. I'm bright enough. I ended up here this time from drugs and for being out of control. I've been off drugs a few months so drink is my main problem now. It always reels me back in.

I love drink. The day before I came here I got kicked out of my house. Me and my mate bought two slabs of drink and had one each. There are twenty-four cans in a slab. I didn't get any sleep and was drinking right through the night. I was still pretty pissed walking in here. It's my third time in treatment. I have copped on a little bit now. First time, I just came in here, I was only doing it so I would make people happy. I left after four weeks. I came back then because I relapsed. Then I came back because I was sent to court. If I don't get clean and sober this time, I'm looking at two years in a detention centre. My plan in life is to join the Army and become an electrician. My older brother was in the Navy but got kicked out. A lot of my mates are in the Army.

When I came in here I was talking about the drinking and I said maybe it was a gene because my dad was an alcoholic. Everyone was saying, 'You can't be blaming your dad.' I reckon, though, it was just a case of as soon as I got a taste for it I couldn't stop.

I never had a problem getting served and anyway, I always hung around with lads older who got drink for me. In here I'm not around the streets, starting fights or getting beaten up. I reckon it would be better if there were a few more treatment centres around.

[A] few of the guys I hung around with could end up in here. Some of them will never try to stop and they would have been saying to me when I came in here—'you're a quitter' and that. But I don't give a shit. Their life is going to be ruined and I'm going to get mine back. I have to stay off it this time. I owe dealers money and they have been calling to my house threatening to break my legs and that. I was always hanging around with older people. When I was nine years of age in England I was hanging out with eighteen-year-olds.

Most people in Ireland don't mind the fact I have an English accent. But anyway, fuck them if they do. Whatever happened eight hundred years ago is not my fault. My brother got put in hospital once—someone slashed him a few times. My mum is glad I'm here now. She was always worried where I was. There were times when I wouldn't answer my phone for days and would just disappear. She'd be driving around the whole city looking for me.

The worst thing parents can do, I think, is have a go at their kids when they come back drunk, shouting at them or whatever. That's stupid. Whenever my mam does it, it just makes me want to go out and drink again. I think if parents approach the situation with a little more calm. I have four weeks left here. I do my Leaving Cert Applied when I get out. Think I will stay home and out of everyone's way when I get out and try getting a new crowd to fall in with. If I go back to the way I was, I'm going to end up dead and I know that for a fact.

'Paul' is 19 and from the South. His father has chronic liver disease and introduced Paul to alcohol at a young age.
I was here last year and stayed for eight weeks and was sent home. To be honest I didn't change the places I hung around in or the fellas I hung around with so I'm back here.

When I left the first time, I never thought I'd smoke heroin and I smoked heroin about three months ago. I only smoked it for three or four nights and then I stopped. I had no intention of smoking heroin but when I had eight bottles of Bulmers drank, I thought, 'Here, fuck it, give me the heroin and show me how to do it.'

I'm drinking since I was thirteen years of age. It has had a big effect on my life. My father gave me my first drink. He gave me a can. He was drunk one night and he said, 'Come on in.' He needed someone to drink with so I started to drink with him. The next day he brought me out to the pub and he gave me a pint outside. He just wanted a drinking buddy, as he didn't like drinking on his own. He wanted someone to talk to and have a singsong with and have a few jokes and talk about his past. I have been drinking with him ever since. It got heavier and heavier. First I might have had vodka and a few cans. Drugs got worse. I'd drink a litre of vodka and be drunk so I'd take a line of coke to wake myself up. Drink another litre of vodka then.

On a night out I could have two bags of cans, vodka, whiskey, anything I could get my hands on. Anything I could rob. Anything. I started to rob my family and going through a bad way. I lost my mother when I was sixteen. Three years ago. I couldn't deal with it. That's when I started going on the drugs, you know, to take the pain away. My dad is still drinking. He has cirrhosis of the liver and he was asked to go to the hospital and basically he stuck up his finger at the doctors. He keeps passing blood and his legs are very skinny. He can't sleep and can't eat, just drinking and drinking.

It's Ireland, though, and as far as I can see, everybody drinks. I think the place has gone to the dogs, to be honest. I was drinking in pubs at the age of sixteen with my dad. I used to get money off my dad for drink. Sometimes I'd go robbing CD players out of cars and selling them. I broke into houses and stole plasma TVs. I even broke into my school and robbed four computers out of it.

My dad admitted last year that he is an alcoholic. He went to Bushy Park for three months. The day he got out he told my sister he was just going down to pay the ESB bill. When she went down to the ESB to see what was keeping him, he was in the pub next door. My granddad was a madman for drink too. He passed it onto my father, so it's in the genes. But then, sometimes it's not all about the genes. It's not as if my father held me down and poured that can down my throat. It was my choice. That's the way I see it.

I dropped out of school before my Junior Cert and went straight into FÁS working. I was there for two years. But I'm always getting arrested for theft, burglary and assault. I tried to commit suicide twice. I put a rope around my neck and a friend saved me. Another time I had to get twenty stitches in my hand. I went into my bathroom and got a razor and just started slicing. I wouldn't do it when I was sober. Not once. It's a disease. I have to stop, because if not, the next time I pick up a drink I'll be dead.

Most of the people I know are saying, 'Ah sure when you get out you know you'll go drinking again.' This time, though, I'm going straight into a halfway house for three months. After that I'm hoping to move to Wexford or Waterford and get a flat. You know, get away from the places where I grew up.

The more I look at it it's getting better and better for me. I want to be a mechanic or a mason. I have a failing to appear in court and a bench warrant out on me for assault, but I have a drugs taskforce officer looking into it for me. When I get out it's going to be very tempting. I don't know what'll happen. I might last and I mightn't last. There are adverts on the television, it's on posters and there's a pub on every corner. I'll just have to pick up the phone and call someone. I was in foster care after my mum died. They told me, you get help for you[r] drink or you're getting thrown out. So I decided to come here to this centre. I was only doing it to keep a roof over my head. But four weeks into it I started to realise that my life was a disaster. All the damage I had caused. It hit me. The only person I know that doesn't drink is my brother.

With my dad, though, there's no hope for him. He said he doesn't care. He stays on the couch with his bottle of Paddy and his bottle of vodka and drinks away. He only uses the car to go to the off-licence and back. He keeps saying he has nothing to live for. We have a good relationship since I came in here. He can see me improving. It's very safe in here. You're not afraid of people knocking on your door. You're away from drugs. People in here actually listen to you. If you tried to say what you were feeling on the outside, they'll tell you to cop on or fuck off.

I think the government need to open up more treatment centres. There should be more clubs and organisations to take fellas like me away from the streets or even away for the weekend.

I only went drinking because of courage to talk to boys and girls and go dancing and stuff. I was very shy. Give me about eight cans and I'd talk to anyone and dance and [do] all sorts of things. Nearly everybody I know is like that. It is getting worse if you ask me.

——

Okay, so not every child in Ireland who opens their parents' drinks cabinet or drinks a can of cider in a field will end up in the Aislinn Centre. By choosing to present these testimonies, I could be accused of distorting the general experience for Irish adolescents. But these testimonies are real. They exist.

The fact remains also that for those who take a wrong turn or develop an addiction at a young age, specific treatment services and approaches are wholly underdeveloped and underformalised in this country. With an adolescent drinking problem as well-signed as ours, it seems a glaring oversight on behalf of government not to provide enough treatment facilities. We're very good on reports, not so on rehabilitation, it seems.

Perhaps, though, there is not enough societal pressure to enable a response. In communities such as the one I visited in Clare, the community is aware the society exists. But there is little discussion, few collective efforts made to get to grips with the problem.

Unlike Copenhagen, where 'outside the box' thinking is being applied to the problem of youth drinking, from parental consensus to initiatives such as the Night Ravens, in Ireland we seem to still have a one-dimensional and somewhat wish-based approach.

Government would like for children not to start drinking so young. Secondary school students, like those in Clare, express a desire for something else to do. So, despite arthouse and mainstream cinemas, more theatres and arts centres, specific youth-orientated gigs, an infrastructure of bowling and arcade centres, well funded sports facilities, additional skate parks and more opportunities for international travel, there is still nothing for young people to do except get out of it. Until parents are able to provide an example of life without alcohol abuse, then perhaps youth-orientated thinking will continue to be blurry. The focus therefore needs to be more on parents than policies, more on personal responsibility than limiting access. Generations of Irish children grow up seeing alcohol as part of their parents' lives and experience. The token dialogue we have been having with youths is clearly inadequate and needs to be sharper, more relevant and less preachy. It needs to talk about issues such as emotional need, love, friendship, sexual health, peer pressure, respect and social acceptability.

A recent EU survey pointed out that the cost of alcohol misuse in the EU is estimated at about €125 billion, equivalent to 1.3 per cent of gross domestic product. So in a very real sense, addressing the problem at a young age saves society, financially and socially. With the real cost of alcohol in Ireland dropping at an alarming rate in the past two decades, and youngsters having more disposable income, coupled with the altering of traditional family structure, a perfect storm for the acceleration of alcohol abuse has been raging. Little has been done to have young persons speak to young persons to allow the dialogue between policymakers, health officials and others to include those most in need. The Pioneer movement are calling for abstinence for all under-18-year-olds— yet that already exists in law in Ireland. What's needed is a maturing of attitudes and a stricter enforcement of present legislation. The government sees the problem as parents' responsibility. Parents see it as a government problem. The health lobby sees the problem but can't get action to tackle it. The drinks industry sees the problem but takes small, somewhat insignificant steps to tackle it. In the meantime, the cycle continues.

Niall Toibin, Actor

I started drinking before I joined the Civil Service. I was put in a new section with fellas just discharged from the Army. On pay day they would bring me down to the pub and of course I would be pissed out of my mind, and I wasn't even eighteen years of age.

These boys would really give it a lash, and that was normally on payday, which was twice a month. At a young age it was regarded as absolutely natural that this was what you did. They regarded me as a sort of mascot. Of course, I was also great use as I was the only one who spoke Irish very well. A lot of stuff that came up though the Department would have Irish in it—forms and so on—so they came to rely on me. It was the Statistics Department and the job we were working on was a tabulation of the 1946 census. It was the first time any kind of mechanical information-gathering was in use, at a time when statistics and all that were in their infancy. Everything was punched onto cards and they were fed into machines and so on. Some of the equipment was so new that if you put your foot on the pedal and kept it there for an extra ten seconds, the machine would go on fire. Of course the engineer would have to be called from the firm that supplied the stuff and we would all have three or four hours off. They twigged to that in due course, but is just shows you how basic the whole thing was. I mean, it was like being there at the invention of the typewriter. Here we were two hundred years later at the start of the electronic revolution, and I was beginning my drinking life.

The natural thing to do was to go out on payday and get smashed and that was it.

You might get the weekend out of it, but once you did that and paid your digs you would be broke. It was always pints back then, or you might have the odd half one. Because I was the youngest they would give it to me and have a laugh with it. But the thing was, there was nothing strange about starting to drink almost after you had left school. I had gone straight from school to the Civil Service. So, I became very used to it and it drinking became second nature very early on. I would think nothing of going in and having a pint in a pub on my own at eighteen years of age, if I had the price of it.

Come to think of it, I didn't drink pints that much—I drank bottles of stout. It was only a bit later when I started drinking with Dublin fellas that I started on pints. But then, once I started, I just drank and drank and drank, until I was about forty-three years of age, and then I stopped.

I think on my game, acting, or in any of the arts or in literature, it is a bit of myth that you have this license to drink. There were some very famous examples, such as Brendan Behan, who would be absolutely smashed and was a genuine sort of alcoholic case. I would say with others like Richard Harris it was more of an attention thing. He did drink heavily, okay, but perhaps he exploited that reputation quite deliberately, whereas Brendan had no control over it. If he got pissed he got pissed and the resulting publicity happened accidentally rather than he set out to get attention. Because Brendan was a clever man in his own way, and if he wanted publicity he was sure to be able to control what type of publicity he would get.

I think even still the whole Irish attitude to drink is very stupid. Drink, to my mind, is a fucking curse. It needn't be, but in many cases in Ireland, those who drink have a problem of some description with it. They tend to deny it or cover it up or control it. The whole attitude here is wrong, from the government approach to the GAA sponsorship by Guinness. So you have thirteen-year-olds going out onto a sporting field and sponsored by the biggest drinks company in the country—that to me is . . . outrageous. I think that has been stopped now, but it should have never happened at the very beginning.

The association with drinking in Ireland seems to me to be a Celtic thing. All the Celtic races seem to do it. I suppose an Irishman without a pint is like an Italian without a glass of wine. I regarded it as natural until I began to have big problems with it.

I had big domestic problems with it. Also when I was young and lashing back pints, there was no great problem about it because I wasn't responsible to anybody. Then I got married, and later, when the kids were growing up, my drinking began to be a problem. I wouldn't really drink at home, but having said that, if I came home drunk and if there was stuff there in the house I'd lash into that too.

When I was in New York and the *Borstal Boy* was on and I was a public figure playing Brendan Behan and I would lash into it. And they used it for publicity and so on. At that time I had great health and it wouldn't affect me. I was in my thirties then. In fact, my fortieth birthday in New York, I remember getting very depressed and getting pissed because I was going to be an old man!

Eventually, I had to stop. I did so in the end because I had a very sane doctor, who said, 'You can drink the way you drink and you can work the way you work, but you can't do both. It's none of my business, it's up to you.'

That, to me, was putting it right on the line and I just had to face the facts. I stopped drinking and I went to AA for a while. I used to go to meetings, and funnily enough I stopped going to meetings but I never went back drinking. When I made my mind up that was it.

The anonymity part of AA didn't bother me—I know some people with public profiles find that hard. Most people who go there go to help themselves; it's one of the great things about the fellowship. They are concerned about their own problem and the open confession and so forth. I think people trying to stop drinking are not really going to start peering into the secrets of others. They are there to help themselves. You can rely on an AA meeting to help you and guard your secret.

Once I stopped drinking, I lost ninety per cent of my friends. It would be just 'Hello' and they would walk on. Mind you, a lot of that would be helpful, as they would be thinking, 'We can't put him in the way of drink.' Whereas with others it would be, 'Yerrah fuck him, he's only a bore.'

I couldn't not go into bars after I stopped drinking; it was part of my life still. I noticed, though, when I went to England and America, people went into pubs and some didn't have a drink at all. They went in there to have food and they went in there to have coffee and they talked. The only people who deliberately went in there to get hammered were all alcoholics anyway.

I noticed, too, that I got more work when I stopped drinking, once people realised I was sober, then I used to get plenty work. For instance, I got an awful lot of work in England on television and stage and so on because people in the business knew I was reliable now and not a drunken Paddy. If you had an Irishman who didn't drink, not only would he be talented, but sober as well.

And to be honest once I stopped and once I began to be very happy being sober, I never gave it thought again, simply because I was happier. Now, if I had been more miserable I probably would have gone back to it.

The only thing, and I had to realise this quickly, is that you have to cut out your mates. Fuck them. Because if they want to drink, they want you to drink. You have to cultivate a whole new circle . . . of people who are not going to be dragging you in for a pint. You develop a different range of social experiences or meet people who like you because you don't drink or have stopped drinking.

It very easy to say pub friendships are useless but in many cases I found that they were, really. When the time comes and you want to go back to one of your old drinking mates for a hand in something, he doesn't want to fucking know you. I'm only talking about people who themselves have a basic problem even though they may not know it.

The majority of ordinary drinkers, people who go in for a pint, two or three nights a week, well, they are a different story, then. I'm talking about people who I used to drink with and who expected me to drink and then when I didn't I was a lost cause.

If I look at Ireland today the patterns of drinking is a sort of bravado. If you ask me what do I think of Irish society at the moment, I think it's a fucking awful country. I think there [is] no respect whatsoever for people or sensitivities or rights. If you have the money you can do whatever you like and ride roughshod over everybody, until you fall off the horse and then fuck you, then they'll kick you around. I mean, this is strong talk but I react very strongly to the way anybody with money seems to have the right to do whatever they like.

The old pub scene, too, is gone completely. When you went on holidays down to Lahinch or Crosshaven or towns like that, at certain times of the night, maybe three or four pints in, someone would be called on to sing. People had their party piece which they did and it was all very low-key and humorous and civilised. You'd hear the same jokes every night about the same people and it was relaxed and very rarely was there pugnacious behaviour. That is not the case now, I don't think.

I'll leave you with one of my favourite drinking stories:

I used to serve at twelve o'clock Mass, and I was supposed to serve Mass for the Bishop one Sunday. I got a call that one of the lads in AA . . . was after breaking out and he wanted to see me. My problem was that if I got to see him I wouldn't be able to go and serve Mass for the Bishop. I thought about it and said, 'The Bishop can always find someone else to serve the Mass.'

Not only did I not serve the Mass, I didn't even go to Mass, which at that time was a heavy thing to do. I thought that I had helped the guy and said to myself the man above would understand and would forgive me . . . that is, if there is anyone up there. And there fucking well better be, because otherwise it's an awful fucking waste of drink . . .

Chapter 8

The State of Us

A 2008 HSE report into alcohol-related harm in Ireland found that between 1995 and 2002, alcohol-related hospital discharges increased by 92 per cent, while liver disease increased by 148 per cent during a similar 10-year period. The report also found an 85 per cent increase in alcohol-related injuries between 1995 and 2003, with a staggering 133,962 alcohol-related discharges between 1995 and 2004, or just over four per day. These are telling statistics, putting huge pressure on Ireland's already stretched health service and underlining the social costs associated with the drunken Irish.

We know also that between 1986 and 2006, the sale of alcohol in Ireland increased across all beverage categories (Hope, A. (2007) 'Alcohol consumption in Ireland 1986–2006'. Health Service Executive—Alcohol Implementation Group). Beer sales increased by 32 per cent while spirits increased over the same period by 46 per cent, although, in a new trend, the report states that the 'most dramatic increase by volume was in wine sales with an increase of 8,121,225 litres of pure alcohol representing a 523 per cent increase, although this was from a relatively low base. The sale of cider increased by 3,195,013 litres of pure alcohol, which represents a 647 per cent increase.'

It's worth noting, though, that during the 20-year period this report takes account of, Ireland's population increased by almost 20 per cent. Bearing this in mind, alcohol consumption per capita increased over the 20 years by 48 per cent, and this increased per adult (persons aged 15 years and over) from 9.8 litres of pure alcohol in 1987 to a high of 14.3 litres in 2001. Figures for 2007 indicated that this level stood at 13.37 litres. The average level of consumption per adult in the EU is 10.2 litres of pure alcohol, meaning that Ireland consistently ranks in the top five of European countries in drinking leagues. The latest figures available for 2008 come from within the industry, and point to a decline in alcohol consumption of 5.9 per cent in 2008. The report, issued in March 2009, stated that 'Per adult consumption decreased by 7.3 per cent in 2008, while per capita consumption went down by 7.7 per cent. These rates are equal to the decline in consumption that was recorded in the entire seven year period between 2001–2007. As a result average consumption levels are back to 1997/98 levels.'

Yet it is unclear whether or not these figures take into account the large amount of alcohol bought in Northern Ireland (taking advantage of lower VAT rates) during the same period, with suggestions that up to 10 per cent of sales had migrated across the border. Emigration out of and migration into Ireland was also higher during that period. With the economic recession, income over the last year has fallen more sharply than it has done for a decade or so previous. In 2009 the value of the alcohol market in Ireland, despite a 2.9 per cent drop, was still a staggering €6.9 billion, with the government taking in somewhere in the region of €1 billion in taxes annually. In financial terms, the booze is one of Ireland's most reliable cash cows.

One of those at the forefront of trying to get a handle on Ireland's alcohol epidemic is Prof. Joe Barry, who divides his time between work with the Health Service Executive (HSE) and Trinity College Dublin. Prof. Barry was initially lending his expertise as part of the HSE drug services, starting in 1991, when the focus was on heroin and methadone treatment. As time progressed, alcohol was seen more and more as a substance frequently abused, and Prof. Barry's attention was re-directed. Alcohol consumption in Ireland peaked in 2001, before coming down in 2002 and 2003, coinciding with an increase in government tax on spirits and cider. Trends show that consumption remained steady up until 2007, when there was another drop. Prof. Barry points out that while alcohol consumption is lower now than it was at the turn of the noughties, in European comparisons, Ireland still ranks quite high and is not shifting all that much. The second report of the Alcohol Strategic Taskforce noted that 58 per cent of male drinking in Ireland was binge-drinking. While the bingeing definition is modest by Irish standards, there is now widespread European consensus that people in Ireland, the UK and to a certain extent Northern Europe tend to practise fairly heavy episodic drinking as opposed to drinking with meals or on occasion. 'There are a lot of cultural issues in Northern Europe as opposed to Southern Europe,' says Prof. Barry. 'In Ireland, we have to look at what patterns we have here. Europe is so culturally diverse, not just for drinking policy but for many things. You can have some macro-EU policies, but with something that is so culturally specific as alcohol, you have to have locally based national policies as well.'

But the big question is, what are those national policies in Ireland? And is there consensus between the public health lobby, the government and the drinks industries on the extent of the problem firstly, and the manner in which it should be dealt with? Prof. Barry thinks there is huge disparity between all three sectors on how to tackle Ireland's drink crisis. The longer that divided approach remains, the less likely it will be to get a handle on our drinking patterns. 'There isn't consensus among what might be called the stakeholders,' says Prof. Barry. 'The drinks industry doesn't accept the view that there is a relationship between per capita consumption and drink-related harm. The public health and World Health Organisation view is that a rise in per capita consumption will lead to a rise in drink-related health [problems] and social harm. The industry does not accept that. So therefore they will lobby the government not to have any change in our drinking levels. The government isn't unified on this either. The Strategic Taskforce in 2004 recommended that we reduce our overall per capita consumption to the European average, which at the time would have been an eighteen per cent reduction. So that is the premise on which public health practitioners are working. Minister Harney in the Dáil last year agreed that we need to reduce our overall consumption.'

I was keen to get the drinks industry view on per capita consumption, so put this point to Kieran Tobin, chair of the Drinks Industry Group of Ireland. On paper, at least, there seems to be a clear parallel over the last two decades between the rise in per capita consumption and the rise in alcohol-related harm statistics, from liver failure to A&E admittances. I asked Mr Tobin whether or not *he* believes a rise in per capita consumption and a rise in alcohol related harm were related.

'Not necessarily. I don't believe there is an absolute and direct link between the two. You can have misuse of alcohol at low and medium per capita consumption. If you are saying that by driving down consumption you are going to do away or reduce alcohol-related harm, we don't believe that will work. What might happen is as people get more informed and more educated about alcohol-related issues, then we might see people more careful. That might result in a slight decline. But I don't think driving down the average consumption will do anything to inform and educate people. We always work on the basis that the vast majority of people enjoy alcohol in a sensible manner and that alcohol-related harm is not an issue for the vast majority.'

But if studies show that 58 per cent of the adult male population takes part in binge-drinking, then how true is it that the 'vast majority of people enjoy alcohol in a sensible manner'?

And in a country of our size, does 133,962 alcohol-related discharges between 1995 and 2004 not signify a widespread problem relationship with alcohol?

If we side-step the drinks industry views for a moment, and assume that reducing per capita consumption is government policy, then it's worth asking, how does the state currently try to achieve this policy? With the economy in freefall since 2008, the government is looking to gather all revenue it can to balance the books; therefore, reducing the drinking levels may not be in the best interests of the Department of Finance, for example. For any government policy to work, there needs to be a clear idea within government on where the responsibility falls to tackle the issue—

be it the Department of Health or Justice. Perhaps the most successful State intervention in the area of alcohol misuse has come in the form of drink-driving campaigns, specifically with the introduction of random breath testing. This has seen a reduction in deaths on the road. Yet the majority of government legislation on alcohol emanates from the Department of Justice, as opposed, say, to the Department of Health, meaning that alcohol misuse is still seen primarily as a law-and-order issue as opposed to a health one. 'The problem is there isn't really a national strategy in relation to alcohol as there is, for instance, in illicit drugs,' says Prof. Barry. 'So if you are asking me what's the policy, well, that depends on who you ask.'

————

I wanted to put some of these issues to the Irish government and hear firsthand what exactly is being done to tackle the issue of alcohol abuse in Ireland. Having heard already from public health campaigners like Prof. Joe Barry and Dr Chris Luke, from frontline staff in places like the Aislinn Centre, where treatment beds for youngsters are at a huge premium, it was clear that government in Ireland has a huge role to play. And it's not as if they can plead ignorance on the issues, with so many government-funded surveys pointing in the same direction. Having put an interview request to the Department of Health to speak with Health Minister Mary Harney, I was instead directed to the Minister of State at the Department of Health and Children with special responsibility for health promotion and food safety, namely Minister Mary Wallace. This was the person tasked by the government to comprehensively draw together existing strands of government thinking and policy and bring about a positive legislative impact on alcohol misuse. I met with Minister Wallace in her office in Leinster House, while her Department advisor Robbie Breen sat in on the interview. The following is a transcript of our conversation and an indication of government efforts, thinking and insight.

BO'C:

The graphs indicate that the issue of alcohol abuse in Ireland has been steadily rising over the last two decades. Does the government acknowledge that? And what is the government's approach to tackling this area?

Minister Wallace:

From our point of view in the Health Promotion Unit we'd be very concerned about the situation and I suppose one of the big steps taken last year was the Intoxicating Liquor Act. We do feel that the whole availability of alcohol in areas such as off-licences and supermarkets is a problem. The whole increase in the number of off-licences in the country has had a huge impact. So a couple of things have happened. The fact that people can't buy drink in these places now past ten p.m.—that has been useful. The price of getting a licence for an off-licence was one hundred euro, we increased this to three hundred euro, because, again, of this whole forecourt access to alcohol and the presence of alcohol. We've also had the separation of alcohol and food in supermarkets and the removal away from the front door. We see this as very important, because whether we're talking about alcohol or indeed if you look across all the addictions, including obesity, the same principle applies. The principle is that the environment in which we all do our business needs to change.

BO'C:

Are the changing of licensing laws and the changing of alcohol placement in shops merely just tinkering around the edges of Ireland's alcohol problem? For instance, what are the underlying issues in Ireland that make our society so prone to alcohol abuse, and is government doing anything to tackle those underlying issues?

Minister Wallace:

We would look at the whole issue of advertisement and sponsorship also. The government decided in April 2008 to set up groups to look at these issues. Now, again, when you go into looking at these issues, things may seem straightforward at the beginning but then you see all the complexities with it. But we would certainly be saying if you look at rugby and the Heineken Cup and if you look across all the different sports you discover there is alcohol involved in the sponsorship of sport. We would see that as being an issue that we will be having a good look at. We can talk about statistics all day but one of the big concerns we have is the increase in younger women involved in alcohol and we have a graph we can show you which is actually frightening. In terms of alcohol-related discharges from hospitals seventy-five per cent will be men, twenty-five per cent will be women. But when you look at the seventeen-year-olds you discover forty-seven per cent are women and fifty-three per cent young men. The younger women issue as, indeed, the teenagers and the whole youth aspect to alcohol, is becoming more and more of a concern to us.

BO'C:
Just on that, I was in the Aislinn Centre recently in Kilkenny. They tell me they have fourteen beds, and that, as far as they are aware, it is the only residential centre in Ireland where juveniles under the age of twenty-one can be treated for addiction. When you take out HSE-owned beds and probation beds, it leaves four to six beds for the treatment of children for the whole of Ireland. So, if the government acknowledges there is a rise in alcohol abuse in Ireland, particular[ly] amongst young people, how come there are only fourteen beds in the whole country to treat young addicts?

Minister Wallace:
Treatment is a big issue across all the sides of it. There is a lot of treatment in communities and I'd be aware of a lot of treatment issues. But the big problem first of all is the early age with which people are actually starting to drink. One of the most important messages is that I'm not quite sure that parents have embraced the seriousness of a fourteen- or fifteen-year-old drinking. If I were writing a chapter in any book I would write a chapter on the

importance of delaying the first drink. If we could delay it from fourteen to over twenty it would make such a huge difference. There are people who say to me they can't understand why their loving child in primary and post-primary school didn't do as well in the Leaving Cert and then dropped out of college. They don't seem to see the link between the impact of alcohol on the young brain. So if there were to be one strong message, I would say the whole importance of knowing where children are. So government can do x, y and z, but way back at the very beginning of it—if I was to say I have a priority as Minister on the alcohol side—that priority would be the younger teenagers and in relation to the whole delaying issue.

BO'C:
So how do you get that message to parents?

Minister Wallace:
Well, I suppose through publications like yours, through the media and whatever. There are some excellent books available through the HSE in relation to teenagers and alcohol and I would direct parents to the booklet on teenagers because again, where are teenagers getting alcohol? Frequently the first access to alcohol is actually in the home and it may be in the presence of parents. It may be a case of, 'Well, I'd rather have my children having a glass with a meal on Christmas Day,' or whatever. But in fact, that's missing the point that the delay is so important for the child. For a number of reasons: for the child's brain, for the education and for the fact that the younger people commence drinking alcohol the more likely they are to have problems later on.

BO'C:
Do we have any idea how much an untreated addict costs society? I know for example in Northern Ireland they have produced a figure of half a million pounds sterling.

Minister Wallace:

Not necessarily in terms of money costs but we do in terms of the impact on the whole of society. I can give you some quick figures if you want. So for example in hospital discharges, there was a ninety-two per cent increase between 1995 and 2004. So we looked through statistic[s] in that period. Also in relation to liver disease, an increase in the same period by one hundred and forty-seven per cent. In relation to deaths it increased from 3.8 to 7.1 and again this issue of it being a contributory factor in road fatalities. There was a very interesting piece of research done in the northeast. It looked at the issue of accidental suicide and injury and fifty-five per cent tested positive for blood alcohol. A closer look, we find that forty per cent of traffic fatalities, fifty-five per cent of suicide[s] and thirty per cent of drowning[s] were all alcohol-related. So what does that tell you? There's a kind of carelessness creeps in. Suicide is such a tragedy for young people but maybe theirs is an element of hopelessness in relation to the link with alcohol that leads to these deaths. So again it comes back to the delay is hugely important.

BO'C:

The accusation that is often [levelled] is that the drinks group is such a strong lobby in Ireland, creating so much employment, that it is very difficult for government to form a policy that will impact on their business model. Would you agree with that?

Minister Wallace:

From our point of view on the health promotion side our biggest issue is individual responsibility. Again with all the figures we have concerns in relation to the units. This business of 'Am I a binge-drinker or not?'. A lot of people don't actually realise that they are binge-drinking. So the current recommendations are that women should have no more than fourteen units and men have twenty-one in terms of weekly consumption. To me that would appear to be high. There's a report due out shortly where the HSE are talking about reducing that to eleven for women and seventeen for men.

What's a unit? Do people realise that a unit is not a pint? It's a small glass of wine, a measure of spirits. The whole affluence society we have gone through, when you go back through the years in the 1970s and 1980s, a glass of wine was a small glass of wine. Now there are big glasses of wine. Even if you go into a restaurant and order a glass of wine, what's the measurement of it? Order a bottle of wine and you know it's one hundred and seventy-five millilitres, but you order a glass and it's hard to know. We would have concerns. In relation to what we're doing about it, we are looking at another piece of legislation, the Sale of Alcohol Bill, which we expect to hopefully publish before the summer (2009), but again it's not on our side, it's on the Department of Justice's side.

I personally think the Intoxicating Liquor Act was a great day in terms of the impact, because if I were to say to someone last May or June, what had the biggest impact, they all would have said the development of off-licences in every little village in Ireland. The whole culture of that. Once again we are talking about small steps making a difference. But the fact that in a village if they feel they have enough with one or two off-licences they can object to the District Court.

BO'C:

Is the point not this, though: that it's still acceptable in Ireland for a father or mother to bring their son or daughter into a bar at fifteen or sixteen and buy them their first drink?

Minister Wallace:

Well, it isn't acceptable and it shouldn't be acceptable. It's against the law. My understanding is if that was to be happening it is more likely to be at the kitchen table. Certainly the publican or barman should not serve alcohol even with the parent present.

BO'C:

Can we go back to the treatment side of things, given that we know the problems exist? It's my understanding that someone cannot present to a psychiatrist and be admitted for alcohol-related problems unless there is a risk of suicide. All cases now have to be referred back through family doctors. So I'm wondering on the treatment side are there enough beds to treat adults and are you satisfied that if someone presents to their local GP or psychiatrist with a problem, are there proper processes in place to treat that person?

Minister Wallace:

I'm over twenty years in public life and would have dealt with a lot of people across the table that really wanted to do something about their difficulty and thankfully I have a met small percentage that have had success. Chiefly, my experience is that the individual themselves have to be committed. Without the commitment you can have two hundred family members that can afford the Rutland Centre or the best private care and nothing might change. It's really about the culture of support around that individual, the messages we're giving about the unacceptability of their behaviour. A family can be committed in the best of ways but if the individual isn't committed then it just doesn't succeed.

BO'C:

Specifically in relation to the Aislinn Centre in Kilkenny, they say [they] are strapped for cash and trying to get government recognition and support for their work. They have fourteen beds with over ninety persons on a waiting list late last year to try and get in and avail of their services. These are young kids who have taken that first step and admitted they have a problem and need help. So what does that say in terms of government's acknowledgment of the problem of young drinkers when these kids cannot get treatment?

Minister Wallace:

I'm not familiar about what happens in Kilkenny; I can only talk about my own community. I know there is a one in three success rate for treatment programmes. I'm delighted for the one in three who makes it but what I'm actually more worried about is those who never got into the group of three. Those who never got beyond the step of going for treatment and it wasn't for the lack of services. It was for the fact they changed their mind as an individual and they will be the people I would come across most in community settings. I'd have the family around them saying to me, we had everything set up, the appointment was made for next Thursday morning, say, we were all systems go, he or she has been off it for the last couple of weeks, and then Thursday morning comes and he or she wouldn't get into the car. I think that's the tragedy of the culture and so I think . . . you're lucky to be the three that go across the threshold. From my point of view it is how do we get people into the situation of going for treatment? Some people can have alcohol in their lives, others can't.

BO'C:
Would you be in favour of raising the legal age to twenty-one years?

Minister Wallace:
I would be in favour of it. What really saddens me was story I heard about a community where a twelve-year-old birthday party was held. One twelve-year-old was able to say to the other twelve-year-olds, 'Listen, do you need any alcohol?' That happened in a community in this city. I think really it's the twelve to fourteen is such a fragile age group. Their parents have a duty to protect them.

————

I decided to meet with Dr Moosajee Bhamjee, a consultant psychiatrist, in his offices at Shannon Health Centre. Dr Bhamjee entered the national consciousness following his General Election win in 1992, when he took a surprise seat for the Labour Party in the Fianna Fáil stronghold of County Clare. He was the first Muslim TD elected to Dáil Éireann (or, as many remarked at the time, the first Indian among the cowboys). When I bumped into him outside the West County Hotel, shortly after his election win, he himself summed up the electoral win with the memorable phrase 'O'Connell, it is a black day for Fianna Fáil'. His day-to-day work is as a senior clinical psychiatrist, and over the last 20 or so years he has worked at the frontline of substance and alcohol abuse in the mid-west. He has experience, then, of working within both the health lobby and the political one and I was interested to hear from someone born outside Ireland, who perhaps could cast a more detached eye over our societal habits.

Having grown up in County Clare in the 1980s, I knew there was a huge stigma attached to seeking treatment for alcohol-related problems. Bushy Park was the nearest treatment centre and had the cultural associations of a place where you went at your lowest ebb. In-jokes between Ennis revellers had us all going to Bushy Park on many a shaky Monday morning following a heavy weekend session. 'Jesus, I should be in Bushy Park,' was the general gist. It was more or less held in the same light as Our Lady's Psychiatric Hospital was a generation earlier—a place for the hopeless and those who were cast out by general society. Needless to say, words such as 'rehabilitation', 'counselling', 'support groups', 'making amends' and so on never got a look in. So, have times changed and is there an acceptance now among the wider community that alcohol abuse is an illness like any other?

'I think people have come around to realise alcohol can be a problem and so it's good to see all these new alcohol treatment centres for adults opening all throughout Ireland,' says Dr Bhamjee. 'But most of them are private, and a lot of people with medical cards don't have access to the facilities. So the State has been negligent in a sense. The State has also been negligent in treating a person for alcohol withdrawals. It used to be done in psychiatric units before. The situation now is that the Inspector of Mental Hospitals and Mental Health Commission don't want withdrawals in psychiatric units, so they asked us all to stop treating people for alcoholism and to refer them to the medical wards. It is now for medical people to treat people for withdrawals. But medical beds are in short supply, so people only stay one night or two nights and there is no proper detoxification process taking place. There is certainly nowhere to detox young people, unless they say they are suicidal; then they can go into [a] psychiatric unit for seven to ten days. The State is talking one thing and at the same time it is not providing the service for people, including drug addicts.'

Dr Bhamjee has seen Irish society change from a pub-orientated culture to one where drinking has become far more commonplace in the home.

'The pub atmosphere has changed a lot since I came to Ireland. More shots are being drunk now towards evening time and because of things like the drink-driving people are now drinking at home, where they tend to drink more. Price has also become a factor—alcohol really is twice the price in a pub, so the off-licence trade has increased and increased. Being able to buy drink from a supermarket is also a huge cultural shift. I know that a lot of housewives with their daily shopping are now buying wine, and wine has now attracted massive sales. Some are drinking a bottle as part of their supper and feel quite normal.'

He agrees with Minister Wallace that alcohol abuse is a societal problem that requires a poly-pharmacy response. At the point when persons present for treatment, it is vital, he says, that they receive the proper supports.

'Adults need to take responsibility. We all of us have to share in this problem. We need to bring in a certain amount of control in drinking. There are people who know nothing else except the pub, so once they come off the alcohol they need a life change. That means getting a new social life, new friends, new hobbies and new interests. There has to be a whole mindset change. I think the amounts people are drinking are the same, but the style of drinking has changed. The problems with it are also starting much younger; we're now seeing full-blown alcoholics at twenty-two or twenty-three.'

When I mentioned my visit to a local secondary school, where no major discussions around alcohol use were taking place, Dr Bhamjee became animated. 'People always talk about issues to do with school—these issues are parental issues. They are not school issues. We see that more and more nowadays when any problem is being talked of as the responsibility for schools. It's parents that are supposed to talk to children and train them. We need to encourage children to play games and look at leisure time so that it is productive, and they don't say, "We are bored," which is a major excuse that is used.'

Speaking of the positives in the past few years, Dr Bhamjee feels now, at least, there is a greater awareness in society that alcohol can be a problem and that treatment is available. He says more and more he comes across families encouraging one of their members to seek treatment, whereas in the past in Ireland the problem would have been kept within the home and hidden from view. Yet he, too, refers to the apparently haphazard way in which alcohol addiction is treated in Ireland at government level. 'There is no proper planning in Ireland for treatment of alcohol and drugs. There is no system in place. If someone presents to me, then the process is that they have to be referred back to their GP, who might send him or her to a day hospital. They then try to treat the [person] as an outpatient and will refer them to an addiction centre. But between all the different strands, there is no networking and no cohesion.'

Irish society, he believes, is still defining itself too closely with drink, simple as that.

'Ireland has to learn that if you have a problem, alcohol isn't the answer. We are still doing that; we did fifty years ago. If you had a problem, you avoided it and used drink to try [to] sort it out. We have a lot, too, of what I call the JR Ewing style of drinking. This is where people come in after a long drive or a journey and the first thing they do is reach for a glass of whiskey or a glass of wine. Those are bad habits. We need to bring the pot of tea back.'

————

One of the main problems when looking at the issue of alcohol abuse in Ireland is that no one central agency or public health body is responsible for either research into the area or suggesting ways to deal with it. Several different sectors of society are conducting research into the causes and effects of alcohol abuse, but there are often disparate approaches, aims and objectives between the drinks lobby, public health and government.

At any one time several different reports are in the process of being published or about to be undertaken, whether it's the drinks lobby looking at consumer trends, public health looking at alcohol-related harm, or individual institutions such as the Gehry Institute looking at wider sociological issues. There can't be any joined-up thinking, because there is no coherent strategy to deal with the problem of alcohol abuse in Irish society. Government lacks the political will to seriously tackle the issue, preferring instead to speak in general terms about society's responsibility. The voices of public health professionals are often muffled by the marketing juggernaut of the drinks industry. For instance, in one report by the Health Research Board (Mongan D, Reynolds S, Fanagan S and Long J (2007) 'Health-related consequences of problem alcohol use'. Overview 6. Dublin: Health Research Board) looking at the health-related consequences of problem alcohol abuse, the recommendations highlight just how lacking the response to the problem has been thus far. The report called for a comprehensive strategy to reduce alcohol-related harm with a strong public health base. It went on to say that taxation, regulating the physical availability of alcohol and drink-driving countermeasures were only part of the solution.

One of the main recommendations was to 'delay in the initiation to drinking among young people. It is important to decrease the easy access and availability of alcohol to young people and to increase the provision of alternative alcohol-free social activities.'

In terms of available data, the report acknowledged serious gaps and called for 'accurate and complete data on the numbers receiving treatment for alcohol use' as well as 'greater integration of alcohol and drug treatment services'.

This call was made in recognition of the fact that one in five people receiving treatment for problem alcohol use also report problem use of at least one other drug.

As well as this, calls were made for strong health promotion campaigns to inform and educate women about the dangers of alcohol, especially during pregnancy; data on people with alcohol-related conditions who attend accident and emergency units but are not admitted to hospital; and accurate data on alcohol-related deaths, including those where alcohol was a contributory factor.

Much work needs to be done also in the area of alcohol-related suicide. At a recent conference in Cork, Dr Jane Marshall, consultant psychiatrist at the Maudsley Hospital, London, said alcohol was implicated in one in six suicides in Ireland but she believed the rate was much higher. She said, 'Suicide rates are lower in women because of lower rates of alcohol and substance abuse, but as women drink more, we will probably see a corresponding increase in suicide among young women. It's the chicken-and-egg syndrome. Usually, the alcohol problem comes first, but in some people, particularly women who have experienced traumatic life events such as sexual abuse, alcohol seems to be secondary to their depression problem.'

Also addressing the conference, Barnardos chief executive Fergus Finlay said the organisation was dealing with an increasing number of children whose lives had been 'blighted by suicide' where alcohol and drugs had been involved.

Finlay outlined the case of one 10-year-old boy whose father left him a letter telling him he was now the head of the household after taking his own life. 'The number of people who commit suicide fortified by drink and drugs is staggering but a ten-year-old child cannot understand this link. Every single kid we work with carries guilt—sometimes for the rest of their lives or until they are lucky enough to get help—and believes they are responsible in some way for their mother or father's suicide,' said Mr Finlay.

Dr Declan Bedford, public health consultant with the HSE North East, whose study Minister Wallace referred to, pointed out that 16–17 year olds in Ireland spend a staggering €145 million per annum on alcohol.

He said: 'The Irish suicide rate increased consistently from 1980 to 2006 with a slight drop in recent years. The alcohol consumption rate mirrors the suicide rate, i.e., the more a nation drinks, the more alcohol-related harm there will be.'

In a study of coroners' reports on suicide deaths, Dr Bedford found that 90 per cent of those under 30 had alcohol in their blood, 58 per cent were drunk and nearly all were men. 'I can tell you suicide was far from their minds when they went out that night,' he said. Dr Bhamjee in Clare, too, had thoughts on the link between suicide and alcohol. 'If you look at the time when many suicides occur among young people it is often Friday, Saturday and Sunday nights. I think it's hard for young people to separate alcoholism from drugs these days as the two of them are nearly always linked. We see them together in at least sixty per cent of cases and both are major factors in suicides.'

Currently, research and targeted campaigns into the area of suicide, and all the other areas highlighted by the 2007 Health Research Board report, are lacking. It makes for a bleak if somewhat compelling insight into just how little concerted action has been taken to tackle the alcohol abuse epidemic in Ireland over the past two decades.

'The two taskforce reports had about a hundred recommendations between them,' says Prof. Barry. 'If we're waiting for unanimity then nothing will ever happen. Obviously the drinks companies will vigorously oppose in public and in private any attempts to reduce our overall consumption. So then any partnership between the industry and public health doesn't make any sense. The ways you reduce consumption include tax and pricing. Taxes are relatively high here; prices are not, certainly in off-licences. Most of the cheap drink sold here is sold in multiples, such as supermarkets. There have been recommendations for a minimum pricing structure, which government haven't to date implemented. That would be one way. Drink-driving [restrictions] will reduce consumption. [Reducing] availability of outlets could reduce consumption. Like anything, the more outlets you have the more alcohol will be sold.'

As previously mentioned, the drink-driving campaign in the past few years is an example of the positive role legislation can play in the alcohol debate. Public awareness campaigns, including stark television advertising, were having little effect in decreasing road deaths. The problem needed to be tackled, as behavioural changes were not occurring voluntarily among the public. Yet it took almost a decade before government took the advice of the public health lobby in this instance. Public health campaigns had been calling for mandatory breath testing since 1997, and it wasn't introduced until 2007. A year after its introduction, 100 lives were saved, which makes you wonder how many could have been saved had the public health lobby been listened to much earlier.

'The government is like everybody else—they respond to pressure,' says Prof. Barry. 'So they're getting some pressure from the public health lobby. But the access the industry has to government is greater than public health. They're very powerful companies, big corporations. It's a globalised industry. They lobby at European level. They lobby locally. They give government ministers seats at Croke Park for international matches. You know. And the government have freely accepted and admitted that. You give somebody a ticket for Croke Park, it's that little bit less likely that they will do anything tough.'

In general terms, though, aside from public houses, where numbers are declining (most notably in rural areas), there hasn't been any reduction in points of sale for alcohol in the last decade. In fact, in contrast to a decade ago, the majority of supermarkets and petrol stations now sell alcohol. Coupled with this, the marketing spend by the drinks industry has risen considerably, with some observers putting the annual 'over the radar' marketing spend at somewhere in the region of €70 million per annum.

The current programme for government has plans to initiate discussions with sporting bodies with a view to phasing out alcohol sponsorship in sport. But so far there's little sign that the appetite exists or any concrete discussions are taking place in this regard. Advertising revenues continue to increase. 'The industry will say advertising does not increase overall consumption,' says Prof. Barry. 'If not, then why spend that kind of money?' It's an important point and one that the government will have to tackle in the years ahead. The simple fact is that the industry spends so much on advertising because they believe it works and it gets people drinking their product. 'There is a cultural dimension,' says Prof. Barry. 'There has been a few reports commissioned on the impact of advertising. Young people see and hear and experience the advertising. Alcohol adverts are brilliant ads, very clever. I heard a story of some Danish teachers who were visiting a national school in Ireland, and were talking to the twelve-year-old kids. One of their teachers asked, "Any questions now for the visitors?" And one of the kids asked, "Is it true the Danes don't like Carlsberg to leave Denmark?" So those advertisements impact on young people.'

————

Established in 2002, MEAS (Mature Enjoyment of Alcohol in Society) is a group whose origins lie in the Drinks Industry Group of Ireland, and was set up, as it says itself, 'in order to better support the development and implementation of social responsibility initiatives'. The member companies of MEAS are Beamish and Crawford, C&C group, Diageo Ireland, Drinks Industry Group of Ireland, Edward Dillon & Co., Heineken Ireland, InBev Ireland, Irish Distillers Ltd, Licensed Vintners Association and Vintners Federation of Ireland. The society has a code of practice including guidelines on marketing and packaging of alcohol, and also holds an annual conference and issues a variety of publications. It also highlights individual bars and outlets who breach its code of ethics. One of the main offshoots of the organisation is the drinkaware.ie media campaign and website, which was launched in November 2006. The site is interesting and eyecatching, obviously aimed at a younger market, and includes features such as a 'drinks diary', facts on 'alcohol, sport and you', and various other bits of information and consumer polls. The largest aspect of the website, when I clicked on in mid-March 2009, was a box highlighting 'The Morning After Cure'. This basically turned out to be a chatty guide to how to minimise hangovers, from drinking water to telling people to have '48 hours without alcohol if it was a heavy session'. The tagline says that, in respect of hangovers, 'time is the only cure'. Moderation doesn't get a look in.

As with the general drinks industry response to Ireland's issues with alcohol over the past two decades, there is a real sense of closing the stable door long after the horse has bolted. In another section entitled 'Top Ten Booze Myths', it looks at whether or not milk should be drunk to line the stomach before a night out. The site, and by association the drinks industry who fund it, offer the following advice: '. . . eating before you drink is way better than scoffing a bag of greasy chips after a skin full. You'll avoid puking on the dance floor because you drank on an empty stomach and you won't succumb to overpriced burgers, which you'd rightly avoid under normal circumstances. Milk on its own won't do much for you though.' Is this really the manner in which responsible drinking should be promoted? Does it not raise issues about the suitability of self-regulation within the drinks industry and its ability to carry the public health agenda?

I raised the subject of MEAS and drinkaware.ie with Professor Joe Barry. At the very least, the drinks industry were attempting to raise important points of public health through the media; surely that should be welcomed? 'The coverage in the media has taken on the public health view, by and large. Which is unusual, given that historically journalists (like doctors) would have strong relationships with alcohol. You read the business pages, though, and you see a completely different agenda from drinks companies. If they're on about corporate social responsibility, it's a meaningless phrase. The difficulty with MEAS is that they are funded by the industry. MEAS are not going to do anything that will harm the industry. I don't believe that they work independently. They have the same views as the industry on any topic. Okay, so MEAS will get tough with some poor publican down the country who goes against their codes, but in general, MEAS don't criticise. They're not independent. Full stop. They have slogans such as "drink responsibly." We have asked the industry, "What does drink responsibly mean?" and we haven't got an answer. It's meaningless.

The public need information, but I would prefer to see it coming from the health sector than the drinks industry.'

Fionnuala Sheehan, Chief Executive of MEAS, rejects criticisms of the organisation and says that the drinks industry has provided a €20 million funding commitment over the next five years towards the organisation. She points to the fact that MEAS is run by an independent board appointed by member organisations and that she and her team work separately from the drinks industry. She says the industry became concerned with establishing a code of ethics in 2001/2002 and that the work of MEAS is very much research led. Her comments, below, though would seem to underline the view held by some in the public health lobby—that the drinks industry has the ear of government, more so than those pushing the health agenda: 'Our point of view in MEAS is that we recognise the sensitivities involved and are conscious of the funding we receive. We also believe we would be very much open to the HSE involving itself in a direct way into the area of drink responsibility as was done with the drink-driving campaign. I have to say, though, the response of government so far has been very positive. I'd refer you to the comments made by [the] Minister for Health Promotion a year ago, where he referred in warm and positive terms to the work of MEAS and expressed a desire to see greater collaboration between us and the HSE.' She agrees with the view that drinking patterns are shifting, and when pressed on whether or not MEAS agrees that alcohol consumption levels are too high, Sheehan says the following: 'MEAS is on record many times saying our alcohol consumption levels are at an internationally high level. We referred to a reaction occurring in recent times and we said that is a positive development.'

As already mentioned, the Irish industry does not differentiate between beers and spirits and its approach to the problem of alcohol abuse is one of a united front, unlike in Denmark, for instance, where the industry has fractured.

'We are strongly of the view that alcohol is alcohol is alcohol. Our view is that it would not be useful in helping to promote responsible drinking if we differentiated between the products. We don't believe one product is benign as opposed to another one.'

Of the current deficiencies in the overall approach to problem drinking in Ireland, MEAS, though, accepts there are shortcomings in the current societal approach: 'I think there is recognition that this is a complex problem that needs a multifaceted approach. It's something we don't have at present. There is a lot of consensus that we need a national policy towards alcohol involving all the relevant departments. There are some individuals opposed to us all getting around a table, as they see it purely as a public health issue. That will have to change.'

———

It's clear from the current body of research that Ireland has high levels of problem drinking which is costing society. Our per capita consumption levels continue to rank among the highest in Europe. It's worth bearing in mind also that the Total Abstinence Association (or Pioneers) still claim membership of close to 200,000 individuals in Ireland, committed to abstaining from alcohol. When that group is taken out of the adult population, then the statistics paint an even starker picture. The binge-drinking levels, particularly among young adults, are placing huge burdens on health services, and will continue to do so through the life of each drinker. More studies are needed on the links between alcohol, suicide and depression, and there is also a need for more accurate information with regard to coroners' reports and the collection of alcohol-related harm statistics. The government, for their part, are in a difficult position, with a powerful drinks lobby employing close to 100,000 individuals at a time of economic stress. There are different viewpoints within government as to how best to tackle the problem and indeed the responsibility falls, sometimes, between different departments.

It remains to be seen whether or not self-regulation within the industry is the best way to approach the issue. During the 1990s and into 2001, when research was showing drinking levels to be reaching critical proportions, the industry took very little concrete action to tackle the issue, aside from internal discussions. It wasn't until 2002, after damning statistics on binge-drinking had been released the previous year, that efforts were made to publicly address the problem. MEAS, despite its protestations, is a drinks industry body, and rarely if ever criticises the direction of Ireland's drinking patterns in public. There is a cosy feel to its literature and stance, and it comes across as more of an 'after the event' body than one seriously committed to tackling the underlying issues of Ireland's drinking patterns.

A failing of the State has been identified in the area of treatment, particularly among young persons. The Minister's failure to address this issue will do little to reassure those at the front line—the addiction counsellors, the psychiatrists, the worried parents and the doctors—that there are adequate supports in place to effectively treat our increasing class of young problem drinkers.

With over 100 recommendations, the Strategic Taskforce on Alcohol had some useful and timely suggestions, such as accurate data gathering, investment in treatment services and a look at minimum pricing. Many of these suggestions remain to be implemented, as does a serious look at the issue of alcohol sponsorship in sport. Meanwhile, the government point to measures such as raising the cost of an off-licence by €200 and pulling back off-trade opening hours as measures of success. Such 'signal policies', as they were called elsewhere, fail to tackle the underlying behavioural issues at the core of Ireland's problematic relationship with alcohol.

It is clear also that a division exists between the public health lobby and the drinks industry on how best to tackle the issue, with government moving between the two groups. Government needs to adopt a clear, singular approach, and without a National Alcohol Policy, it is unlikely that this will ever happen organically.

Even the Taoiseach, Brian Cowen, has adopted a laissez-faire attitude in public on occasion. During an interview with 'Hot Press' magazine, he was prompted to give his tuppence on our binge-drinking levels, and instead of offering a clean break with past tolerances, he seemed to indicate it was okay for young people to let their hair down now and again. He claimed that young people 'should be able to go out and enjoy themselves' with alcohol, as long as they 'find a balance and keep the head', while adding that he was 'all for people enjoying themselves', but wouldn't 'welcome a boozing sort of culture' coming into the country. Coming into the country? All the evidence says it's already here. Who is advising him and how blinded can he be to the realities of Ireland's association with alcohol?

As journalist Gemma O'Doherty noted in a follow-up article, 'There isn't a pocket of the planet where Ireland's reputation as a "boozing culture" isn't seen as part and parcel of our national identity.' And it's not as if Cowen is alone in his observations. When his predecessor, Bertie Ahern, was confronted with a survey that showed Irish schoolchildren as the third-highest substance samplers in the world, his response was 'They're just experimenting. Just because you smoke a joint doesn't make you a druggie.' So if that is part of the higher ranks of government thinking (and we've already heard the Minister of State's views on a lack of awareness outside her own community), where will the pressure to tackle Ireland's drinking culture come from? Certainly not from the estimated 80,000–100,000 workers dependent on the Irish drinks industry, more precious now as the country enters into a prolonged downward economic cycle.

Perhaps not from the industry themselves, who promote 'drink responsibly' and 'drink aware' campaigns while simultaneously offering solutions to irresponsible drinking and its consequences on their websites. It's akin to speaking with clarity out of the one side of their mouth while slurring through the other. And therein lies the Irish complex. What we say and do are two different things when it comes to alcohol, and the industry is a strong lobby determined to maintain the status quo. The public health lobby has to fight for attention, but with our health service under constant strain and scrutiny for a host of other deficiencies, from cancer screening to cystic fibrosis treatment, organ transplants to proper community healthcare packages, tackling the alcohol issue doesn't seem all that high on the policymakers' agenda.

Conclusion
Where to Next?

When money's tight and is hard to get
And your horse has also ran,
When all you have is a heap of debt—
A PINT OF PLAIN IS YOUR ONLY MAN.

The story of Ireland and its people, as told through literature, song and poetry, is often soaked in alcohol. Behan, Kavanagh, O'Brien, MacGowan, the Dubliners, Richard Harris, Donal McCann, Luke Kelly, Phil Lynott and Rory Gallagher were all marked by an overdependence on the booze at various times in their lives, which informed and shaped their artistic output. They were products of their environments, and alcohol was seen as a fertiliser of artistic freedom, as allowing creativity to flourish, despite the cost in human terms. The only filmed interview with Flann O'Brien that is known to exist shows a desperately shy, insecure, half-shot and inarticulate individual, decidedly the worse for wear. It's rarely shown on Irish television and the image doesn't make it onto posters or stamps. 'Great Irish Writers Who Pissed Their Lives Away' has decidedly less market value than 'Great Irish Writers' full stop. Yet behind every drinking writer and artist, there are surely days of empty retching and starvation, mental anguish and trauma. Those stories, with a few notable exceptions (such as Nuala O'Faolain's *Are You Somebody?*), are largely left untold and almost completely written out of Irish popular culture. It's much the same with Ireland itself. As a country we rely on the drinks industry for revenue and employment, we rely on the image of ourselves as a booze nation to attract tourists, and we rely on alcohol to paper over the cracks of our emotional longing. The romanticism of excess thrives in Ireland, where the problem drinker is often harboured by society, sheltered in his or her forgiving bay for longer than would be the case in most other countries. For a non-drinker, the pervasiveness of alcohol within society can be alienating and socially marginalising.

During the research for this book, and having lived sober in Ireland for almost half a decade, I see few signs of a reduction in the relationship between Ireland and alcohol emerging. The terms of reference between the two might be shifting, with the decline of the bar trade and the rise in domestic drinking, yet that in itself merely reflects a more insular and less community-orientated society which has emerged in the past two decades. Communities are also witnessing the closure of independent local shops and post offices, so that the decline in the rural bar trade, in particular, can be seen as part of a wider move towards urbanisation. There are other reasons for the shift to off-premises drinking. Over the past five years, many have paid over the odds for homes they are now intent on enjoying. The pub experience is easily reproduced in a home setting with modern audiovisual appliances and a better range of take-home drinks. Therefore, less numerous and less populated bars in Ireland should not be confused with a maturing of our relationship with the gargle. It is revealing that the two events publicans point to as reasons for a decline in the trade are the smoking ban and the stricter enforcement of drink-driving laws. Yet the smoking ban has been mimicked all over Europe, while the drink-driving enforcement was a necessary focus on implementing existing laws at a time when road deaths were spiralling. Still, those two events are seen less for the impact they have had had on reducing illness and death and more for their supposed effect on drinks revenue. Too often when it comes to addressing issues associated with alcohol in Ireland, money talks.

———

In April 2009, during our most recent economic woes, the 'Late Late Show' decided to invite actor Eamon Morrissey on to the show to recite Flann O'Brien's 'The Workman's Friend'. This was prime-time Friday night entertainment, with the actor reciting the poem behind a mock bar erected on the floor of the studio. The last refrain goes: 'In time of trouble and lousy strife,/You have still got a darlint plan,/You still can turn to a brighter life—A PINT OF PLAIN IS YOUR ONLY MAN.' Morrissey had adapted the poem for his play, *The Brother*, in the early 1970s, and on cue at the end of the poem downed a pint in one, before wiping his brow and taking a seat next to the host, Pat Kenny. Generally, the 'Late Late Show' is an irony-free zone. Therefore, in a country where statistics over the past few decades consistently point to high incidences of problem drinking, where the alcohol-related harm figures have soared, where binge-drinking is prevalent among our teenagers, where per capita consumption stays ahead of the EU average, the question is: how acceptable is it for a Friday night chat show to host an actor downing a pint in one and heralding the pint as the answer to all of life's problems? Will the startling facts and figures we now possess do anything to dislodge the symbiotic relationship between Irish culture and alcohol?

The imaging was similarly myopic when the Ryder Cup, the largest golf tournament in the world, was held on Irish soil in 2006. As a celebratory nod to the host country, European captain Ian Woosnam was seen by millions around the world downing a pint of the black stuff in one and presenting the empty glass to the cheering attendees. He did it because this is what you do when you are in Ireland. There was little or no comment in the media afterwards on the suitability of the image—indeed, many papers and news bulletins had it as their lead item. It's a similar tale when visiting dignitaries come here. Ex-Taoiseach Bertie Ahern felt the need to bring then US President Bill Clinton round to his local in Drumcondra for a pint during a visit. The images went around the world. No one at home batted an eyelid; in fact, there would have been questions had Bertie *not* introduced Bill to the black stuff, given that it is a long-established tradition for American presidents on Irish soil.

What I'm trying to get at is that, despite increased legislative approaches to tackling the issue of alcohol abuse in Irish society, despite a greater awareness by those in the drinks industry that problems exist, and despite the documenting of those problems and their cost to Irish society, the underlying relationship between Ireland and alcohol continues to have deep psychological and cultural roots. Throughout the ages, travellers to Ireland, from the seventeenth century onwards, perpetuated the image of the drunken Paddy, recounting their experiences and perhaps exaggerating certain aspects for political purposes. In the twenty-first century we don't need others to do the stereotyping for us—we've become experts at fuelling the image of the drunken Paddy all by ourselves.

Having just come through a period of financial giddiness, Irish society is now suffering the mother of all monetary hangovers. While economic moderation might be the future, alcoholic excess very much remains the present. How the economic straitening will affect our relationship with alcohol remains to be seen. On the one hand, disposable income will not be so readily available, which should have a knock-on impact on per capita consumption. The alarming spikes in binge-drinking and per capita consumption directly reflected the rise in prosperity during the Celtic Tiger years. It was a period of abandonment and recklessness, and it will be interesting to see whether or not tighter economic times lead to behavioural changes in relation to alcohol. Responsibility starts at home, though, and as many in this book have commented, parents need to take the lead in allowing moderation and maturity to determine their children's relationship with alcohol.

The government, too, have a role to play in helping modify behaviour and acting on available data, although whether or not a strong legislative hand would have any impact on drinking patterns remains to be seen. Despite taking the lead in inaugurating the workplace smoking ban, smoking numbers in Ireland have crept up in recent years, putting us above the UK and US in percentage terms (29 per cent of the adult population in Ireland smoke, compared to 20 per cent in the US and 24 per cent in the UK). So while wider society may regard smoking in public places as totally unacceptable, smokers, it seems, are carrying on regardless and the legislation has had little positive effect on actual numbers smoking in Ireland. The smoking lobby point to the fact that once the ban had been introduced, areas such as establishing smoking helplines and promoting education and awareness lapsed, thereby allowing numbers to creep back up again. So there is a debate as to whether a similar crackdown on drinking hours and availability would in any way change drinking levels in Ireland.

But something has to be done, and at the very least a concerted effort made to form a consensus approach within government. As it is, different departments appear to be skirting around the fringes of the issue, without actually grasping the bigger issues or acting on a coherent policy.

As things stand, government doesn't seem to have the political will to take on the drinks industry and row in behind the health lobby's stance. Indeed, the government set out their stall in a recent emergency budget (April 2009). When presented with a chance to raise the price of alcohol, they declined. While cigarettes and diesel rose by 25c and 5c respectively, alcohol remained unchanged. The reason? There was 'no scope for increases in excise duties on alcohol or petrol because of the substantial risk of loss of revenue by the purchase of these items in Northern Ireland', explained Minister for Finance Brian Lenihan. We're still justifying alcohol policy in financial rather than health or social terms. In the weeks prior to the budget the drinks industry had lobbied hard for excise on alcohol to remain unchanged. The government, it seemed, listened. At the time of writing, plans are afoot by government to tackle loss-leading alcohol promotions and cut-price deals. This is in recognition of the fact that the cost of alcohol has fallen sharply in recent years while the number of outlets selling alcohol has increased dramatically. For instance, between 2001 and 2007, there was an increase of almost 70 per cent in the number of off-licences and shops selling alcohol. In some outlets it is now cheaper to buy a bottle of beer than a bottle of water. Tesco was one of the stores criticised for promotions in recent times, when it ran a St Patrick's

Day offer of 48 cans of beer for €24. Many off-licences now have volunteered to close their stores for part of St Patrick's Day, yet public disturbances and large-scale street drinking continue to go hand in hand with celebrating the national day of Irishness.

During the course of this book I'd like to think I have exposed some of the reasons, from issues of circumstance to those of emotional need, that lie behind our problem drinking. Those underlying issues, coupled with a degree of uncertainty on how best to tackle them, have created something of a perfect storm for problem drinking in Ireland over the past few decades. Ironically, the current generation is the first to emerge free from past oppressions such as widespread poverty, religious persecution and questions of national identity. Yet still, there is often a need to dilute everyday experience and life events through large-scale abuse of alcohol.

———

On a personal level, I am content with my sobriety. It can be challenging living in Ireland and not drinking alcohol. It can also be difficult to identify whether or not you have a problem in the first place, given that we live in a culture where tolerance levels and drinking volumes are so high. I believe it's not by comparing ourselves to each other that we will address our drinking; it will come more from making international comparisons. Simply put, my sobriety is far less of an issue and rarely discussed when I am in another country. In Ireland, passing on wine at dinner or ordering a mineral water in a bar on a Friday night will often be marked, especially in new company. My experience is that this doesn't happen nearly as much elsewhere.

I am still proud to be Irish, still enthralled and excited by many aspects of this country and its people. I'm just less enamoured with the manner in which we engage with other socially. I find it frustrating, depressing and often off-putting. I know that after I came out of rehab, people would say, 'Oh, he had a problem with drink.' But I don't feel as if I'm the one with the problem. I look more critically at society since I got sober and often find myself unable to relate. Yesterday, stopped in traffic lights at 4 p.m. in Cork city centre, I saw a group of teenage girls vomiting outside a bar where they were being served. They were clearly underage and drunk. Ahead of me was a tour bus of what looked like American golf tourists. They took pictures. So, *this* is Ireland?

Whether or not the current generation will redefine Ireland, free from alcoholic associations, remains to be seen. There are signs that a café culture is beginning to take hold in cities and towns around the country. This will take time to root and flourish, and affect in a substantive way the manner in which we engage with other socially. Alcoholism is still something of a taboo in Ireland, its sufferers still often seen as damaged goods, socially scarred and emotionally fragile. At least that's the feeling you can allow yourself to succumb to, unless you search for an Ireland without alcohol. Such an Ireland does exist, it's just that it is a little slow in revealing itself.

Of all the people I spoke to for this book, those Irish I met in Cricklewood have remained in my mind the longest. There, in dingy Dickensian hovels, clutching onto fragments of an Ireland long gone, is a version of ourselves and our overdependence on alcohol almost too shocking to contemplate. I think of those men, many dead, others on the way, and hope that the next generation will note their dependencies, self-delusions and struggles. There's dignity in their desperation, as well as resignation and insight and an acknowledgment of the grip alcohol can have over self and society. Often, when I reflect on the good things sobriety has brought me, I replay the interview with Séamus. The fizz of a single-bar heater is audible in the background, and between cups of cider, he examines what is left of his life and his environment.

'At the same time all me mates were all heavy drinkers. Jesus— they're all dead now. Tom is the only survivor. Some of them would knock on the door at two or three o'clock in the morning. And sure I'd answer the door straight away for them no problem at all. Jesus, they're dead now. The man other side that wall there. Billy

Simpson. He was sixty-eight. And Patsy was in the room across, he was sixty-nine. And Eóin in the back room was from Achill Island. But Jesus, we were all the one gang, a crazy gang. All great mates. Nobody would see each other wrong. It's a different ball game now. It's beating me now and all, I know it is. At the same time I'm fighting a good aul' battle as best I can.'

For me, the above serves as a timely reminder of what can happen when society and self come to rely too much on the social. It always leaves me grateful that I was given an opportunity to redefine my Irishness. Others, I am acutely aware, have not been so lucky.

Acknowledgments

The author and publishers thank the following for permission to reproduce copyright material:

Page 85: Jimmy Crowley for a verse from 'A Sorrowful Lamentation on the recent Price Increases on Ales, Wines and Spirits', from 'The Boys of Fairhill' by Jimmy Crowley and Stokers Lodge, CRO 001 on Freestate Records, freestaterecords@gmail.com.

Page 104: Jimmy MacCarthy for two verses from 'Missing You'.